Wilderness Therapy: Foundations, Theory and Research

Jennifer Davis-Berman, Ph.D.
University of Dayton
and
Lifespan Counseling Associates

Dene S. Berman, Ph.D.
Lifespan Counseling Associates

KENDALL/HUNT PUBLISHING COMPANY
4050 Westmark Drive   Dubuque, Iowa 52002

To our children and for Dad,
who would have bought a million copies.

Photo credits: Illustrations and Wilderness Therapy Program Logo by Greg Lukjanovs. Photographs courtesy of Dene S. Berman

Contents ▽

Preface   v

Chapter One   Introduction **1**

Chapter Two   The Wilderness Ethic **19**

Chapter Three   Early Wilderness Programs **39**

Chapter Four   Recent Programs **61**

Chapter Five   Varieties of Programs **85**

Chapter Six   Theoretical Understanding of Wilderness Experiences **109**

Chapter Seven   Designing a Program **137**

Chapter Eight   Program Evaluation **167**

Chapter Nine   Gaining Perspective **193**

Appendix A   Program Resources **211**
     Mental Health Programs **213**
     Enrichment Programs **227**
     Leadership, Personal Growth, and Training **227**
     Executive Programs **247**
     University-Related Programs **250**
     Court Programs **258**
     School Programs **262**
     Health Programs **270**

Appendix B   Index of Programs **273**

Index   **277**

Preface ▽

Our program, the Wilderness Therapy Program, was conceived in 1982 on a trail on the Bruce Peninsula in Ontario, when one of us (DSB) began what would be one of many dialogues with our wilderness guide, Dave Thobaben, whose academic background was in mental health. Together, we dreamed about the therapeutic possibilities of taking troubled youth on the trail.

Some years after our program was established, we began to think about a book. Naive to the process of writing a full length book, we started down this road with the unbridled enthusiasm of young children, full of optimism, energy, and ideals. At that time, we were very committed to our own program, but were quite interested in the work of others as well. Being affiliated with universities in one way or another for most of our adult lives, we were also quite naturally intrigued with the more "academic" side of therapeutic programs (especially JLD-B, the full-time academician among us). As practitioners and professors, we longed for material and research to read which described the history, research, process, and outcome of therapeutic wilderness programs, and even more specifically, of wilderness therapy programs.

Although we read a number of excellent articles and books, no one source seemed to pull these topics together in an organized and readable way. Hence, one of the strongest motivations for this book—there was a need for it. The literature needed a volume which could serve to provide some background, examine the current status of the field, and project into the future.

We are pleased to say that the journey down the path to this book's eventual completion has actually been fun. We have had a chance to become immersed in a literature that we love, and we have been able to comment on these readings. We have learned so much about the past and the rich historic material surrounding the wilderness. Writing this book has also given us the opportunity to remind ourselves and others how critical process and outcome evaluation are to the success of these programs. Given these experiences, our own program has become richer.

Most importantly, during the writing of this book, we have encountered some enriching people. We served on a national task force which worked on developing standards for residential wilderness programs. During these meetings, we were fortunate to be able to interact with many of the leaders in this field. Additionally, in compiling the resources chapter, we were in contact with the majority of the institutional members of the AEE. For the most part, when asked for information about their programs, these people responded in a generous, unselfish fashion. Many of them went out of their way to write personal letters, and even encouraged us to call. We found that in general, those people running wilderness programs appear to be open, warm and caring, and have been a pleasure to work with.

If some of our comments or positions are controversial and evoke strong responses, we welcome this challenge. We truly hope that our colleagues in programs and organizations across the country will accept and be energized by these differences. We believe that the field of wilderness therapy can be refined only through discussion and debate. If this book plays even a small role in instigating this activity, we will be immensely satisfied.

We would like to thank the large number of people who helped contribute to the successful completion of this book. To all of the institutional members of the AEE and to all of the non-member organizations and individuals who have given their time and energy to us, thank you. You have been a pleasure to work with. To Ms. Laura Hengehold, who spent hours interviewing on the phone, and who essentially compiled our resources, heartfelt thanks. Not only are you extremely competent to work with, Laura, but a lot of fun as well. We truly appreciate your time and talents.

We would also like to thank and acknowledge the talents of some outdoor professionals who read and critiqued our book in its formative stage. Thanks to Mitch Sakofs who gave us candid, constructive feedback about Outward Bound. Your support and materials were extremely helpful. Thanks to Mark Wagstaff for a thoughtful reading of our book, and for being a strong supporter of our writing. Thanks also to David Cockrell for his very insightful suggestions for revision. Your input has played an important role in the completion of this book. Finally, thanks to Maurice Phipps, whose suggestions about the tone and presentation of our material have been invaluable.

To the students from Wright State University and the University of Dayton who have helped with library research, data collection and analysis, you've lightened our load and, hopefully, learned along the way. Special thanks to Michael Anton, Yvonne Baker, Lynne Capone, and Kelly White.

Many companies have aided us in our wilderness endeavor by supplying products, advice, and encouragement. Thanks are extended to the folks at Patagonia, Sierra Designs, Mountain Science Research, HiTec, and Dagger. The Beavercreek Jaycees have generously offered scholarships to youth in need. To our friends and colleagues, especially the Daves, who have spent long hours on trails and rivers as co-therapists and staff, we express our love and gratitude.

Chapter One ▽

Introduction

Adolescents today are recognized as having factors affect them that make adjustment difficult, including changes in family structure and composition, geographic factors like inner city dwelling, socioeconomic factors including poverty and inadequate education, and even the threat of living in a nuclear age (Garcia & Travis, 1985). Add to this the violence that many adolescents face and life threatening illnesses like AIDS, and one can see that visions of adolescence as a time of innocence, security and little responsibility are outdated. Adolescence is not just the time of physical maturation and the process of adapting to this growth. Thus, adolescents have special needs by virtue of the unique developmental issues confronting them and the problems adolescents face in society today.

Of particular concern for our purposes are the psychological problems facing adolescents and a novel approach to working with troubled adolescents: **wilderness therapy.** Wilderness therapy may be viewed as a way in which many adolescents may be helped to overcome their problems. It should be emphasized that, like others forms of psychological counseling, wilderness therapy is not a panacea; rather, it is most appropriately viewed as a constellation of techniques that has the potential of helping some adolescents.

Our interests in wilderness therapy have grown out of our backgrounds as mental health professionals who enjoy the outdoors and began experiencing, firsthand, the restorative and healing properties of the wilderness. As we began to use the wilderness as a setting for providing psychological treatment for troubled adolescents, we noted dramatic changes in the participants. Initially, we were struck by the absence of a place to turn for information about the use of the wilderness as a therapeutic modality. While there were a few articles, they were in scattered sources. Thus, there was not an accumulated, readily available, body of knowledge to which we could turn. This led us to gather what information was available and to collect outcome data on our program.

When we shared our results with other professionals by writing journal articles and making presentations at conferences, we met, either in person or through correspondence, a small number of therapists who were using the out-of-doors as a medium for providing counseling. Others who found our work intriguing were in one of two general groups. The first group included therapists who worked with adolescents and were frustrated with the limitations of traditional modes of counseling for some of their clients. The second was a group of professionals who worked with troubled youth in a variety of settings—as camp counselors, corrections workers, outdoor educators, or residential treatment center staff—and understood the value of the wilderness, but lacked the knowledge of, or training in, psychotherapy.

This book is for all of these professionals. For therapists who are looking for new approaches and outdoor specialists who work with troubled adolescents, we offer an introduction to a new field that is striving to integrate psychotherapy and outdoor adventure pursuits. A framework for conceptualizing this synthesis will be presented, along with ideas for setting up programs. For those therapists who use wilderness settings, we hope to support your efforts by providing information about theoretical models, other programs, ideas about program development and evaluation, and emerging issues in this field. We hope this book serves as both a source of information about the field and a heuristic for further research and discussion.

In this first chapter, we begin by exploring theories of adolescence in order to examine some of the developmental tasks confronting adolescents. We then turn to some of the shocking facts about the magnitude of problems plaguing adolescents. The limitations of traditional counseling with adolescents will then be addressed. At that point, we will begin to present an overview of wilderness therapy. Finally, this chapter ends with a brief overview of the material to be found in subsequent chapters.

Theoretical Accounts of Adolescence

Adolescence, as a distinct stage of development, is a modern concept, barely one hundred years old. Before that time, in pre-industrial society, the family was the primary economic unit. Children shared in the work that was performed in and around the home, and were an integral part of the family unit, assuming apprenticeship roles in childhood and adult roles around the time of puberty (Aries, 1962). This notion of adolescence as a stage different from childhood or adulthood was popularized largely as the result of the writings of psychologist G. Stanley Hall, whose book, *Adolescence*, was originally published in 1904.

America at the turn of the century was being transformed from an agricultural to an urban, industrial society. This led to changes in the functioning of the family and the role of adolescents. In urban areas, youth were often found wandering, seemingly with little to do. Not surprisingly, this led to the creation of social institutions for adolescents (Platt, 1977). Chicago typified this transition from a rural to an urban society, and it was there that the first juvenile court was founded in 1899, along with the first adolescent guidance center, the Juvenile Psychopathic Institute (now the Institute for Juvenile Research), ten years later (1909).

By the 1920s, juvenile courts, guidance centers for children and adolescents, and a host of other reforms typifying the progressive era were evidenced in cities all over the country (Rothman, 1980). This marks the societal acceptance of adolescence as a developmental stage, with unique needs, problems and treatments.

Adolescence is often described as both an exciting time and a tumultuous one, as well. The first psychological theory of adolescence was formulated by

G. Stanley Hall (1916). He suggested that the major physical changes that occurred during this time caused psychological changes. The adjustment to one's body during this time caused *sturm und drang* (storm and stress). Hall believed that one could emerge from this developmental phase emotionally stronger.

Perhaps the two most well known modern theorists on psychological growth and development during adolescence are Peter Blos and Erik Erikson. They, like Hall, adhere to *sturm und drang* notion of adolescence. Blos (1979) conceptualizes adolescence from a psychoanalytic perspective in which the person is individuating for the second time, the first having occurred before age four. This process involves disengaging from the parents in order to prepare for adult relationships. Like other developmental phases, this one involves a drive, an inner conflict, and a developmental task. The drive, for Blos, is sexual, and concerns resolution of underlying conflicts that are primarily sexual in nature. Resolution comes through the taming and redirection of unacceptable primitive urges by identifying with role models of the same gender, and an emulation of their behavior.

Thus, Blos views psychological development, not only in adolescence but throughout the life span, as following biological maturation, and as following a number of phases. These phases are developmental milestones, each containing a conflict to be resolved in order to psychologically mature. When adolescents are involved in the process of individuation, their behavior becomes most tumultuous and unpredictable. Even trained clinicians can find the task of understanding this turbulence difficult, as noted by Blos: "The adolescent in this state presents the clinician with a most delicate task of discrimination as to the transient or permanent or, simply, as the pathognomic or normal nature of the respective regressive phenomena" (1979, p. 167). Adolescent turbulence can therefore either be a sign of normal or abnormal development.

The extent to which the adolescent grows in a healthy manner, from Blos's perspective, depends on a variety of factors. They include whether or not earlier developmental conflicts have been successfully resolved and the adolescent's reactions to physiological changes in puberty. Two external factors affecting growth are the adolescent's family and cultural factors, including the mass media. It is clear that, even under the best of circumstances, turbulent times that include acting-out are to be expected from this theoretical perspective. Under unfavorable circumstances, psychological problems can be expected to be more intense or prolonged.

Erikson (1968) also presents adolescence as a developmental period in which there are conflicts to be resolved, upon which healthy adult functioning depends. Unlike Blos and other psychoanalytic writers, however, Erikson de-emphasizes sexual drives, focusing instead on ego functions. Thus, he is concerned with consciousness and the development of self.

His theory posits that there is a sequence of development stages that characterizes normal development. If the conflict that characterizes each stage is successfully resolved, the individual is then able to move on to the next developmental stage. This follows the *epigenetic* principle, referring to the idea that an organism's structure and its developmental sequence are genetically determined. Erikson theorized that there are eight developmental phases, each characterized by interpersonal conflicts, that follow biological development.

Prior to adolescence, the individual has four major conflicts to resolve. The first, *trust versus mistrust,* involves the infant's ability to bond with nurturing parents during the first year of life. As a result of this contact, the child ideally comes to experience security and the beginning of a sense of identity. At approximately eighteen months, when the child's muscle control allows for mobility as well as self-restraint, a conflict regarding *autonomy versus shame and doubt* arises. Hopefully, autonomy prevails and the child at four or five years of age develops a sense of *initiative*, instead of *guilt*, that grows out of successful play. Finally, the child, during early school years, develops a sense of competence as the outcome of the conflict between *industry versus inferiority*.

These first four normative crises re-emerge in adolescence, corresponding to puberty. In order to resolve these re-emerging conflicts, adolescents often have to create adversaries in their lives. Even after these earlier conflicts are resolved, the adolescent must then begin to address identity issues.

The primary adolescent crisis for Erikson concerns the acquisition of a sense of *identity versus confusion*. Typifying this period is role experimentation. Adolescents must develop a sense of bodily identity, not an easy task given the radical changes taking place at the time of puberty. Then, a sense of social roles is often explored, often by consideration of the roles modeled by parents and others. When these conflicts are successfully resolved, the adolescent comes away with a sense of self in terms of sustained loyalties (*fidelity*) and convictions about values (an *ideology*).

Unfortunately, this positive outcome is not always achieved. When a sense of identity is not achieved, one may see identity confusion in which the individual feels lost, with little sense of family or community relationships that allow individuation and separation. Another unhealthy pattern that is often seen involves *negative identity*. In this case, adolescents identify with things that parents, teachers, or society deem undesirable. These adolescents would prefer to be bad or dead than to be lost or controlled by parents' wishes. In sum, Erikson's theory portrays a developmental period that involves problems, even in the best of cases. When the conflicts are not resolved, the confusion or negativity that all adolescents experience may become pronounced or even dominant.

The theories of Blos and Erikson lead one to speculate that the turbulence found in adolescence is a universal phenomenon, thereby resulting in all families in which an adolescent resides. However, a comparison of these theories with a survey of the research on family conflicts suggests that not all families are fraught with conflict (Montemayor, 1983). Montemayor found that conflicts typify adolescence to the extent that there are challenges to the established order. But in some families, conflicts involving adolescents are successfully resolved. This suggests that the *sturm und drang* notion of adolescence may not represent the exclusive, or even the normative, pattern of adolescent development (Powers, Hauser & Kilner, 1989). Families in which there is a child experiencing the dramatic changes in biological, cognitive and emotional functioning typical of adolescents are often able to maintain equilibrium by making concomitant changes in family functioning. Nevertheless, at least as many adolescents have psychiatric problems as do their adult counterparts (Powers, Hauser & Kilner, 1989).

The Scope of the Problem

While theories may shed light on the types of psychological issues with which adolescents wrestle, they cannot convey the magnitude or variety of psychological problems that affect adolescents' emotional well being in contemporary society. Reviews of epidemiological studies on the prevalence of emotional disorders (Brandenburg, Friedman & Silver, 1990; Kazdin, 1989) group children and adolescents together. This makes it difficult to isolate the prevalence for adolescents as a distinct group. Also making this determination difficult is the fact that studies use different terms and criteria for establishing disorder. Nevertheless, while some estimates of psychiatric disturbance among children and youth vary from 5 to 20%, most estimates suggest that approximately 15% of this population have a psychiatric disorder. This number can be translated into suggesting that almost 4 million of the more than 26 million adolescents between the ages of 12 and 19 have emotional problems severe enough to warrant treatment in the United States.

Tuma (1989), in her review of the literature on mental health services for children and youth, summarized prevalence rates for common childhood disorders. The categories she used were taken from the standard diagnostic manual, the DSM-IIIR (APA, 1987) and are summarized in Table 1-1. These figures are for children under the age of 18. Where Tuma indicated a range, the midpoint of that range was used. Omitted were her results for psychophysiological disorders, any of which generally affect less than one percent of the population of adolescents. The estimates for alcohol and drug abuse are for the general population and not children and adolescents, per se. Anxiety and Adjustment Disorders are listed as "frequent" because many, if not most of children exhibit symptoms in these categories sometime during childhood or adolescence. These statistics are intended to be suggestive in that they are global estimates and are not a comprehensive accounting of all disorders. Instead, they point to the possibility that the 15% overall prevalence rate indicated above may be low. They also hint at the variety of problems facing many adolescents and the seriousness of some of their psychiatric problems.

Figure 1-1. Prevalence Rates for Selected Disorders

DSM-IIIR Categories	**Prevalence**
Developmental Disorders	
Mental Retardation	1%
Pervasive Developmental Disorders	<1%
Specific Developmental Disorders	7%
Disruptive Disorders	
ADHD	3%
Conduct Disorder	5%
Alcohol Abuse	13%
Drug Abuse	8%
Emotional Disorders	
Depression	1%
Anxiety Disorders	frequent
Adjustment Disorders	frequent

from Mental Health Services for Children: The State of the Art. *American Psychologist* by June Tuma, p. 189. Copyright © 1989 by the American Psychological Association. Adapted with permission.

Sometimes numbers cannot convey the extent of a problem. It may be easier to understand the importance of adolescent psychological problems by looking at an index of psychopathology—suicide. A Center for Disease Control survey, recently reported by the press, found that more than one of every four (27%) high school students seriously thought of killing themselves during the prior year (Dayton Daily News, September 20, 1991). Moreover, one of every six high schools students had a specific plan, and one of every twelve tried suicide one or more times during the prior year. The suicide rate for adolescents has tripled in the last 30 years and is now the third leading cause of death (behind accidents and homicide) among adolescents (Berman & Jobes, 1991). Clearly, adolescents experience numerous, often severe, & sometimes life-threatening mental health problems. Let us now turn to how these problems are addressed by the current service delivery system.

Tuma (1989) presents data on the utilization of mental health services for children and youth. Fewer than 1% of this population receives treatment in hospital or residential treatment centers and approximately 5% receives outpatient mental health services. She found that "70% to 80% of children in need may not be getting appropriate mental health services" (Tuma, 1989, p. 190). In conclusion, not only are there millions of adolescents in need of mental health services, the majority of them are not being served.

One solution is to expand the range of settings in which adolescents are served. Currently, the primary service settings remain inpatient and outpatient settings, with the former including both hospitals and residential treatment centers. There are a limited number of hospital beds for adolescent psychiatric care, partially due to the movement to deinstitutionalize public psychiatric hospitals. Although there has been an increase in adolescent beds in private psychiatric hospitals, the cost of inpatient stays in these facilities is often prohibitively high.

Residential treatment centers, like hospitals, are restrictive settings in that the adolescent is removed from the home and some level of control is placed on one's ability to leave the facility. These treatment centers are not hospitals and can range from large institutions to small facilities that resemble group homes. While they are intended to serve emotionally disturbed individuals, they often exclude those most difficult to treat and offer fewer mental health services than may be available in other settings. Here the milieu is the primary mode of treatment.

Outpatient settings include community mental health centers, private clinics and private practices. Because outpatient services are in the community, the adolescent is not separated from family, friends or peers. This is desirable for most adolescents, except when problems with the system are intractable and maintain dysfunctional behavior. It is also a less restrictive and less costly alternative to inpatient care.

A less utilized and more recent alternative to both inpatient and outpatient settings is partial hospitalization. As an intermediate setting, partial hospitalization involves more restrictiveness than outpatient settings, but does not involve 24 hour care. Partial hospitalization can involve day treatment, sometimes at a school, in which the patient receives treatment during the day and goes home at night.

While traditional inpatient and outpatient settings or more recent combinations of the two can provide needed services to many adolescents, others are not served at all or are not well served. As previously mentioned, the majority of adolescents in need do not receive services. There may be many reasons for this: services may not be easily accessed by adolescents because of geographic location, cost, stigma, waiting lists, etc. The solution is not just that we need more of the same traditional services; rather, while more services are needed, with easier accessibility to them, different services are also needed. Moreover, there are limitations to services provided in traditional settings that may result in adolescents not being treated as effectively as possible.

Limitations to Traditional Services

In addition to problems with access to and availability of mental health services, there are limitations inherent in the provision of traditional services for adolescents. It should be apparent from our previous discussion of traditional services that there is a limited range of services available for most youth. Most delivery systems offer outpatient and inpatient services, with few options. This is exemplified by the services reimbursable under most insurance plans, where only inpatient and outpatient services are generally covered. While there are some adolescents in need of the structure and restrictiveness of inpatient hospital psychiatric programs, many adolescents are placed in these programs because they are in need of more intensive or restrictive services than may be available in outpatient settings while still not needing as many restrictions as with inpatient psychiatric care. That is, the lack of a full range of options may lead some adolescents to be placed in more restrictive settings than is necessary. This fact was borne out during the first Wilderness Therapy Program trips, when adolescent inpatients from acute psychiatric hospital units were taken into remote wilderness settings. Not only did the vast majority of residents function well in this out-of-doors setting, but, in general, changes for participants during the trip were more rapid than during other phases of their hospitalization (Berman & Anton, 1988). Based on these findings, one could question the need for the restrictiveness of inpatient psychiatric care for some adolescents being cared for in that setting.

Another limitation of inpatient services is that, like many other forms of hospitalization, they encourage people to be "patients"—docile and compliant—and may even contribute to learned helplessness (Seligman, 1975). Learned helplessness occurs when events are uncontrollable outcomes of our behaviors. Stated otherwise, a person will learn to be helpless when responses and outcomes are no longer paired and the person's behavior is independent of the reinforcements that follow. This can lead the person to give up trying to influence the environment. Docility, hopelessness and depression can ensue. However, when the out-of-doors is used as the medium for providing therapy, each person must take responsibility for self as well as others. There are direct, immediate consequences for one's own behavior. For example, when setting up a tent in the face of an impending storm, participants are reinforced for cooperating with their partners (the tent goes up faster) and for following the instructions of staff (the tent will be set up where the drainage is good).

Adolescents are often difficult to treat in outpatient counseling (Saffer & Naylor, 1988). For the process of counseling to be successful, most approaches require the client to be reflective, verbal, and disclosive. These propensities are foreign to many adolescents in need of counseling. Many of them come from families in which communication is problematic, making for strained dialogue in the therapist's office. Then again, most adolescents are reluctant to see a "therapist" because of issues of trust or because they feel forced into counseling by their parents. Another factor that makes counseling difficult is the fact that adolescents tend to use the defense mechanisms of displacement, in the form of motor action, and denial, reflected in statements like "I don't know" or "I don't care," both of which make talking in a counselor's office threatening.

There are two other difficulties encountered by many adolescents in counseling that should be presented before ending this discussion on limitations. First, most outpatient counseling occurs in 50 minute blocks of time, in an office, once a week. This type of setup can present impediments to growth for adolescents who need time to learn to trust or warm up to a therapist or who need a more intensive therapy experience than these relatively short, infrequent sessions. Second, many adolescents have grown up in a dysfunctional environment in which their behavior is "normal." Thus, they are unable to see that they have problems, primarily because their behavior is maintained by their environment. These limitations hinder efforts to help adolescents change.

Wilderness Therapy

The limitations cited above can be overcome by providing counseling in a different manner. The use of an out-of-doors setting, with a group of adolescents, utilizing adventure education activities and group therapy, over a number of days, or in a number of sessions, overcomes most of these limitations. This "wilderness therapy" experience is at the same time more intense than most outpatient settings and less restrictive than inpatient settings. It separates participants from environments that foster and maintain dysfunctional behavior. It is action oriented, provides immediacy of feedback, and enhances taking responsibility for oneself. At the same time, it depends on interdependence among group members and staff, and the development of effective communication skills.

Problems brought to the program by adolescents (depression, isolation, aggression, etc.) usually become apparent in the process of engaging in activities of the program and are processed as they occur. In this way, when problems occur, they are confronted and resolved in an attempt to enhance daily living on the trail—a more palatable alternative to traditional counseling, which often becomes aversive because both the therapist and therapy become associated with the constant dredging up of problems.

At first glance it may appear that the notions of therapy and wilderness are mutually exclusive, but that is only because therapy is usually conceptualized in terms of its setting (hospital, clinic, office) and not the process involved. Therapy involves a professional relationship in which there is planned change toward desired goals in order to alleviate psychological problems. Viewed in this way, there is no reason why therapy cannot occur in a variety of settings, including the out-of doors. In fact, recent persuasive critiques of the mental health delivery model (Tuma, 1989) have recommended alternative locations for service provision (e.g., within the educational system).

"Wilderness" is a rather ambiguous word. When reference is made to wilderness, it can be literally or metaphorically. Literal definitions attempt to define wilderness in terms of tracts of land with certain characteristics. Other definitions attempt to capture a state of mind. These latter definitions use wilderness as a metaphor for certain experiences or feeling states.

One widely cited definition of wilderness comes from Robert Marshall (1930, p. 141):

> a region which contains no permanent inhabitants, possesses no possibility of conveyance by any mechanical means and is sufficiently spacious that a person in crossing it must have the experience of sleeping out. The dominant attributes of such an area are: first, that it requires any one who lives in it to depend exclusively on his own effort for survival; and second, that it preserves as nearly as possible the primitive environment. This means that all roads, power transportation and settlements are barred. But trails and temporary shelters, which were common long before the advent of the white race, are entirely permissible.

Marshall, like many of the preservationists to follow him, would seem to be trying to achieve a certain state of mind by describing land that has certain characteristics. A person traveling in such an area would see few if any people living there; other people seen would be transient. In having to "sleep out," one would be close to the ground and, presumably, more connected to nature than in the outside world. The area would be "primitive," requiring the travelers to live on their own and travel on trails, without power. The essence of Marshall's definition is for those seeking the wilderness to retreat from the outside world, living as the aboriginal people did, close to nature and depending on their own skills. Clearly, Marshall is trying to distill the essence of the relationship primitive people had with the land into a workable definition so that we can share that experience.

A literal definition of wilderness is as a legally defined area of land so designated by Congressional act. The Wilderness Act of 1964 (Public Law 88-577) defines wilderness as:

> an area where the earth and its community of life are untrammeled by man, where man himself is a visitor who does not remain....(1) [it] appears to have been affected primarily by the forces of nature, with the imprint of man's work substantially unnoticeable; (2) has outstanding opportunities for solitude or a primitive and unconfined type of recreation; (3) ...is of sufficient size...; [and] (4) may also contain ecological, geological, or other features of scientific, educational, scenic, or historical value.

This definition is largely consistent with Marshall's, but is a noteworthy compromise of it. For example, whereas Marshall seems to be advocating for temporary shelters that may be erected and allowed to remain, the Wilderness Act would seem to disallow shelters because they leave noticeable "imprints" of the passersby. The Wilderness Act not only literally defines the physical aspects of wilderness but also attempts to be a figurative definition of the spirit of the wilderness.

Attempts have also been made to define wilderness in terms of inner experience. Brown (1982, p. xi) uses the term in a figurative way:

> Wilderness as a modern term is relative. To the white man when he first came to this country, wilderness was anything that wasn't directly under his control. The wilderness was full of savages and wild beasts. When I use the term "wilderness," I use it as a convenient reference but I don't believe that land uninhabited by man is 'wild.' That kind of land is actually "natural."

Brown (1982, p. xvi) clearly indicates the psychological experience he looks for in this "natural" land when he says, "Seek the wilderness, for there is peace." Scott (1974), writing about the "psychology of wilderness experience," makes reference to altered states of consciousness and peak experiences as characteristics of the wilderness. This approach suggests that, besides the untrammeled earth where people are visitors, other environments may also enhance personal growth, provide a sense of solitude, and help one find peace.

When we refer to the wilderness, we do so with both literal and figurative definitions in mind. To explain this further, we accept definitions, like those of Marshall and the Wilderness Act, as defining some, but not all, of the environments that can create the positive effects that are referred to in figurative definitions of the wilderness. Thus, any outdoor environment that fosters positive change and allows one to gain a sense of peace may be an acceptable location for wilderness therapy, although it is probably easier to find a place of this sort in unspoiled, natural environments where one can get away from the urban, crowded, mechanized world.

In addition to the use of wilderness environments, another characteristic of wilderness therapy is that it uses outdoor, recreational and/or adventure education activities. Many varied terms have been used to describe these activities, with Ewert (1989, p. 2) listing some of these terms: "adventure recreation, high adventure, natural challenge activities, outdoor pursuits, and risk education." He goes on to define these activities as: "A variety of ... activities utilizing an interaction with the natural environment, that contain elements of real or apparent danger, in which the outcome, while uncertain, can be influenced by the participant and the circumstance" (Ewert, 1989, p. 6).

For ease of communication, we will refer to these activities as "outdoor adventure pursuits." Our own use of these activities focuses on physical challenge in the natural environment, group cooperation, and the opportunity for personal growth. We try to eliminate "real dangers" and "uncertain" outcomes because we do not want to expose our clients to unnecessary risks. Instead, we believe that personal change can be stimulated by introducing activities in which there are perceived risks but a very low probability of actual physical harm. This view is consistent with the model of adventure offered by Priest (1993) in which he defines adventure as involving a higher level of competence than risk. For this reason, we feel comfortable with activities like backcountry backpacking and flat-water or mild white-water kayaking or canoeing (after proper training). We also use adventure games and activities to enhance group cohesiveness, improve self-esteem, develop problem-solving skills, and develop an increased sense of trust. Rohnke (1984, 1989) has authored two books filled with these sorts of activities.

In conclusion, wilderness therapy involves the use of traditional therapy techniques, especially those for group therapy, in out-of-door settings, utilizing outdoor adventure pursuits and other activities to enhance growth. Wilderness therapy is a methodical, planned approach to working with troubled youth, although we envision a broader range of applications to other populations. To clarify this last statement, we want to emphasize that wilderness therapy is not taking troubled adolescents into the woods so that they will feel better. It involves the careful selection of potential candidates based on a clinical assessment and the creation of an individual treatment plan for each participant. Involvement in outdoor adventure pursuits should occur under the direction of skilled leaders, with activities aimed at creating changes in target behaviors. Finally, the provision of group psychotherapy by qualified professionals, with an evaluation of individuals' progress and program effectiveness, are critical components of the program.

Overview of Subsequent Chapters

In the next chapter, we will trace society's enchantment with the wilderness. The chapter begins with an historical sketch of early American views toward the wilderness and how they changed with the advent of the Romantic movement. This movement will be discussed, and examples of art, literature, philosophy and poetry will be presented. Two controversial newspaper series at the beginning of this century will be revealed. The origins of our current wilderness ethic will then be shared in the context of modern historical events.

Chapter 3 reviews early programs that utilized the wilderness as a means of promoting healthy youth by virtue of the camp setting and the activities in which the youth engaged. These programs initially took the form of camps, and some can be traced back more than 100 years. This camping movement was followed, around the turn of the century, by the creation of Boys Clubs, the Boy Scouts, and then, the Girl Scouts. The origins of "tent therapy" will then be explored, along with other early programs designed as treatment for those with emotional and/or behavioral problems. This movement was gaining momentum by the 1950s, culminating in the burgeoning of programs like Outward Bound. The theoretical underpinnings of these programs are discussed.

Programs that are therapeutic in nature and more sophisticated in approach began to appear in the 1970s. These more recent programs are presented in Chapter 4. They range from programs in hospitals to those in mental health centers. The first reports of the success of these programs were anecdotal, and we will explore some of these reports. Then we offer a comprehensive review of the research on the efficacy of wilderness therapy programs. Consideration will be given to the problems inherent in this type of field research.

In Chapter 5, the variety of wilderness programs will be presented. There are mental health programs, most of which are designed for troubled adolescents. These programs are to be found in hospitals, residential treatment centers, and outpatient counseling settings. Some are designed for the treatment of specific psychiatric disorders, like substance abuse, while most are more general in the problems they are targeted to treat. Another area of programming concerns court programs serving delinquent youth. Examples of these programs are provided to give a feeling for the types of programming available in this area. School-based programs represent a third type of program. These programs are primarily concerned with experiential learning and general gains in areas of self-esteem and leadership. A more recent area of development includes programs falling within the realm of health-care related programs in that they offer services to those with life-threatening disorders, like cancer, or as an alternative to a hospital-based treatment program for alcohol abuse, or as an adventure-based program for the physically challenged. Finally, we briefly mention programs that deal with executives, enrichment, and other special problems and populations.

The chapters to this point indicate numerous changes that accrue to participants as a result of experiencing a wilderness program, but there are few explanatory models for these changes. Chapter 6 takes a look at theoretical approaches to wilderness therapy. The chapter begins with a rationale for the importance of theories and criteria for evaluating theories. A number of theories are then reviewed, starting with the environment as serving a restorative function. Social learning theory is then considered, with emphasis on modeling and observational learning. Theories that encompass explanations of self-esteem are then reviewed, followed by related theories concerning self-actualization. We next turn to transpersonal theories, epitomized by the theory of Jung. Systems theory is then discussed, with its ability to be used in conjunction with other theories. The chapter concludes with an evaluation of these theories.

By this point in the book, we hope that you are intrigued about the possibility of integrating wilderness therapy programs into your own practice, or, for those of you who have programs, to consider changes in your programs. To help accomplish this, Chapter 7 presents a discussion of program design, development and implementation. The chapter opens with consideration of program needs and the goals of the program. Selection criteria for participants and staff are a part of this discussion. With regard to staff, we present a model for the bifurcation of wilderness therapy staff. The concept of treatment planning is presented as an integral part of the planning process for wilderness programs. Attention is then focused on the components of trip planning: the where, when, and how aspects of the trip. Methods for conducting therapy groups are discussed, along with other techniques for change, with consideration to maintaining changes once participants return home. The final topic of this chapter concerns critical issues for most programs—marketing and funding.

It is not enough to offer programs without an evaluation of the effectiveness of that program. Unfortunately, many outdoor programs lack this component, the topic of Chapter 8. After the basic concepts of, and the rationale for, program evaluation are discussed, we present some ideas for the evaluation of wilderness programs. The general approach to program evaluation is quantitative, but we argue that much of the richness of wilderness programs is lost with this approach. To overcome this shortcoming, we discuss qualitative methods and a method for integrating both quantitative and qualitative approaches to evaluation.

Chapter 9 serves as both a summary of the concepts of wilderness therapy and a discussion of critical issues in this field. These issues include the professionalization of wilderness leaders and the certification of programs. This will be difficult to accomplish, however, unless more attention is spent defining the scope of the field. Finally, we assert research must be an integral component of wilderness programming in order for the field to achieve the level of credibility it seeks.

We end this book with an extensive compendium of programs offering varieties of wilderness programs throughout the country. These offerings are organized into the following categories: mental health, enrichment, court, school, and health programs.

We now invite you to sit back, turn the page, and continue on this trek with us. Not unlike a wilderness trip, we have planned our trip, know our itinerary, and hope that those who share the journey with us do so with a love of the outdoors and a dedicated desire to work with those in need.

References

Aries, P. (1962). *Centuries of childhood: A social history of family life.* New York: Vintage.

Berman, A. & Jobes, D. (1991). *Adolescent suicide: Assessment & intervention.* Washington, DC: American Psychological Association.

Berman, D. & Anton, M. (1988). A wilderness therapy program as an alternative to adolescent psychiatric hospitalization. *Residential Treatment for Children & Youth, 5,* 41-53.

Blos, P. (1979). *The adolescent passage: Developmental issues.* New York: International Universities Press.

Brandenburg, N., Friedman, R. & Silver, R. (1990). The epidemiology of childhood psychiatric disorders: Prevalence findings from recent studies. *Journal of the American Academy of Child & Adolescent Psychiatry, 29,* 76-83.

Brown, T. (1982). *The search: The continuing story of the tracker.* New York: Berkley Books.

Erikson, E. H. (1968). *Identity: Youth & crisis.* New York: Norton.

Ewert, A. E. (1989). *Outdoor adventure pursuits: Foundations, models, & theories.* Columbus, OH: Publishing Horizons.

Garcia, N. & Travis, N. (1985). The adolescent phase of the family life cycle. In M. Mirkin & S. Koman (Eds.), *Handbook of adolescents and family therapy.* New York: Gardner.

Hall, G. S. (1916). *Adolescence.* New York: Appleton..

Kazdin, A. (1989). Developmental psychopathology: Current research, issues, and directions. *American Psychologist, 44,* 180-187.

Marshall, R. (1930). The problem of the wilderness. *Scientific Monthly, 30,* 141-147.

Montemayor, R. (1983). Parents and adolescents in conflict: All families some of the time and some families most of the time. *Journal of Early Adolescence, 3,* 83-103.

Platt, A. (1977). *The child savers: The invention of delinquency.* Chicago: University of Chicago.

Powers, S. I., Hauser, S. T. & Kilner, L. A. (1989). Adolescent mental health. *American Psychologist, 44,* 200-208.

Priest, S. (1993). A new model for risk taking. *Journal of Experiential Education, 16,* 50-53.

Rohnke, K. (1984). *Silver bullets: A guide to initiative problems, adventure games and trust activities.* Dubuque, IA: Kendall/Hunt.

Rohnke, K. (1989). *Cowtails and cobras: A guide to games, initiatives, ropes and adventure curriculum.* Dubuque, IA: Kendall/Hunt.

Rothman, D. (1980). *Conscience and convenience: The asylum and its alternatives in progressive America.* Boston: Little, Brown.

Saffer, J. B. & Naylor, K. A. ((1987). Difficulties encountered in the treatment of outpatient adolescents. *Adolescence, 22,* 143-147.

Scott, N. R. (1974). Wilderness experience. *Natural Resources Journal, 14,* 231-237.

Seligman, M. E. (1975). *Helplessness: On depression, development and death..* San Francisco: W. H. Freeman.

Tuma, J. (1989). Mental health services for children: The state of the art. *American Psychologist, 44,* 188-199.

Chapter Two ▽

The Wilderness Ethic

In this chapter, we will explore changing societal attitudes toward the wilderness. Modern views of the wilderness will be traced back to early American settlers' views. They saw the wilderness as a harsh and threatening environment, with parallels to their primitive conceptions of evil. As America came to be settled, it was viewed as a vast area of richness to be cultivated and conquered. We will then turn to the period of the mid-1800s, when the Romantic view flourished and the wilderness came to be seen as cleansing and divine. This created a clash of values between those who wanted to conserve the wilderness and those who viewed the wilderness not as an end unto itself, but still as a dark and foreboding environment, to be used for our material needs. This controversy is explored as it was typified by events on both sides of the continent before World War I in news stories of the damming of the Tuolumne River in California and the adventures of the first popular survivalist. These stories captured American hearts, paving the way for the creation of protected lands and a reverence for the wilderness.

For most people, it is hard to imagine that societal concerns for the wilderness predate the first Earth Day in 1970. In that year, during a time of war protests and an undercurrent of social revolution, concerns about the environment were espoused by a small number of people. Proponents of a concern for the environment and the wilderness were more likely than not to be on the fringes, rather than the mainstream of society.

Edward Abbey's "The Monkey Wrench Gang" (1975) typifies this movement. The story involves an unlikely collection of environmentally concerned individuals who try to save the wilderness by employing such unorthodox principles as pouring sugar in the fuel tanks of earth moving machinery in order to stop what most thought was "progress." The story and the values of the Monkey Wrench gang continue in a recently published sequel, "Hayduke Lives" (Abbey, 1990). Evidence that Abbey has had a lasting impression is found in the fact that the methods of his gang have now been recognized as "monkeywrenching." Strong (1990) suggests that Earth Day was an outgrowth of a movement that included Congressional support for a number of acts—the Clean Air Act, Clean Water Act, Wilderness Act, National Environmental Policy Act—and even the creation of the Environmental Protection Agency. In his view, "Earth Day (1970), celebrated on college campuses across the nation, provided a catalyst for environmental awareness and legislation" (p. xvii).

The second Earth Day, in 1990, was an event that was celebrated by a much more representative sample of the population. Even Abbey's nemeses, major corporations, touted environmental consciousness with ads of wilderness scenes and vanishing oil tankers. They were appealing to the vast number of people who see themselves as advocates for keeping the environment unspoiled.

It would be easy, but erroneous, for one to assume, based on events like Earth Day, that society's interest in the wilderness and the environment represents a current movement, or that conflicts about preservation versus utilization represent new debates. To better understand the current movement, it is important to place our conceptions within their historical context.

Early American Conceptions

The New World was explored and then colonized because of the richness it promised in both material goods and freedom. The early settlers, however, experienced this new land as a forbidding wilderness that threatened their very survival. In this vein, the Jamestown colonists came in 1607, searching for gold, but quickly had to focus on survival. Their survival was tenuous for years, until the cultivation of tobacco gave them a viable commodity to trade and an infusion of new settlers arrived, including women and slaves (Nivens & Commager, 1967).

Leaving the religious persecution of Europe for the new world in search of religious freedom, the Pilgrims, contrary to popular belief, landed in Provincetown (not Plymouth) in December of 1620. The winter was so harsh that half of their group died. The Pilgrims finally travelled across the bay to Plymouth, seeking a more hospitable environment. William Bradford was a passenger on the Mayflower and the first Governor of the Massachusetts Bay colony. Contemplating this new land and the need to move from Provincetown, he wrote (Bradford, 1952, p. 62):

> But here I...pause and stand half amazed at this poor people's present condition...they had no friends to welcome them, no inns...no houses.... And for the season, it was winter, and those that know the winters of that country know them to be sharp and violent and subject to cruel and fierce storms, dangerous to travel to known places, much more to search an unknown coast. Besides, what could they see but a hideous and desolate wilderness full of wild beasts and wild men?

Within ten years, hundreds of settlers left England for the Massachusetts Bay colony, which was still viewed as wilderness, but less inhospitable than experienced by the Pilgrims. Hundreds of Puritans settled in Salem and no fewer than 11 ships with 900 settlers settled the colony in the spring of 1630. By this time, at least some of the coastal regions of Massachusetts were no longer viewed as wilderness, unlike other areas just miles away. For example, the noted historians, Nevins and Commager, commenting on the expulsion of Roger Williams from the Massachusetts Bay colony, refer to his being exiled to the wilderness: "Roger Williams, a minister of Salem who courageously taught the separation of Church and state, with other radical views, was driven into the Rhode Island wilderness" (1969, p. 7).

This early image of wilderness was one of foreboding. Early America was a wilderness, where one found wild lands and animals. This was also the land of native Americans, who were initially viewed as pathetic creatures who were in need of the white man's religion and culture. But as threatened Indians defended themselves and their land, they came to be viewed, along with the rest of the environment, as a threat. The wilderness was viewed as an enemy to be vanquished, and once conquered, its riches could be taken. Trees were felled, ground cultivated, Indians defeated and pushed west. Discussing this westward expansion, Huth stated (1990, p. 2): "Then the breaking of ground was all important and the broadaxe considered the most essential tool. Later, the axe was even accepted as the appropriate symbol of the early American attitude toward nature".

Thus, we see early conceptions of wilderness as a dark and dangerous setting, at first to be struggled against merely for survival. As settlers gained a foothold in the New World, the wilderness became a place to be conquered and tamed. When this was accomplished in the eighteenth and nineteenth centuries, the newly created urban areas were often found to be dirty, dangerous places with few opportunities. This led to the beginning of change in views of the wilderness and receptivity to European Romanticism.

Romanticism

The Romantic movement began in Europe in the eighteenth century, with the tenets of this movement revealed in the art and literature of the time. An example of Romanticism in art is presented by Rosenblum (1975) who suggests that Caspar David Friedrich's "Monk by the Sea," painted in 1809, is the first work of this movement. It depicts a monk standing in the foreground on a beach, with an empty sea behind him. The largest part of the painting is of a dark sky, broken by lighter clouds at the top of the work. Rosenblum describes this work thusly (1975, pp. 12-14):

[It] strikes an alien, melancholic note, strange not only in the presence of so dense, so haunting, and so uninterrupted an expanse of somber, blue-grey light above a low horizon, but in the disturbing absence of any of the expected component of conventional marine painting...the picture is daringly empty...devoid of everything but the lonely confrontation of a single figure, a Capuchin monk, with the hypnotic simplicity of a completely unbroken horizon line, and above it a no less primal and potentially infinite extension of gloomy, hazy sky...the individual is pitted against, or confronted by the overwhelming, incomprehensible immensity of the universe, as if the mysteries of religion had left the rituals of church and synagogue and had been relocated in the natural world.

Aspects of Romanticism that can be seen in this painting[1] and characterize the movement include that which is "strange, remote, solitary, and mysterious" (Nash, 1967, p. 47). Other important concepts include the enormity of the environment and the association of God and the wilderness. There is even the appeal of the primitive in Romanticism. Romanticism was popularized in urban areas by the educated and cosmopolitan. It received impetus from the galleries and libraries of major cities, first in Europe and then America. It is ironic that the wilderness was transformed from its earlier dark, evil and dangerous image to the Romantic notion of being attractive and even Godly, not by the individuals who travelled in it, but by those inhabiting its antithesis.

Other paintings characterizing this movement include American works, such as "Niagara Falls" by Frederic Church (1857) and Albert Bierstadt's "The Oregon Trail" (1869). Church's "Niagara Falls" reflects the majesty of the wilderness in its sheer size (62" X 112"). Bierstadt helped popularize the west with his paintings, with their suggestion of the deification of wilderness travel.[2]

---

[1]"Monk by the Sea,"by David Caspar Friedrich, 1808-10, Staatliche Museen zu Berlin—PreBischer Kulturbesitz Nationalgalerie. Reproduced by permission.

The Romantic movement and its relationship to the wilderness is also evident in the literature of the time. While this body of writings has as its roots the works of European authors such as Chateaubriand and de Tocqueville, both of whom visited and then wrote about the American wilderness, there is a rich tradition of American writings about this period. There were travelogues, monthly magazines, and novels and poems that depicted the wilderness from within the Romantic framework. Consider the poems of Whitman and Longfellow, the writings of Emerson, or the novels by Cooper, all of whom were contemporaries in the first post Revolutionary War generation.

Longfellow's writings during the middle nineteenth century reflect the growing national interest of the time in our wilder, more aboriginal past (Canby, 1967). The poem that most enhanced Longfellow's reputation was Hiawatha. Longfellow used Indian legends, replete with factual errors, but this did not seem to matter to the public, captured as it was by the romantic images conjured up in the telling of stories. An example of the Romantic notion of deism in nature is conveyed in the following lines, taken from "Hiawatha," originally published in 1855 (Longfellow, 1967, p. 197):

---

[2]"The Oregon Trail,"by Albert Bierstadt, 1869. 31x49 oil on canvas. Acquired 1946 from Vose Galleries, Boston. Obtained from and reproduced by permission from The Butler Institute of American Art, Youngstown, OH.

Once, in days no more remembered,
Ages nearer the beginning,
When the heavens were closer to us,
And the Gods were more familiar,
In the North-land lived a hunter....

Other Romantic concepts, such as the healing qualities of the wilderness,
the knowledge conveyed therein, or the mysticism of nature are suggested in
this passage from "Hiawatha" (Longfellow, 1967, p. 221):

Froth then issues Hiawatha,
Wandered eastward, wandered westward,
Teaching men the use of simples
And the antidotes to poisons,
And the cure of all diseases.
Thus was first made known to mortals
All the mystery of Medemin,
All the sacred art of healing.

Whitman, too, popularized the appeal of the wilderness. He gave us
images of the peace to be achieved by leaving civilization behind, as revealed
in this passage from "Song of Myself," originally published in 1855
(Whitman, 1940, p. 43):

Alone in the wilds and mountains I hunt,
Wandering amazed at my lightness and glee,
In the late afternoon choosing a safe spot to pass the night,
Kindling a fire and broiling the fresh-kill'd game,
Falling asleep on the gather'd leaves with my dog and gun by my side.

In leaving the cities behind, and heading westward, Whitman suggested
that happiness, and not hardship, would result for those pioneers who braved
the wilderness. One wonders how many idealistic pioneers were caught
unaware when they travelled west expecting to find the idyllic images
portrayed by Whitman, as in this passage from "Song of the Open Road"
(Whitman, 1940, p. 5):

I think heroic deeds were all conceiv'd in the open air, and all free
    poems also,
I think I could stop here myself and do miracles,
I think whatever I shall meet on the road I shall like, and whoever
    beholds me shall like me,
I think whoever I see must be happy

Turning from poetry to literature, one only needs to look at the writings of James Fenimore Cooper to see how the wilderness was popularized. As a biographer of Cooper put it, "There is no doubt that, as a man of thought and feeling, more than any other writer of his generation, Cooper understood the time and place in which he lived and gave them voice and meaning" (Spiller, 1965, p. 5). If this is indeed the case, Cooper's writings reflected an interest in the wilderness.

In 1850, Cooper published *The Leather-Stocking Tales,* a collection of five stories about a wilderness scout, Natty Bumppo, also known as Leather Stocking. These five stories had previously been published as *The Pioneers* (1823), *The Last of the Mohicans* (1826), *The Prairie* (1827), *The Pathfinder* (1840) and *The Deerslayer* (1841). The hero of these stories, Bumppo, was depicted as skillful and at ease in the wilderness. The stories are themselves "a dramatization of the past... And they are candid efforts at mythmaking about the common man in America" (Van Nostrand, 1961, p. vi).

Also to be considered are the works of American writers cum philosophers, such as Thoreau. Thoreau was certainly not the only influential writer about the value of the wilderness, but he is perhaps the best known Romantic writer on this subject, even more so in recent times because of current attempts to save Walden Pond as a protected sanctuary from the hands of developers. It was Thoreau who said, "in wildness is the preservation of the world."

Thoreau, born in 1817, grew up in Concord, Massachusetts, the neighbor of Ralph Waldo Emerson. Emerson was influential in the development of Thoreau's views of the wilderness. Emerson was at the center of American Transcendentalism, espousing the importance of a spiritual reality that corresponds, and yet is higher than, physical reality. Emerson established Brook Farm as an experimental cooperative devoted to the Transcendental ideal that nature symbolizes the spirit. Surely, the fact that he lived with and worked for Emerson for a number of years was influential in Thoreau's own sense of reverence for the wilderness (Krutch, 1962).

Perhaps best known for *Walden Pond,* Thoreau actually only lived there for two years, and that was interrupted by at least one extended trip to Maine. But while in the small cabin he built there, he began to write about concepts that are still of great significance to us today. This book contains four main themes (Krutch, 1982): (1) most people lead desperate lives that are maintained in silence; (2) this condition is brought about by a fallacy that has to do with materialism; (3) happiness comes from leading a simple life close to nature; and (4) leading this kind of life results in the understanding of higher, spiritual principles. Thoreau's famous quotation about his reason for going to Walden Pond suggests many of the aforementioned themes (1854/1982, pp. 172-173):

I went to the woods because I wished to live deliberately, to front only the essential facts of life, and to see if I could not learn what it had to teach, and not, when I came to die, discover that I had not lived. I did not wish to live what was not life, living is so dear, nor did I wish to practice resignation, unless it was quite necessary. I wanted to live deep and suck out all the marrow of life, to live sturdily and Spartan-like as to put to rout all that was not life, to cut a broad swath and shave close, to drive life into a corner, and reduce it to its lowest terms, and, if it proved to be mean, why then to get the whole and genuine meanness of it, and publish its meanness to the world; or if it were sublime, to know it by experience, and be able to give a true account of it in my next excursion.

Thoreau's style may have been the impetus to a whole genre of outdoor writers who have extolled the virtues of the wilderness in their stories of life and travel in the untrammeled out-of-doors. A book on the lives and writings of a number of these authors, including Thoreau, Muir, Sevice, Marshall, Rustrum and Olson has been written by Vickery (1986).

As the popularity of outdoor writers grew, there was a concomitant movement in favor of governmental intervention to preserve the wilderness (Nash, 1967). Thus, the Hot Springs of Arkansas were designated as a national reservation in 1832. In 1864, President Abraham Lincoln signed the federal legislation granting to the state of California the Yosemite Valley and the Mariposa Grove of sequoias "for public use, resort, and recreation" as a park (Runte, 1991). While the Yosemite Valley area was small (only 10 square miles), its designation as a park area led to the proposal of other areas to be so preserved. An area around the Yellowstone River in Montana Territory was set aside in 1872 as Yellowstone National Park. This was accomplished largely through the efforts of a small group of eastern intellectuals, one of whom, Nathaniel Langford, published two articles in a national magazine advocating for the creation of the park. This created public interest that was supported by a Congressional act designating the region as a "public park" to be enjoyed by visitors at the same time it was to be preserved. The park area set aside was over two million acres.

In 1885, approximately 700,000 acres was set aside in the Adirondacks of New York as a "forest preserve." The public was behind this proposal as well, not only because this area was widely written about for its unspoiled wilderness, but also because it was believed to ensure the watershed to protect water supplies and river commerce (Nash, 1967). Uniform support for the preservation of the wilderness did not continue unabated. Soon a conflict began to stir between forces for preservation and those who advocated for the use of the environment to fulfill the public's increasing material needs. As this conflict grew, so, too, did the public's interest in issues concerning the wilderness. Long before television and radio provided us with news and entertainment pertaining to nature, the print media carried stories about the wilderness that had mass appeal. A look at two events, on opposite sides of the continent, as depicted by the media prior to the first world war, reveal the extent to which most people were enthralled by the wilderness. These events sparked the public's growing interest about environmental issues.

Hetch Hetchy

In 1913, in California, a debate was raging about the use of a valley, Hetch Hetchy, located in the Sierras, approximately 150 miles from San Francisco. The Tuolumne River ran through Hetch Hetchy Valley. Its scenic beauty made it appealing to nature lovers of the time, while its flow of water presented the potential for generating hydroelectric power and supplying water to the San Francisco area (Nash, 1967).

In the early 1880s, engineers in San Francisco suggested damming Hetch Hetchy to create a reservoir. These efforts seemed foiled when, in 1890, Congress passed an act that created Yosemite National Park and designated Hetch Hetchy as a wilderness area. The future of the area seemed secure. April 14, 1906 was the date of the great earthquake that leveled San Francisco. With it came fires that destroyed much of what the earthquake left standing. This event led city planners to again request the use of Hetch Hetchy as a source of water for the city. From 1907 to 1913, two vocal groups argued about the best use of Hetch Hetchy (Cohen, 1988).

On one side of this argument were men like John Muir, a staunch preservationist. Muir and his friend, Robert Underwood Johnson, Editor of *Century Magazine,* had been influential in lobbying for the bill that was to create Yosemite National Park. Muir was also at the core of a group of professors, lawyers and business leaders who met to discuss the enjoyment and preservation of the wilderness. This group was incorporated as the Sierra Club in 1892. On the other side were men like Gifford Pinchot, who became Chief of the Forest Service in 1905. Pinchot was a utilitarian conservationist, whose view was that the demands of the local community took precedence over other concerns. According to Cohen (1988, p. 23), Pinchot felt that natural resources should be "available to the home-seeker, the prospector and miner, the user of timber, the user of range, and the user of water."

This controversy between preservationists and conservationists was of national proportion. At its center was President Theodore Roosevelt, an ardent lover of the wilderness. During his tenure in office, he spoke to both sides of the issue when, at different times, he referred to: "the fundamental idea of forestry is the perpetuation of forests by use" and, in a seemingly contradictory fashion referred to forests as "preserves for the wild forest creatures" (as cited in Nash, 1967, pp. 162-163). The issue of how to use Hetch Hetchy symbolized the importance of the wilderness conception in the collective American mind of the time. No one could have anticipated the fervor that would surround both sides of the argument, either in terms of the specific issue of Hetch Hetchy or the larger issue regarding the value of the wilderness. Despite the fact that Roosevelt camped in Yosemite in 1903 with Muir and praised the Sierra Club, he chose Pinchot as his principle advisor regarding the use of Hetch Hetchy as a reservoir. Roosevelt was also advised, by a group of consulting engineers, that this was the only viable site for a reservoir.

By the spring of 1908, the granting of a permit made the damming of Hetch Hetchy seem imminent. Those aligning themselves with Muir took their argument to the public. This took shape, over the next 5 years, in the form of articles, speeches and even pamphlets. Magazines like *Outlook* and *Century* published articles by Muir and Johnson on the preservation of wilderness and used Hetch Hetchy as a symbol of this perspective. Others, like J. Horace McFarland of the American Civic Association and Henry Gregory of the American Scenic and Historic Preservation Society, spoke at governmental hearings on the Hetch Hetchy issue. And organizations like the Sierra Club and the Appalachian Mountain Club distributed pamphlets on the prevention of the destruction of Yosemite National Park and the Hetch Hetchy Valley within it (Nash, 1967).

The Hetch Hetchy debate reached a new level of controversy when Woodrow Wilson became president in 1913. A bill was introduced to Congress that would finally clear the way for the dam to be built. In response, the opponents of this bill sent letters and articles to more than 1400 newspapers nationwide, bringing this controversy to every corner of the country. Meanwhile, Congressional hearing and debate continued, ending with a vote passing the bill in September 1913. Subsequent to the bill's passage, Congress still had to approve San Francisco's application to build the dam.

In a final stand against the dam, the debate was taken to the public, primarily through the newspapers. According to Nash (1967, p. 176), "[h]undreds of newspapers throughout the country, including such opinion leaders as the *New York Times,* published editorials on the question, most of which took the side of preservation." This, no doubt, sparked the volumes of mail sent to politicians all over the country, as well as the public protests in settings as diverse as women's groups and college campuses.

Finally, the vote on whether or not to grant San Francisco the right to build the dam was held on December 6, 1913. That morning, a special edition of the *San Francisco Examiner* depicting an idyllic view of the Hetch Hetchy valley as it would look dammed, was placed on the desk of each Senator. This bill passed the Senate that night and was signed into law by President Wilson two weeks later.

Although the preservationists lost the battle to stop the dam from being built, the controversy surrounding it may have contributed to the public's appreciation for the creation of protected lands in America (Cohen, 1988).

Public acceptance of a more preservationist perspective must certainly have been influenced by Muir's writings. A clear example of Muir as the preservationist and romanticist is his article in the January 1908 issue of the Sierra Club Bulletin on Hetch Hetchy:

> It is impossible to overestimate the value of wild mountains and mountain temples as places for people to grow in. They are the greatest of our natural resources, God's best gifts... (1993, p. 58).

John Muir died a year after his defeat on this issue. Cohen (1988, p. 31) maintains that Muir's death "was perceived almost universally as a personal martyrdom." It was as though there was a sense of national guilt to be atoned for after the passage of the dam bill and Muir's death. Certainly, there was rapid growth of organizations like the Sierra Club as a result of this controversy. In this vein, the National Park Service was created in 1916 with the charge of protecting the parks (Wellman, 1987).

Joseph Knowles

The headlines of the Sunday edition of the *Boston Post,* on August 10, 1913, read: "LIKE CAVE MAN, HE DEFIES NATURE." The caption continued: "The Sunday Post Gives Today a First-Hand Account of a Most Extraordinary Experiment Never Before Attempted by Civilized Man—Boston Artist Knowles Tells Here How He Will Live, as Did Our Primitive Ancestors, Without Implements, Clothing, Food or Any Other Aid to Life."

This provocative headline was followed by a series of pictures and articles. In one, there is a report on the physical examination of Knowles by a Harvard professor that also lauds this effort on scientific terms, and references the "getting back to nature movement" and the fact that "[o]ut-of-door life is today being demonstrated as the ideal and natural life for human beings." Centered on the page is a picture of Knowles disrobing before entering the woods six days before, and next to it, a signed statement by witnesses who saw him enter the woods. Another picture shows him naked, entering a forest in Maine.

The challenge taken on by Knowles was to spend 60 days in the woods, with no clothing, food, or human contact. He planned to make his own tools, by which he could make clothing and hunt. Periodically he agreed to send reports and pictures by using charcoal on birch bark, hiding it in a cache to be brought out by a local guide. Interest in the Knowles' story blossomed. He was hunted in the woods by sportsmen who wagered that he could not stay there for two months. After he wrote of catching a bear in a pit and killing it, game wardens also pursued him. Readers found Knowles' reports of how he ate berries, caught fish, made clothes and tanned hides fascinating, leading the circulation of the *Post* to swell (Holbrook, 1948). Editors of the *Post's* rival, William Randolph Hearst's *American,* not to be outdone, attempted to discredit Knowles' solo efforts by reporting that Knowles was actually in a cozy cabin. Other *American* stories reported him in a chateau in Quebec, a hotel in Portland, and in a private home (Kenny, 1987).

Circulation of the *Post* rose to over 400,000 copies. The story was also being followed by papers all over the Northeast. On October 4, 1913, the day Knowles was to emerge from the wilderness, the story was front page news at the *Post.* This story so captivated the public that numerous letters supporting his efforts, and even proposals of marriage were sent to the editors of the *Post*

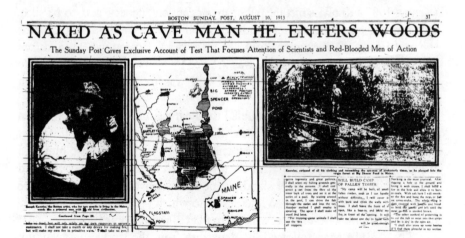

BOSTON SUNDAY POST, AUGUST 10, 1913

NAKED AS CAVE MAN HE ENTERS WOODS

The Sunday Post Gives Exclusive Account of Test That Focuses Attention of Scientists and Red-Blooded Men of Action

TAKES ABSOLUTELY NOTHING WITH HIM

"In fact, the casting off of civilized life will be complete. From the moment when I eat my last breakfast at King and Bartlett Camp I shall be entirely independent of the rest of humanity. I shall accept no aid from any source, unless accident or illness compels me to emerge from the woods, and in that event my experiment would terminate.

"I shall keep a record of time, and on the fourth day of October I shall walk out of the forest at the same point where I parted from civilization. If civilization or accident compels me to seek aid I shall not hesitate to terminate my stay in the woods.

"When I emerge in October I shall be sufficiently clothed to walk the city streets. I shall be as comfortably clothed as any human being. From cap to heels I shall be fitted out with at least one equipment, and may possibly have a variety to suit weather conditions.

"I shall go before medical experts for examination immediately after I come out of the woods. This examination will show the effect of my independent life, and I am willing the doctors shall submit me to any tests.

WILL EMERGE CLOTHED IN SKINS

"I have been through the section of the region in which I shall live. That was 15 years ago, when I guided parties of sportsmen and lived at the hunting camps. Since that time I have never entered the territory. However, I remember its topography, and am told that the section still abounds with game of all kinds and is an excellent forest for my experiment.

"I know that I shall find there conditions that will best suit the conditions of my experiment. It is surrounded in all directions by hunting and fishing camps on the many lakes that border my domain. I am unable to show myself in any direction, for every camping party in the region is aware of my experiment and the conditions under which I am to live. That fact will aid me to sustain my claim, in the event I complete my experiment without accident, that I did not seek or accept aid or comfort from those who lived nearest to me.

"I want to be subjected to the most severe observation. I want all doubters to satisfy their curiosity, and am open to any observation that will not interfere with my efforts to secure the food, skins and other things which I shall need.

LIKE CAVE MAN, HE DEFIES NATURE

The Sunday Post Gives Today a First-Hand Account of a Most Extraordinary Experiment Never Before Attempted by Civilized Man---Boston Artist Knowles Tells Here Just How He Will Live, as Did Our Primitive Ancestors, Without Implements, Clothing, Food or Any Other Aid to Life.

NAKED HE PLUNGES INTO MAINE WOODS TO LIVE ALONE TWO MONTHS

Dr. Sargent of Harvard
Lauds Scientific Attempt

(Kenny, 1987). Knowles met the public in Megantic, Quebec—and, to be sure, the press was also there. He returned to Boston on a special train, and greeted the public on "Newspaper Row," that area of Boston where a dozen newspapers had their offices. Joe was greeted by a crowd that some estimate might have been as large as 400,000 and was the largest ever seen on Newspaper Row (Kenny, 1987).

The story of Joe Knowles doubled the *Post's* circulation in a year. Even when he returned from the woods, the story continued. The *American* continued to question Knowles's veracity and promised to expose him as a fraud. The *Post* responded with an injunction against the *American* and followed it up with a suit for slander. Knowles published his account of the experience in "Alone in the Wilderness," to which the public responded by making the book a best seller, with more than 300,000 copies sold.

The Nature Man followed his departure from the woods by spending almost six months on the vaudeville circuit, where he capitalized on the controversies surrounding his adventure. The controversy continued to be fueled by Hearst's *American,* by trying to produce affidavits proving Knowles claims false.

The controversy over Hetch Hetchy came to a head in 1913. And the Nature Man, Joe Knowles, became famous in the same year. The former involved what might have been perceived as a west coast issue and the latter, hardly an issue except for the public-interest aspects of the story, took place on the east coast. Somehow, however, these stories captured American hearts. Clearly, Americans revered the romantic stories about the rugged individualists who traveled through and conquered the majestic untamed environment. It was as though society loved what it had largely lost, and tried to recapture it through a love for stories about the wilderness, the creation of parks, and even through the promulgation of this love of the wilderness in the creation and growth of organizations aimed at taking youngsters into the woods.

Evidence that the country was ready to embrace the wilderness may be found in a number of places. As will be discussed in the next chapter, camp programs expanded to include girls and even the mentally ill. Visitors to National Forests grew from 3 million in 1911 to 11 million in 1924, reflecting the interest in the wilds (Wellman, 1987).

That the country was ready to embrace the wilderness is also evident in the publication of the first *Boy Scout Handbook* just a few years earlier (1910). The wilderness was no longer to be feared or in need of taming, at least not to the same proportions evident before. Instead, it was to be largely appreciated for its perceived healing and restorative qualities. That this was the case is perhaps nowhere more evident than in the popularity of another book that made its appearance in 1911, *Tarzan of the Apes.* Nash (1967) convincingly makes the point that by the 1890s, the continent had been largely tamed, and the wilderness reduced. The public's image of the city became one of corruption, disease, and exploitation. The hostility that had once been reserved for the wilderness was now directed toward urban areas. Refuge was to be sought in the wilderness. In this way, Joe Knowles was fighting the common person's battle against civilization and Hetch Hetchy symbolized the basic conflict between civilization and wilderness. This represents an important shift in popular views of the wilderness. No longer was the wilderness to be harnessed; it was now to be protected and enjoyed. This symbolizes an acceptance of the wilderness for its healing and restorative powers, and parallels the growth of camps created to provide healthy recreation for youth (see Chapter 3).

The Primitive Man Moves West

William Randolph Hearst obviously knew what the public wanted and tried to deliver it, for instead of continuing his refutation of Joe Knowles and the veracity of Joe's story, Hearst hired him! Thus, in July of 1914, Joe, again naked and without tools, entered the Siskiyou Mountains of Oregon. There, he essentially replicated his experience in the Maine woods.

Up and down the west coast, Joe's adventure made front page news in papers with large circulations, such as the *San Francisco Examiner* and the

Portland Oregonian. According to one source (Holbrook, 1948, p. 9): "There hadn't been such a local story since the San Francisco 'Fire,' and it was going great guns as July crept into its last week." At the same time that Joe was living off the land—eating nuts and berries, hunting, and fishing—and again sending reports out to the public via charcoal messages on bark, events in Europe were reaching a peak. On July 28, 1914, war erupted and, as one can imagine, Joe's story was relegated to obscurity. By the time Knowles successfully emerged from the wilderness, few knew or cared in the shadow of World War I.

A variation on this same attention-getting stunt was tried a third time, in the summer of 1916 in upstate New York. This time, Joe was characterized as "Dawn Man" and was paired with "Dawn Woman," who was also to enter the woods naked. Dawn Woman could last only seven days in the wilderness before she emerged, leading to the collapse of the sensationalism behind this story. Joe had little reason to remain in the woods and returned to civilization soon thereafter. While Knowles slipped into isolation in a small village on the Washington coast where he died in 1942, he was still a symbol for the nature movement and the ability of people not only to survive, but also thrive, in the wilderness (Holbrook, 1948).

The Legacy of Hetch Hetchy and Knowles

While Hetch Hetchy may have been dammed and Joe Knowles faded into obscurity, the movement for preserving the spirit of the wilderness continued. An example of this movement was the passing of the National Park Service Act in 1916. Another voice for preserving the wilderness came from Aldo Leopold, who began working with the Forest Service in 1909. He argued for keeping parts of the forest undeveloped, a position that was often received with hostility for almost 20 years after he began his career with the Forest Service (Runte, 1991).

In 1921, Leopold wrote an article, "The wilderness and it's place in forest recreation policy," that was influential in the establishment of the Gila Wilderness Area in 1926 (Wellman, 1987). Other important events in the 1920s included the appeal for the Appalachian Trail and President Coolidge's call for a National Conference on Outdoor Recreation (NCOR) in 1924 (Nash, 1967). Subsequent NCOR meetings in 1926 and 1928 led to support for Leopold's idea of inventorying and preserving wilderness areas. In 1929, the Forest Service officially issued a regulation ("L-20") to preserve wilderness regions in the National Forests (Runte, 1991). The movement created by Leopold and the Forest Service in the twenties continued into the next decade.

During the Depression, the Civilian Conservation Corps (CCC) employed thousands to work on the creation and maintenance of trails, reforestation, and a host of other projects. CCC workers and their camps were supervised primarily by the Department of Agriculture (of which the Forest Service is a component) and the Department of the Interior (the parent agency of the National Park Service). It is difficult to imagine the scope of the impact the CCC has on our current woodlands. For example, in 1936, over 11,402 miles of new trails were created and an additional 69,920 miles of trails were maintained by the CCC. Similarly, by 1936, over 500 million new trees had been planted by CCC workers (Salmon, 1967).

CCC projects were often aimed at forest preservation by creating trails that would allow fast and effective responses to fires (also by creating fire breaks, water storage basins and lookout towers). They also created hundreds of campgrounds and numerous parks (Salmon, 1967). While not all of their work was designed to facilitate an appreciation or use of the outdoors, much of their effort remains to foster forest lands that are both accessible and preserved. In this way, the CCC created trails serve as the backbone for the current trail system used for backpackers all over the United States.

These earlier efforts were strengthened when Congress passed Public Law 88-577, designated as the "Wilderness Act," on September 3, 1964, after a seven year struggle that involved 18 Congressional hearings and 6,000 pages of testimony (Iker, 1989). At that time, 9.1 million acres were designated as wilderness, prohibiting such acts as logging, grazing, mining and development. Twenty-five years after the passage of the Act, that area has grown ten-fold to more than 91 million acres. There are now 474 units of land designated as wilderness under the National Wilderness Preservation System, ranging from a 6 acre island in Florida to an almost 9 million acre area in Alaska. In fact, there are 20 proposed wilderness areas being considered in Colorado alone (Fayhee, 1991). There are other protected areas as well, including national seashores, lakeshores and wildlife sanctuaries.

This is not to suggest that the wilderness is no longer endangered; in fact, threats to wild lands abound. Many organizations have taken strong preservationist stands. Among them, the Sierra Club, so central to the fight to save Hetch Hetchy, is still fighting to protect the wilderness. As its name implies, the Wilderness Society has a commitment to preserve the wilderness.

At the same time as this effort to protect the wilderness, a set of values developed that would foster individual growth and harmony within the wilderness. This took many forms. One need only compare different editions of the *Handbook for Boys,* published by the Boy Scouts of America, in order to trace this changing value system. While the earlier handbooks depicted trail blazing with axes, those after World War II discouraged this use but advocated other destructive practices, like chopping trees to make a reflector for one's fire. The latest handbook conveys a very different message, discussing the concept of low impact camping—"leave nothing but footprints, take nothing but pictures."

While many aspects of our conception of the wilderness have changed over time, as we have documented in this chapter, one component has remained—the healing, restorative quality of nature. This view is consistent with the Romantic notion of the environment, as discussed earlier. So popular was this belief that even 200 years ago, when it was not easy to travel, numerous individuals and families would leave more urban areas for seashores and mountains, especially during the summertime (Huth, 1990). Gradually, this movement spread westward.

Not only was there uniform acceptance of the value of leaving the cities for more natural surrounds one hundred years ago, but this ethic is still embraced today. Consider the popularity of wilderness treks and the writings of those who have made these treks. Calvin Rustrum's prominence is an example of this popularity. He wrote 15 books on living happily in the wilderness. His writings typify this genre, as when he says, "We need the joy of living optimally, where every natural force is playing on one's being...Th[e] exquisite pleasure of being an integral part of the natural universe...makes one ecstatic about just living" (Vickery, 1986, p. 172). Regarding the therapeutic aspects of the wilderness for the emotionally troubled, or even those looking for psychological growth, Rustrum is quoted as saying: "Only intimate and prolonged contact with the wilds seems to allow any significant revelation of inner secrets" (Vickery, 1986, p. 161).

This view is also consistent with the underlying assumptions of many out-of-door camping programs for youth. In this vein, the next chapter traces the origin of the earliest camping programs and also discusses the growth of Outward Bound which was based on the belief that the environment has within it the inherent ability to heal, soothe, and foster growth.

References

Abbey, E. (1975). *The monkeywrench gang.* New York, Avon.

Abbey, E. (1990). *Hayduke lives: A novel.* Boston: Little Brown.

Bradford, W. (1952). *Plymouth Plantation, 1620-1647.* New York: Knopf.

Canby, H. (1967). Introduction. In H. Longfellow, *Favorite poems of Henry Wadsworth Longfellow.* Garden City, NY: Doubleday.

Cohen, M. P. (1988). *The history of the Sierra Club: 1892-1970.* San Francisco: Sierra Club.

Fayhee, M. T. (1991). Double exposure: The two sides of John Fielder. *Backpacker, 19,* 32-38.

Holbrook, S. H. (1948). *Little Annie Oakley and other rugged people.* New York: Macmillan.

Huth, H. (1990). *Nature and the American: Three centuries of changing attitudes.* Lincoln: University of Nebraska.

Iker, S. (1989). Struggle for the great wild. *National Wildlife, 27,* 50-58.

Kenny, H. (1987). *Newspaper row: Journalism in the pre-television era.* Cluster, CN: Globe Pequot.

Krutch, J. K. (Ed.) (1982). *Walden and other writings by Henry David Thoreau.* New York: Bantam.

Longfellow, H. W. (1967). *Favorite poems of Henry Wadsworth Longfellow.* Garden City, NY: Doubleday.

Muir, J. (1993, September-October). The Hetch-Hetchy Valley. *Sierra.* 58-60. (Originally Published 1908).

Nash, R. (1967). *Wilderness and the American mind.* New Haven, CT: Yale.

Nivens, A. & Commager, H. (1969). *A pocket history of the United States.* New York: Washington Square.

Rosenblum, R. (1975). *Modern painting and the northern romantic tradition: Friedrich to Rothko.* New York: Harper and Row.

Runte, A. (1991). *Public lands, public heritage: The national forest idea.* Niwot, CO: Roberts Rinehart.

Salmon, J. A. (1967). *The Civilian Conservation Corps, 1933-1942: A New Deal case study.* Durham, NC: Duke.

Spiller, R. (1965). *James Fenimore Cooper.* Minneapolis: University of Minnesota.

Strong, D. (1990). Introduction. In H. Huth, *Nature and the American: Three centuries of changing attitudes.* Lincoln: University of Nebraska.

Van Nostrand, A. (1961). Introduction. In J. Cooper, *The last of the Mohicans.* New York: Washington Square.

Vickery, J. (1986). *Wilderness visionaries.* Merrillville, IN: ICS Books.

Wellman, J.D. (1987). *Wildland recreation policy: An introduction.* NY: John Wiley.

Whitman, W. (1940). *Leaves of grass.* Garden City, NY: Doubleday, Doran. (Originally published 1855).

Chapter Three ▽

Early Wilderness Programs

A logical extension of the early beliefs about the restorative powers of the wilderness was the development of organized ways of encouraging and promoting people's experiences with these environments. One such structured experience was the camp experience. The idea of sending children and adolescents to camp seemed to have a natural appeal, and served to provide the participants with a novel and stimulating way to spend a portion of their summer vacations.

Thus, the earliest organized camping programs in the United States were geared toward adolescents, and were recreational in nature. It was generally thought that the out-of-doors was healthy for children, especially those from urban environments. In keeping with the more philosophical ideas on the value of the outdoors, this environment was seen as restorative and healing in and of itself. Thus, the primary reason for going to camp at this time was to experience a respite from the stress and strain of city life, and to have some fun in a wilderness setting. It should be stressed that learning camping skills, or working on self-improvement were not goals of these early camping programs.

It is generally agreed that the father of modern camping in the United States was Thomas Hiram Holding, who put forth his ideas in 1853. His notions about the role of the camp as recreation for youth formed the basis for the development of all of the camps in this early period. One of the first organized camps in the world, however, was begun in 1861 by Frederick William Gunn. He called this camp the Gunnery School for Boys, and incorporated school experiences into an outdoor setting (Mitchell, Robberson, & Obley, 1977). Although capturing the recreative role of the camp, the Gunnery School also focused heavily on the place of academic coursework in the camp experience. With less of a focus on academics, the Fresh Air Camp for children was established in 1872 in New York on Staten Island. Once again, the healing aspects of the outdoors, especially for urban children, formed the foundation of the program.

These same ideas about the value of retreating to the woods were applied to adult women in 1874, with the development of "vacation projects" for tired women. Basically, women who had been taking care of families, households and children with very little respite came to camp for recreation. The first camp of this sort was established in Asbury Park, New Jersey, and was called "Sea Rest." (Gibson, 1973).

Many of these early camps were affiliated with agencies, so the introduction of private camping was a novel approach to the camping experience. The first private camp was established in 1876 by Joseph Trimble Rothrock, and was named the North Mountain School of Physical Culture. Dr. Rothrock was a physician, and believed that the health of the campers would improve if they could live outdoors. Interestingly, Dr. Rothrock was not referring to physically sick children; he simply believed that living outdoors would improve even further the health of normal children, and would optimize their levels of functioning. Unfortunately, the program was found to be prohibitively expensive to operate, and Dr. Rothrock soon went out of business (Mitchell, Robberson, & Obley, 1977).

Two additional private camps had more financial good fortune. The first was the Good Will Farm for Boys in Hinckley, Maine. This camp was a private church camp developed in 1880 by the Rev. George W. Hinckley. The second private program was a camp which specifically focused on the education of wealthy boys. This camp was established in 1881, by Ernest Berkely Balch, and was located on Burnt Island in New Hampshire from 1881-1889. The campers in this program were to focus on developing a sense of responsibility to themselves and to others, and an appreciation of the worth of work (Mitchell, Robberson, & Obley, 1977). Based on the goals of this program, it appears that the Burnt Island Camp was a very early attempt to effect behavioral change among the campers, as it clearly went beyond the sole purpose of recreation.

One of the more famous early camps, which is still in existence today, is Camp Baldhead. In 1885, Sumner Dudley took YMCA members on a trip to Orange Lake, New York and established a base camp. The camp was named Camp Baldhead because in preparation for the trip, the boys shaved their heads. The initial trip was a success in that the boys reported a great deal of benefit from being in the natural environment. The next summer, Mr. Dudley took 23 boys to the same camp, once again, returning from camp with positive reports from the participants. As word of the success of this program spread, so did the numbers of boys wanting to participate. By the year 1891, 83 campers were part of the program (Gibson, 1973). Later Mr. Dudley organized a camp on Lake Champlain, which was renamed Camp Dudley in his honor (Mitchell, Robberson, & Obley, 1977). During his lifetime, Sumner Dudley became so enthralled with the notion of camping for boys that he gave up his job as a businessman and began working full-time with the Boy Scouts. Thus, in the history of American camping for youth, this man has been a major influence and demonstrated a great deal of commitment to camping programs for youth (Gibson, 1973).

At this point in the chronology of early camping programs, one encounters an interesting diversion. Clearly, during this early period, the vast majority of camping programs were developed and run for boys. Interestingly, the early literature does not discuss the rationale behind the exclusion of girls. Rather, no mention is made of this omission. The early years of the 1900s, however, saw the emergence of a few programs for girls. Luther Halsey Gulick's camp for girls was originally founded as a camp for his daughter and her friends. The intent in founding this camp was to give the girls somewhere to go, and to provide a refreshing alternative experience to city life. Obviously, since there were no established camps, this father decided to develop one for his daughter.

Interest in this camp grew in completely unexpected ways. In an attempt to accommodate the interests of the girls in outdoor experiences, Mr. Gulick later went on to found the Camp Fire Girls. Finally, in 1902, Laura Mattoon founded the first organized camp for girls at Wolfeboro, New Hampshire, called Camp Kehonka for Girls (Mitchell, Robberson, & Obley, 1977). These camps were important in that they allowed for the recognition of the importance of camping for girls. However, the vast majority of the programs, especially the long-lived camps were geared toward boys.

An example of such a camp still in existence today is Camp Shand. In 1894, Dr. J. W. Stewart took 15 boys camping near Lancaster, PA. Later, the camp was moved to Gretha, PA and was named Camp Shand. Camp Shand represents the third oldest association camp, and it is still operating today (Gibson, 1973). Following these camps, The first Boys Club camp was formed in Salem, MA in 1900, with the founding of the Boy Scouts and the first Boy Scout camp in 1908 and 1909 respectively. Finally, young girls were officially included in organized camping with the founding of the Girl Scouts in 1912 (Gibson, 1973). Obviously, the Boy and Girl Scouts have had a tremendous impact on the popularity of camping for children and teenagers. Even though these early scouting programs were recreational in nature, they focused on citizenship and character development (Reynolds, 1942).

Generally speaking, however, these early programs mark what has been called the recreational stage in the development of the camping movement (Mitchell, Robberson, & Obley, 1977). It has been suggested that some of the benefits of these early camps included that they provided adventure for the children, a sense of status with their peer group, and an outlet for having fun (Ashcroft, 1957). In addition to this emphasis on outdoor enjoyment and fun, however, responsibility and virtue were also stressed.

Nowhere is this more apparent than in the early thoughts of Robert Baden-Powell in his ideas about the formation and operation of the Boy Scouts of America. In fact, the goal of the Boy Scouts, according to Baden-Powell was "the development of a community of good citizens" (Reynolds, 1942, p. 156). In accomplishing this end, boys were taught a code of honor, responsibility, and were encouraged to perform service for others. These virtues were taught and reinforced through a focus on the "giving of responsibility to the individual" (Reynolds, 1942, p. 157). In order to accomplish this individual work, the boys were divided into "patrols" of five boys each. Thus, instead of working in large groups, the boys received individualized attention and took responsibility for themselves and others in small patrol groups (Reynolds,

1942). Although not truly therapeutic, the Boy Scouts do provide an example of a movement away from a solely recreational focus in camping programs.

Another significant deviation from the recreational philosophy and design of the early camping programs were the Tent Therapy Programs. According to Caplan (1974), the "tent therapy" movement was born in 1901, at Manhattan State Hospital East. Initially, 40 tuberculosis patients were put in tents on the hospital grounds in order to isolate them from the other patients in the hospital. Improvement in these patients was dramatic. Not only did their physical conditions improve, their mental attitudes and outlooks seemed to improve immeasurably. Due to this improvement and to the rather critical space problems evident at the state hospital, it was suggested that other patients be tried in the "tenting program." Thus, 60 nontubercular psychiatric patients were put into tents. Once again, fairly dramatic improvements were seen in the patients, in both the physical and psychological arenas. In fact, the majority of the patients improved in weight gain, control over destructive habits, and in incontinence, with some improving even to the point of discharge from the hospital. This is especially significant given the fact that this early tent program was a trial program over the summer. Such change over a period of three months truly did seem to be remarkable (Caplan, 1974).

After the summer season, the tents were taken down and patients returned to their usual routine. This was necessary due to the lack of equipment with which to provide heated "outdoor areas". As a result of the discontinuation of the program, many of the patients regressed in their behaviors, becoming incontinent and withdrawn. Unfortunately, there is little academic writing on this fascinating program. The *American Journal of Insanity* in the early 1900s reported on a few of these tent therapy programs. In 1906, Dr. Andrew Hoisholt wrote a letter to the editors of this journal speaking of the condition of the patients in the tents. He said: "They all seemed more comfortable and contented in the tents and on the open grounds, where a nurse on guard here and there was the only restraining influence, and very few made attempts to escape" (*American Journal of Insanity, 63,* 1906, p. 131). Another issue of this early journal describes a camp built on the Susquehanna River for patients of Binghamton State Hospital. It was thought by the staff that this camping program was a "valuable part of the treatment of the recoverable patients" (*American Journal of Insanity, 67,* 1910, p. 445). Tents were replaced by cottages in New York at the Bloomingdale Hospital in White Plains. The benefits of this program are described most effectively by the words of a patient who said: "The Beach Cottage part of the summer of 1915 was the beginning of my improvement, and we all felt that it was the lift we otherwise would not have had" (*American Journal of Insanity, 73,* 1916, p. 334).

These early reports of applying fresh air environments to the treatment of psychiatric patients were certainly revolutionary. However, these programs were also short-lived. Relying on anecdotal reports of success, the actual efficacy of this approach was never documented. However, all of the early reports were quite positive, and suggested that tent therapy may be an important vehicle for the treatment of psychiatric patients. Almost mysteriously, however, discussion of these programs withered, and by the year 1920, reports in the *American Journal of Insanity* and others were non-existent, never again to resurface in the professional literature. Thus, it appears that an innovative approach to working with psychiatric patients was experimented with in the early 1900s, only to vanish a few years later as quickly and unexpectedly as it had originally appeared.

Early Therapeutic Approaches

These early "Tent Therapy" programs were extremely important, however, as they formed the foundation for the later thinking on the therapeutic use of the outdoors. In fact, the introduction of the tenting programs actually marked the beginning of a real attempt to give the camping movement a therapeutic focus. This therapeutic stage begins in the 1920s with Camp Ahmek, which was established in 1929. Camp Ahmek is especially important in that its philosophy was inherently therapeutic in nature. Thus, it has been suggested that the development of this camp actually marked the beginnings of a "therapeutic approach" to camping. In this regard, Camp Ahmek was founded with two major goals: to provide a recreative function for the participants, and to assist in the process of the socialization of the camper's behavior (Dimock & Hendry, 1939). This second goal was unique in that never before had the socialization of camper behavior been specified as a camp goal. Prior to this time, the only real references to any therapeutic change had involved vague notions about character building and individual responsibility, mainly associated with the Scouting movement (Reynolds, 1942).   The first goal of Camp Ahmek involved recreation. Camp was designed to be fun and to provide a source of carefree enjoyment for the participants. This involved getting away from urban life and the strife involved in everyday living, and above all avoiding "spectatoritis". Campers were encouraged to be active and to participate in camp activities. This kind of activity was seen to rekindle the imagination, and refine the emotions. During this time, there was a very strong belief that city living was not necessarily healthy for children, as it restricted their ability to engage in physical activities and to encounter the natural world. Going to camp, therefore, provided these children with an environment within which to experience and play to their hearts' content (Dimock & Hendry, 1939, p. 5). This type of enjoyment of the natural environment was seen to contribute to the overall well being of the participants.

The goal of assisting in the socialization of the boys was even more critical at Camp Ahmek than the recreative function of the camp. As such, the following elements of the camp experience were seen to contribute to such socialization, and thus, set the "therapeutic" tone for the program: (1) In a camping setting, cooperation was a must if the experience were to be successful; (2) Temporary emancipation from parents was experienced as a result of camp attendance; (3) Attitudes of "good citizenship" were essential to successful functioning at camp; (4) A great deal of peer pressure existed to conform to the rules and the standards of appropriate behavior at the camp; (5) The larger camp group becomes a critical reference group in the molding of the child's behavior; (6) The camp counselors become role models for appropriate and desired behavior for the campers; and (7) The camp experience engulfs the whole boy (Dimock & Hendry, 1939, pp. 4-9).

Obviously, the camp capitalized on the importance of the group in the lives of children and young adolescents. By living and functioning in such a group at camp, the desired behaviors became socialized into the campers. In failing to learn and exhibit these desired behaviors, the campers would alienate themselves and would fail in the program. This approach was important in that it also incorporated some critical aspects of the outdoors into its treatment approach. First, the immediacy of the consequences in the outdoors was recognized. This is a concept that was not actually articulated until later in the camping literature. However, the Camp Ahmek program appeared to have capitalized on the fact that cooperation in the outdoors is essential, and that the lack of such cooperation would be met with natural consequences from the environment itself.

Secondly, this program recognized the critical importance of positive role models in the lives of children and young adolescents. Again, the early literature does not specifically discuss counselor characteristics and qualifications as does the later literature. However, Camp Ahmek is impressive in its early recognition of the importance of the counselor as role model.

Finally, Camp Ahmek is unique in that it was one of the first camps to actually try to document its effectiveness in meeting its goals. Unlike the early camps which relied on purely anecdotal reports from campers, the staff at Camp Ahmek attempted to be more objective in their evaluation. Camp outcomes were measured in three different ways: weekly reports of progress by the counselors, direct observation of the campers' behavior, and completion of a behavior frequency rating scale for each camper upon admittance to camp, and again at the end of camp (Dimock & Hendry, 1939). The interested reader is referred back to Dimock & Hendry's detailed accounts of the daily outcomes of Camp Ahmek. In general, the outcome data suggested that following participation in Camp Ahmek, changes in initiative, social skills, responsibility, cooperation, and self control were seen (Dimock & Hendry, 1939, p. 281).

It is important to note that Camp Ahmek was designed to deal with normal, mentally healthy children. Thus, its purpose was to improve the functioning of children who were already functioning fairly well. In a sense, it was an example of "therapy for the normal". A little later, we can find a fairly rich literature devoted to the application of therapeutic camping for mentally healthy, but physically challenged children (e.g., Ash, 1945; Clark, 1937; Crawford, 1956; Howelt, 1945). These kinds of programs are still evident and are increasing in frequency, as evidenced by special programs by groups like Outward Bound.

Concurrent with this application of camping to disabled children was the development of programs geared toward those with mental health difficulties. The use of "camping as therapy" with those with mental health problems was significant, in that the only prior attempts at program design were those early "tent therapy" programs which had seemed to have disappeared. Thus, the idea of designing camping programs for those with mental health needs was fairly revolutionary. Dr. Ernest Harms, editor of the journal *The Nervous Child,* was a strong advocate for the mental health benefits of camping, but at the same time, was an ardent critic of the early programs. In an issue of the journal that he devoted solely to the mental health aspects of camping, Harms criticized the involvement of psychology in analyzing the impact of camping programs on mental health. He continued his comments by suggesting that a "camp-centered" psychology be developed, rather than simply applying psychological theory or concepts to camping (Harms, 1947). Harms did develop and run a camp of his own called The Broadview Farm Camps; however, his role in the therapeutic camping movement appeared to be more of a scholarly critic than an actual program organizer. Dr. Harms, although a strong critic of the early programs, was nevertheless instrumental in their continued development. In spite of his critiques, he was clearly a strong supporter of the philosophy behind developing therapeutic camping programs, and did much to promote their development and implementation.

Interesting early application of these therapeutic principles to the camping experience can be found in the literature. Many of these programs used visiting consultants, usually social workers or psychiatrists as mental health workers. The work of Scheidlinger and Scheidlinger (1947) serves as an example. They reported that in working with campers, some of their goals were: to facilitate the development of emotional ties to the group and to the leader, the relaxation of the Superego, and regression of the campers to earlier levels of behavior (Scheidlinger & Scheidlinger, 1947). These decidedly therapeutic goals were developed and implemented by outside consultants in their capacity as psychiatric social workers in a camp setting (Scheidlinger & Scheidlinger, 1947). In addition to being one of the early reports on therapeutic camping goals, the writings of these social workers clearly demonstrated a psychoanalytic orientation to therapy with the campers. This was important in that it was the first real application of clear cut theory to the specification of therapeutic goals for campers.

Therapeutic influences were also discussed by Zander (1947) in his report on a Midwestern camp. Although not necessarily suffering from mental health problems, the campers in this program were largely sent to camp by parents who wished for improvement in parent-child relations. According to Zander, (1947), the campers grew and developed by confronting their fears, and by sharing with others who may have the same fears. Although not specifically detailed, Zander's (1947) comments appear to support the notion of the centrality of the group experience as was seen in the earliest reported literature. Backus (1947) also highlighted the importance of the group experience as therapeutic for the campers. "Because children live together in camp in an extremely interdependent relationship, there is a unique opportunity for the growth of group feeling, and for each child to come to a greater awareness of the way in which what he does affects the group" (Backus, 1947, pp. 132-133). Thus, campers not only receive support and comfort from the experiences of the group, they actually influence and are themselves influenced by the group. This early perspective appears to suggest a recognition of the significance of peer pressure and support in the lives of adolescents.

Finally, Backus wrote of another distinguishing feature of the therapeutic use of the wilderness, which he referred to as the intensity of the camping experience. He illustrated the effects of the intensity of camping through the following description given of a typical camper: "He is in camp for a twenty-four hour day. He cannot save up his troubles, tears, or tempers until he goes home. If he is to have satisfaction, consolation, praise or triumph, he must find it with the campers and counselors" (Backus, 1947, pp. 131-132). Again, although unknowingly, Backus (1947) seems to discuss elements of the use of the wilderness that will resurface with the increasing sophistication of the literature.

These early writers contributed significantly to the literature on the therapeutic aspects of camping. However, most of this writing was theoretical, or at best, based in the subjective observations of the writers.

Although the early writings were not sophisticated, in-depth reports, they did serve to direct the study of the use of the wilderness. They also defined issues of interest and concern to be addressed by later writers and program planners. One of these issues involved the use of the group and group process in affecting personality and behavioral change. The group was seen to contribute to the growth of the campers in a number of different ways including: a vehicle for engaging in activities, a source of mutual understanding and support, and a setting in which the campers could evaluate their behaviors and attitudes against the standards of their peers. Although the early writings were largely theoretical and based on observation, the centrality of the group experience prevailed.

Another critical issue identified by the early writings was the recognition of the uniquenesses of the natural environment in its ability to stimulate growth and change. This quality was generally referred to as the intensity of the natural environment. It was suggested that this environment affected the campers twenty-four hours a day, and that one could not avoid its impact. It was also a strange and challenging environment for most of the campers; thus many of their past coping skills were rendered ineffective, and alternative behaviors were developed. Finally, the healing and restorative powers of the natural environment were also written about quite frequently in the early literature. As was previously discussed, these healing aspects seemed to be especially significant in the lives and experiences of urban youth.

In addition to the identification of the uniquenesses of the wilderness as therapeutic, the early literature began to take a critical look at some of the problems encountered with applying therapeutic principles to camping. Two of the primary problem areas identified at this time were lack of trained staff and the stability of change. The vast majority of the camp leaders and counselors employed in the early camping programs were not trained professionals, nor did many of them have any mental health training or experience. It was suggested that this kind of specific training was essential and thus the leaders should be experts in both camping skills and human behavior (Perlman, 1947; Zander, 1947).

Finally, the issue of stability of change over time was discussed. Many of the early studies, although largely anecdotal in nature, did suggest that the camping programs were effective in stimulating growth and change in the campers. In spite of these results, Perlman (1947, p. 158) cautioned about too much optimism regarding change, suggesting that such change may be temporary. He advocated for intensive follow-up after the summer camp experience to help to solidify the changes made. Thus, it was recognized that a child could experience change and growth in the camp setting, but that there was no guarantee that these changes would "follow this child home." It was also suggested that any decent studies on the effectiveness of outdoor programs must include a follow-up component to assess the stability of change over time.

Mid-1900s Approaches

Using these early therapeutic programs as a springboard, and keeping in mind the primary benefits and problems identified in the early therapeutic period, the mid-1900s saw the development of more sophisticated camping therapy programs. The University of Michigan Fresh Air Camp and the Salesmanship Club of Dallas will be used as examples of the growing sophistication of the programs. The Fresh Air Camp developed by the University of Michigan was begun as a camp for "normal" boys aged 7-14 years, who participated in 4 week sessions. This camp was not designed to be particularly therapeutic; however, the importance of the group and the training of the counselors were both highly stressed (Morse, 1947). Over time, the camp did seem to evolve into a more therapeutic camp.

According to Morse (1957, p. 15), the final stage of the program represented a "psychiatrically oriented, diagnostic and short-term treatment facility". Thus, this camp in its final stage was explicitly psychological and diagnostic in its purpose. Boys were involved in 7 week sessions, which focused on observation, diagnosis, and psychotherapy (Morse, 1957). This Fresh Air Camp was critical to the development of therapeutic camping in that it was clearly devoted to the diagnosis and treatment of mental health problems. In addition to trained counselors, staff psychologists were utilized on a regular basis. Finally, campers were selected who were suffering from mental health problems, and who otherwise would not fit into regular summer camp. Clearly, this camp moved from a camp for well adjusted boys with a recreational focus to a camp for those with mental health problems with a strong therapeutic focus.

As was the case with all of the early programs, The University of Michigan Fresh Air Camp did not publish much outcome data on its programs, and thus, reports of the camp dwindle and eventually die in the literature. This lack of research is especially unfortunate because it appears that this program did focus on diagnosis and short term treatment, and thus could have been effectively evaluated.

The Salesmanship Club of Dallas, however, represented a longer lived example of a therapeutic camp which is still in operation today. The camp was first developed in 1946, and was directed by Campbell Loughmiller from that time until 1966. The early program was a summer program, and in 1948 the summer component was discontinued and a year round program was begun. This camp, originally named Camp Woodland Springs, only focused on meeting the needs of boys with clear emotional problems. This was different from the Fresh Air Camp whose original purpose was to serve "normal" campers. The name of the camp was later changed to the Salesmanship Club Boys Camp in 1957 (Smith, 1958).

The Salesmanship Club Camp was important in that it incorporated clear guidelines for working with emotionally troubled children into its program including: (1) creative listening, (2) non-judgmental attitudes, (3) empathetic unearned love, (4) strong emotional support, (5) environmental modification, and (6) responsibilities for the parents (Smith, 1958). As the program developed, its focus became more refined and additional offerings were developed. Examples of some of the programs included: The Adventure Trails Program, Parent Groups, and the Town House. The Adventure Trails program was designed for both boys and girls, focused more on prevention, and involved 5-6 weeks of a variety of outdoor experiences. The Parent Groups met regularly when the children were attending the camp program. The intent of this program was to educate and involve parents in the treatment of their children, and to facilitate the generalization of change to the home environment. Finally, the Town House was a residential program utilized by campers for a few months prior to the final discharge from the program. The aim of this Town House program was to facilitate the transition from camp to home, and to assist in the generalization of change.

As with almost all of the programs discussed thus far, one of the flaws of the Salesmanship Club Camp was the lack of empirical research done on its effectiveness. Anecdotal data from the Club suggests that the majority of participants experienced improvement in social adjustment, school performance, and reduced court involvement following their participation in the camping programs (Smith, 1958). Unfortunately, even these vague references to outcome do not differentiate between the various programs offered within the Salesmanship Club. Thus, we have no idea as to the effectiveness of the parent groups and the residential component in addressing the issue of stability of change over time.

Most interesting about the Salesmanship Club however, were Loughmiller's own ideas about what a therapeutic wilderness program should involve. Loughmiller believed that the wilderness environment facilitated change in that it contained many real dangers and threats. By requiring boys to confront these dangers, their feelings of self worth would increase. Additionally, Loughmiller believed that the wilderness environment was ideal in that the consequences for behavior in this environment were immediate and intense. Thus, if a child refused to cooperate and wash dishes, he had to eat from dirty dishes the next day. Importantly, these were natural consequences, not those imposed by adults on the youth.

Finally, Loughmiller focused on reinforcing a sense of control and effective decision making power in the boys. He believed that this would help them transfer the changes made in the camp environment to their everyday lives (Loughmiller, 1965). Loughmiller was one of the first to develop his ideas about the therapeutic aspects of the wilderness in a systematic fashion. As such, he became a leader in the field, and is still widely cited today.

Clearly, in the 1940s and 1950s, there was a surge of more refined thinking and program responses geared toward working with troubled youth in wilderness environments. This era was more sophisticated than prior times, however, in that writers and camp directors realized that although the wilderness may in fact be curative, good programs needed to incorporate solid counseling techniques in order to impact the campers' lives. Thus, the strength and immediacy of the wilderness environment were coupled with early attempts to build self-esteem and change behavior. The Loughmiller model illustrated these developments and distinguished itself as the most sophisticated model of the time.

These early programs also articulated some critical problems with wilderness therapy that would be grappled with for years to come. As was previously mentioned, the two primary problems identified at this time were the lack of outcome data on effectiveness, and the lack of follow-up work with campers after the end of their wilderness programs. Interestingly, these problematic issues are not new, as the reader will remember the reference to them in the critique of the early programs.

Despite the continued dialogue about the need for outcome data, the evaluation of outcome in wilderness programs during this time period continued to be inadequate. Although Camp Ahmek and the Salesmanship Club of Dallas provided some effectiveness data, most of it was based on subjective reports, often of the counselors involved in the program. Such reporting by those who have a vested interest in the success of the program may be considered to be biased.

Importantly, the use of standardized measurement instruments had not yet become commonplace in any psychotherapy outcome research, much less in such an innovative approach to treatment (Watson, 1952). Thus, without evaluation data, we are left to examine and reflect on a number of interesting and creative approaches to working toward change using wilderness settings. Such anecdotal reports, however, do not support the effectiveness of these programs as viable treatment options. As a result, many of these programs lost their funding and were terminated.

The other issue discussed during this time period was the lack of follow-up work with camp participants. As this issue is clearly related to the evaluation of outcome, one could correctly expect that the early ideas on this subject were not developed in any detail or depth. Often the anecdotal reports mentioned in the literature referred to the need for a continuation of the work done at camp in order to maintain the changes experienced over time. Once again, it is likely that the lack of such rigorous follow-up data contributed to the demise of the therapeutic programs of this time. Continuation of programs may well have been contingent not only on their immediate effectiveness, but on the ability of the effects to be generalized over time and in related situations.

Thus, by the end of this "therapeutic period" in the development of wilderness approaches to therapy, we see some interesting and innovative programs come to the forefront. These programs are distinctive because they work with youth with emotional or mental health difficulties, and are built around solid psychotherapeutic principles. These early programs do indeed seem to be effective and suggest that the decades of the 1950s and 1960s will further explore the relationship between the wilderness and treatment, and will see the development and evaluation of refined programs.

1950s and 1960s Approaches

One cannot discuss relatively modern wilderness programs without spending some time on the development and implementation of Outward Bound. Although developed prior to the 1950s, this program came into prominence during the decades of the 1950s and 1960s; thus, its beginnings and some of its philosophies will be discussed within the context of this time period.

Outward Bound was originally conceived from the educational ideals of Dr. Kurt Hahn. A comprehensive discussion of the contributions of this rather remarkable individual is beyond the scope of this book, therefore, we will only highlight some of his philosophies and ideas.

Kurt Hahn was a devoted educator. In 1920, he became the Headmaster of the Salem School, which was located inside the castle of Prince Max Von Baden, for whom Hahn had been serving as a personal secretary. The significance of this school is that through this experience, Hahn was really able to begin to formulate his ideas about education, many of which were quite revolutionary for the time. Even in these early educational endeavors, Hahn was an innovator. He incorporated non-competitive physical activities with social cooperation in his school program. Another central feature of the school was the importance of service. Finally, Hahn introduced the notion that learning requires periods of solitude (James, 1993, 33-34).

Kurt Hahn expressed his moral convictions when he spoke out against Hitler in the early 1930s. As a result, he was imprisoned, and later released and sent to England (Miner & Boldt, 1981). Following this experience, he founded the Gordonstoun School in Scotland, further refining his philosophies on education.

The actual birth of Outward Bound occurred in 1941 in Aberdovey, Wales, in cooperation with Lawrence Holt, who actually named the school Outward Bound (Miner & Boldt, 1981). At this time, Hahn noted that many of the young, physically fit British seamen were not surviving conditions at sea as well as some of the older, less fit men. This observation led him to further apply his ideas about attitude and philosophy, and to suggest that bolstering both the physical and psychological components of the individual could facilitate coping with adverse conditions (Katz & Kolb, 1967; Stich & Gaylor, 1983).

Then, in the late 1940s, Hahn traveled to the U.S. to gain support for his notions about the post-war "restoration" of the German people. The American-British Foundation for European Education was formed to assist in this task, with the result of these efforts being the creation of scholarships to four German schools, and to assist in the creation of three other schools in Germany (Miner & Boldt, 1981).

Kurt Hahn and his dedicated followers worked tirelessly to affect the educational process both within the United States and in the world community. In fact, Hahn worked toward the establishment of an international Atlantic College (Miner & Boldt, 1981). Hahn's impact in the United States, however, is best seen with the establishment of Outward Bound in this country.

In 1962, the Colorado Outward Bound School opened. These early courses included ropes work, physical conditioning, climbing, and included the expertise of Paul Petzoldt. Following the establishment of this school, Bob and Jerry Pieh suggested that a school in Northern Minnesota would be desirable. Thus in 1963, the Minnesota Outward Bound School (now called the Voyager School) was born, followed in 1965 by the Hurricane Island School, and in 1966 with the Pacific Crest School. Finally, the North Carolina School opened in 1967 (Miner & Boldt, 1981).

Clearly, it is important to present some of the chronology of the development of Outward Bound. The interested reader is referred to Miner & Boldt (1981), and to the writings of James (1993) for compelling accounts of this historical development. More important for our purposes is to highlight some of the philosophies and values which underly this educational approach.

"Community"

Kurt Hahn believed in community, and he instilled this into his students through goal setting and community service. Importantly, these elements remain central today. Students make a pledge to a "training plan", which forms the "moral basis of the community" (James, 1993, 46). Students also perform community service which provides a linkage between the school and the larger society, and which reinforces the connection between self-discovery and service (James, 1993, 34). In summarizing Outward Bound as implemented in the U.S., the following educational goals might be considered (Katz & Kolb, 1967, p. 44):

1) To encourage personal growth
2) To develop courage and willpower
3) To live efficiently and rely on one's natural resources
4) To develop interpersonal competence
5) To develop a desire and the ability to serve others

As one might imagine, the actual structure and implementation of Outward Bound has changed as it has grown and become successful in this country. This growth has not been without some controversy. Bacon (1988) has written rather extensively about different models Outward Bound has used to develop and run their program. He begins by discussing the "Mountains Speak for Themselves" (MST). This approach was deemed to be for all purposes, and could be applied to any situation or any participant group (Bacon, 1988).

From this perspective, one could assume that the out-of-doors was therapeutic in and of itself, and nothing more even needed to be said. In fact, to discuss therapy in the outdoors, or to even try to develop therapeutic methods would serve to detract from the ultimate power of the wilderness. Thus, participants were to grow and develop physically, spiritually, and socially, without needing specific structured methods (Bacon, 1988). This approach was more non-directive than many of the therapeutic programs of the 1940s and 1950s, and clearly reflects Hahn's passion for introspection, experience, physical condition, solitude and social responsibility.

The MST approach also assumed that the generalization of the participants' experiences on the trip to their everyday lives would also occur, and that there was no real need to work on refining these skills or facilitating this generalization (Bacon, 1988). Once again, this is in contrast to the early therapeutic programs which recognized the importance of "talk therapy" in solidifying and maintaining change.

Another interesting difference between the earliest therapeutic programs and the Outward Bound early program was the use of the trip leaders. With the increasingly therapeutic flavor of the early programs, discussions about the qualifications and roles of the leaders necessarily arose. Writers like Morse (1957) advocated the use of trained professional counselors in therapeutic programs. In fact, as was previously mentioned, many programs even employed consulting psychiatrists and social workers.

Outward Bound, however, embraced the notion that reflection and insight were primarily the responsibility of the students, not the trip leaders. One of the important goals of the trips was to work toward an "affective high"; however, students were to accomplish this on their own. As a result of this philosophy, even when trips were designed for specialized groups (e.g., troubled youth), the regular staff served as trip leaders. Special needs courses were simply seen as courses with a homogeneous group of participants (Bacon, 1988). Thus, the role of the instructors was to coordinate and execute the physical aspects of the trip, assuring that all participants were safe and were successfully completing activities.

This discussion of the MST approach has been debated and disputed within Outward Bound itself, and these dialogues on the extent of reflection and the role of the instructor continue to exist. Bacon (1988) actually refers to the MST and other approaches as models, whereas James (1980) presents a different perspective. According to him, the phrase the "Mountains Speak for Themselves" was never meant to be construed as a model, but rather, was coined by a course director, in reaction to pressures to increase reflection experiences on trips. James (1980) identifies this division between those who support greater reflection and those who opt for a more purely outdoor experience as a "defining tension" in the field (James, 1980).

As the reader will see, these kinds of fundamental debates were present at the inception of the early programs and continue to the present day. We will encounter these issues again when we briefly discuss present day Outward Bound in the next chapter. At this point, we turn to further discussion on the early Outward Bound program, by examining its research literature.

In fact, very little rigorous research was done on the early Outward Bound programs. However, one study did suggest that delinquents who participated in an Outward Bound program experienced lower recidivism following treatment than did the traditional treatment participants (Kelly & Baer, 1968). This study compared 60 delinquents sent to Outward Bound with a control group of 60 boys. Nine months after the program was completed, the recidivism rate for the Outward Bound group was 20%, as compared to a recidivism rate of 34% in the control group. Additionally, as measured by the Jesness Inventory, at post-test, the Outward Bound group showed significant positive changes in alienation, asocial behavior, aggression, social maladjustment, and value orientation (Kelly & Baer, 1968).

Another study evaluated one of the Outward Bound schools directly, utilizing 50 non-delinquent subjects who had participated in the Colorado Outward Bound School's programs. All subjects completed a self-rating scale, a self description scale, an ideal description scale, and a word meaning test. These measures were given upon arrival, before training, and at the end of the program. The results suggested that the participants improved in their self images, especially those who began the program with low levels of self esteem (Clifford & Clifford, 1967).

These two studies are very important in that they utilized generally accepted principles of research in their design and used standardized measurement instruments to collect data. They also suggest that Outward Bound may be successfully applied to at-risk populations, such as juvenile delinquents. Although these two studies suggest that the Outward Bound Program was effective, the early program in the 1960s was characterized by a lack of research in general, and more specifically, by a lack of control groups and standardized instruments. Biased samples in this research also limited the validity of the findings. Thus, one is left with very subjective evaluations of the effectiveness of these early programs.

Despite these problems, Outward Bound was and continues to be one of the primary outdoor programs in the United States and in many other areas in the world. The present day program and its influence on the therapeutic use of the wilderness will be discussed in the chapter on recent programs. It is important at this point, however, to emphasize that the early program was not really therapeutic in nature and featured leaders who were not trained in mental health interventions.

Although Outward Bound certainly was a prominent program during the 1950s and 1960s, it was not the only wilderness program. In fact, during this decade, the notion of the out-of-doors as a setting for education and personal growth burgeoned. In 1955, the American Association for Health, Physical Education and Recreation established the Outdoor Education Project. The purpose of this project was to focus on the development of both outdoor programs and outdoor leaders. This program was held in conjunction with the Michigan State University, and was responsible for the outdoor education of thousands of American students (Smith, 1973). Obviously, this program was not therapeutic in nature, but rather, served to educate potential outdoor leaders. The success of this program, however, does attest to the significant interest in working in outdoor settings which developed during this time.

In addition to a surge in interest in general camping and outdoor activities during the 1950s and the 1960s, a number of therapeutic camping programs emerged. One of the most exciting aspects of these programs was their diversity, and the variety of settings within which the wilderness approach to treatment was applied. Programs developed during this time included offerings for juvenile delinquents (Kelly & Baer, 1968), and psychiatric day treatment programs, to name a few (Reitman & Pokorny, 1974). Finally, a number of wilderness programs were developed in conjunction with inpatient hospital programs (Ackerman, Mitsos, Seymour & Smith, 1974; Remar & Lowry, 1974; McDonald, 1974). Since the inpatient programs appeared to be most common, a short description will be given to provide an idea of the types of programs operating during this time.

Reports on inpatient programs in the late 1950s at the Evansville State Hospital in Indiana and the Texas State Hospital described a recreational program without any formal therapy provided to participants. The camping experience in these programs was seen as more of a stepping stone to release into the community than as a therapeutic modality (Ackerman, Mitsos, Seymour, & Smith, 1974).

A program offered at the Oregon State Hospital, however, appeared to be more therapeutic in nature, although no real psychotherapy was provided to the participants. An equal number of patients and staff went on a 2-week camping trip, with most of the patients being hospitalized for at least six months prior to the trip. Again, although no specific therapy occurred, it was assumed that the high staff-to-patient ratio would be therapeutic in and of itself. Although no outcome data were presented from this program, it was suggested that the rafting, hiking and climbing had a healing effect on the participants. In the words of one of the patients after completing a difficult rock climbing session, "If I can do this, I can solve my own problems, can't I?" (McDonald, 1974, p. 30).

Other interesting programs could be found in the 1960s in the state of Massachusetts. Programs for epileptics were formed at the Monson State Hospital in 1961. In addition, the Boston State Hospital instituted a camping program for their patients which ran from 1966 to 1972. The camping component generally involved chronic patients and was short term in nature. Although no formal evaluation data was collected, patient reactions to the experience tended to be generally very positive (Remar & Lowry, 1974).

The early attempts at utilizing the healing powers of the wilderness were indeed fascinating. The earliest programs were designed largely for high functioning boys, and were recreational in nature. The goals of these camps were to provide the campers with a recreational outlet while also noting the value of the outdoors as a restorative environment. It was believed that the urban youth would benefit from such an escape from the city. The noted exception to this recreational focus was seen with the tent therapy programs, which represented an experimental treatment for psychiatric hospital inpatients.

Following this recreational period, the early therapeutic programs were developed. Camp Ahmek and others represented innovative attempts to apply principles of therapy and behavior change to outdoor programs. These initial attempts were understandably quite crude, and the programs were criticized for the lack of evaluation research done, the absence of trained trip leaders, and the lack of follow-up to solidify change. During the mid 1900s, many of these criticisms were addressed as programs became more sophisticated in their designs and evaluation of program outcomes. The Dallas Salesmanship Club developed by Loughmiller was the finest example of a program at this time. Unfortunately, many of the issues which plagued the past programs continued into this time period, with the lack of objective evaluation data being one of the most critical.

Despite these shortcomings, by the decade of the 1950s, therapeutic outdoor programs had come a long way in their development and implementation. The early Outward Bound Program in the U.S. focused less on the role of reflection, and thus seemed less "therapeutic" in its approach.

During the late 1950s and 60s, however, innovative programs were developed that were, by nature, therapeutic. These programs ranged from treatment for delinquents to inpatient hospital programs, with the majority being housed in hospital settings. Thus, the history of the use of wilderness as therapy encompasses a diverse range of program responses and critical issues. The following chapter begins with the 1970s, and details for the reader the development of some of the more prominent recent wilderness programs.

In addition to describing some of these programs, we will report on the research that has been done on evaluating both the process and outcome of wilderness programs. Finally, we will attempt to identify issues of concern, and areas for further discussion found in the literature.

References

Ackerman, O., Mitsos, S., Seymour & Smith, B.K. (1974). Some camping therapy programs in Indiana and Texas. In T.P. Lowry, (Ed.), *Camping therapy: Its uses in psychiatry and rehabilitation* (pp. 39-45). Springfield, IL: Charles C. Thomas.

American Journal of Insanity (1906), *63.*

American Journal of Insanity (1910), *67.*

American Journal of Insanity (1916), *73.*

Ash, F. (1945). Sometimes the handicapped give more than they receive. *Camping Magazine, 7,* 11.

Ashcroft, H. (1973). The attitude of children toward outdoor education. In D. Hammerman & W. Hammerman, (Eds.), *Outdoor education: A book of readings* (pp. 371-375). Minneapolis, MN: Burgess Publishing Co.

Backus, R. (1947). Where the new camping tasks begin. *The Nervous Child, 6,* 130-134.

Bacon, S. (1988). Paradox and double binds in adventure-based education. Eric Document Reproduction Service No. 296832, Greenwich, Conn.: Outward Bound, USA, 4-30.

Caplan, R. (1974). Early forms of camping in American mental hospitals. In T. P. Lowry, (Ed.), *Camping therapy: Its uses in psychiatry and rehabilitation* (pp. 8-12). Springfield, IL: Charles C. Thomas.

Clark, A. (1937). Camps for diabetic children. *Camping Magazine, 9,* 10.

Clifford, E., & Clifford, M. (1967). Self-concept before and after survival training. *British Journal of Social and Clinical Psychology, 6,* 241-248.

Crawford, M. (1956). Provide the handicapped with a rich camp experience. *Camping Magazine, 28,* 18.

Dimock, H., & Hendry, C. (1939). *Camping and character: A camp experiment in character education.* New York: Association Press.

Gibson, H.W. (1973). The history of organized camping: Establishment of institutional camps. In D. Hammerman & W. Hammerman, (Eds.), *Outdoor education: A book of readings* (pp. 69-76). Minneapolis, MN: Burgess Publishing Co.

Harms, E. (1947). Camps as mental health institutions. *The Nervous Child, 6,* 173-177.

James, T. (1980). Can the mountains speak for themselves? Unpublished manuscript.

James, T. (1993). The only mountain worth climbing: The search for roots. Unpublished manuscript.

Katz, R., & Kolb, D. (1967). *Outward Bound and education for personal growth.* Reston, Virginia: Outward Bound, Inc. (Mimeograph).

Loughmiller, C. (1965). *Wilderness road.* Austin, TX: Hogg Foundation for Mental Health.

McDonald, M. (1974). Adventure camping at Oregon State Hospital. In T. P. Lowry, (Ed.), *Camping Therapy: Its uses in psychiatry and rehabilitation* (pp. 16-31). Springfield, IL: Charles C. Thomas.

Miner, J., and Boldt, J. (1981). *Outward Bound U.S.A.: Learning through experience in adventure-based education.* New York: William Morrow and Co.

Mitchell, A.V., Robberson, J.D., & Obley, J. (1977). *Camp Counseling,* (5th Ed.). Philadelphia: W.B. Saunders Co.

Morse, W. (1947). From the University of Michigan fresh air camp: Some problems of therapeutic camping. *The Nervous Child, 6,* 211-224.

Morse, W. (1957). An interdisciplinary therapeutic camp. *Journal of Social Issues, 13* (1), 15-22.

Perlman, J. (1947). Camps for maladjusted children. *The Nervous Child, 6,* 155-160.

Reitman, E. & Pokorney, A. (1974). Camping at a psychiatric day center. In T. P. Lowry, (Ed.), *Camping therapy: Its uses in psychiatry and rehabilitation* (pp. 63-67). Springfield, IL: Charles C. Thomas.

Remar, E. & Lowry, T. (1974). Camping therapy in the commonwealth of Massachussetts. In T. P. Lowry, (Ed.), *Camping Therapy: Its uses in psychiatry and rehabilitation* (pp. 13-15). Springfield, IL: Charles C. Thomas.

Reynolds, E.E. (1942). *Baden-Powell.* London: The Oxford University Press.

Scheidlinger, S., & Scheidlinger, L. (1947). From a camp of a child guidance clinic: The treatment potentialities of the summer camp for children with personality disturbances. *The Nervous Child, 6,* 232-242.

Smith, B. (1958). *The worth of a boy.* Austin, TX: The Hogg Foundation.

Smith, J. (1973). A decade of progress in outdoor education. In D. Hammerman & W. Hammerman, (Eds.), *Outdoor education: A book of readings* (pp. 107-111). Minneapolis, MN.: Burgess Publishing Co.

Stich, T., & Gaylor, M. (1983). Outward Bound: An innovative patient education program. (Report no. RC 014830). Eric Document Reproduction Service No. ED247047. (1-18).

Watson, R. I. (1952). Research design and methodology in evaluating the results of psychotherapy. *Journal of Clinical Psychology, 8,* 29-33.

Zander, A. (1947). The influence of the summer camp on personality development. *The Nervous Child, 6,* 161-165.

Chapter Four ▽

Recent Programs

From the decade of the 1970s to the present day, we have continued to see a proliferation of interest in outdoor activity in general, and specifically in the therapeutic uses of the wilderness. This interest is easily supported by the "return to the woods" of middle class, middle aged adults, those individuals who were young teens during the 1950s explosion in outdoor interest.

Coupled with the interest in the outdoors, there appears to be a renewed commitment in the helping professions to addressing the issues confronted by today's youth. Recognizing the increasingly complex society in which we live necessitates the development of alternative and creative approaches to dealing with youth. Many of these approaches are geared toward prevention and/or treatment, such as chemical dependency programs.

Additionally, there have been a few books published which address issues related to the therapeutic use of the outdoors. *Islands of Healing* (Schoel, Prouty, & Radcliffe, 1988), written by the Project Adventure staff, discusses the application of adventure based counseling to outdoor programs. The interested reader is referred to the Project Adventure staff for additional readings, as they have been very prolific in their writing in this area.

During the 1970s, a few interesting edited volumes were published. Hammerman & Hammerman's (1973) volume focused largely on the use of the outdoors as a component of a variety of educational programs. Lowry (1974), on the other hand, considered the history and application of the outdoors to the area of mental health treatment and rehabilitation. More recent publications have included a volume focusing on the application of the wilderness educationally (Teschner & Wolter, 1984), addressing the wider topic of adventure education (Miles & Priest, 1990), adventure therapy (Gass, 1993), and on processing adventure experiences (Nadler and Luckner, 1992). Finally, Ewert (1983; 1989) has made important contributions to the literature. In addition to his work on self-concept, he has written a book consolidating research and theory in the field.

Many creative programs have been developed since the 1970s which attempt to combine outdoor experience and preventive and therapeutic programs for youth. The professional literature during this time period is full of references to innovative programs. What seems to be still lacking, however, are well designed and executed research studies which actually examine the efficacy of these approaches although valient attempts have been made. Much of this literature is indeed interesting, and does significantly add to our understanding and reflection on the philosophy behind the use of the wilderness, and to the meaning gained from wilderness experience. However, it does not effectively contribute to the development of empirically based therapeutic programs.

In addition to reports on small wilderness programs, the literature abounds with both formal and informal writings on Outward Bound Programs across the country. Although the majority of these writings are also not research based, some empirical evaluations of these programs are presented.

In keeping with these themes, this chapter will discuss some of the literature written on wilderness programs developed and implemented since the 1970s. Included in these programs will be evaluation data on our own Wilderness Therapy Program. Due to the number of reports and studies that are published each month in the journals, we are unable to present a comprehensive account of the research literature. However, we believe that this chapter presents many representative studies. Finally, the Outward Bound literature will be examined in some detail, as this program certainly represents one of the most renowned recent programs.

General Philosophy

The recent decades have maintained many of the same basic philosophies about wilderness experiences discussed in the previous chapter. Predominant is the belief that the wilderness environment is curative and healthy, especially for urban youth. Additionally, it is felt that meaningful behavioral and cognitive change can occur using this environment as a vehicle for change. Although we seemed to "know" the benefits of the wilderness in earlier decades, recent years have seen more attempts to document these philosophies.

In an attempt to ascertain what campers gained from outdoor experiences, the Fund for the Advancement of Camping asked 200 government and privately supported camps to participate in a study. These camps were asked to share the unsolicited comments on the value of camp that they had received over the years from campers themselves, parents, teachers, and social workers. A total of 1500 comments were received which served to shed some light on the perceived benefits of the camping experience.

After analysis, the comments appeared to be clustered into the following five general categories: (1) individual growth and development, (2) interpersonal relationships, (3) widening horizons, (4) the development of activity skills, and (5) education and environmental awareness (Clarke & Eells, 1974).

Individual growth benefits of wilderness experience were also identified by Klocke and Wichern (1980). In an interesting and lively article, these two high school counselors report on their own hike of a portion of the Appalachian Trail. According to them, the purpose of the trek was to address their own feelings of stagnation in their lives and to expose themselves to a new challenge. At the end of a successful trip, they reported that their problem solving skills had been fine tuned, and their self images and motivation were improved (Klocke & Wichern, 1980).

The process of personal growth was identified as an actual program goal of the Awareness Adventure Program in Philadelphia. Given the name of the program, one can also easily determine that one of the philosophies behind this program is that growth and insight can occur through outdoor adventure. This awareness can then be utilized in the everyday life experiences of the participants, and is adeptly illustrated by the following statement: "The philosophy behind Awareness Adventure is that what is learned on a rock face, on the trail, and around the campfire has applications in the family, at school, and in the community" (Broida, Proudman, & Magee, 1978, p. 30).

Finally, the impact of the wilderness on self esteem, and the use of the group to facilitate this growth is beautifully illustrated in the following description of a camper: "He learns to see himself as he really is, reflected in a relationship with a protective group, supported and cared for when needed but held to a responsible role within the group. He may feel for the first time in his life that he is a useful individual who has potential for growth and achievement. He may, in effect, learn to cope with life and its problems on a new and constructive basis" (Hughes & Dudley, 1973, p. 49).

These statements of philosophy continue in the research articles cited in the literature. As was previously mentioned, this literature reports on a number of small programs developed since the 1970s in a variety of different settings. Consistent with the movement toward hospital based programs in the 1960s, Hughes and Dudley (1973) report on a camping program for adolescents in the Texas state hospital system. Rather than providing any empirical outcome data, this article adds to the literature by detailing the rationale behind the program, and specifying the psychological dynamics inherent in the treatment program. Some of the positive aspects of the program were identified as: making separation from home easier; taking the "sting" out of the institution; a more informal, physically less restrictive setting; destructive behavior tended to decrease because of the realistic consequences of the environment; and finally, it was suggested that camping provides the opportunity for effective problem solving, including problems or issues involving relationships with other campers (Hughes & Dudley, 1973, pp. 45-47).

The rationale behind the effectiveness of experience as education was reported in an entire issue of the *Journal of Experiential Education* which was devoted to this topic. Stich (1983, pp. 24-25) suggests that the following factors comprise the rationale behind the therapeutic properties of physical activity:

1) Activity increases conditioning, which leads to self confidence.
2) Control of the body encourages control in other life areas.
3) Exercise releases aggression and anxiety, and promotes self expression.

4) Self expression gained from exercise leads to a greater ability to communicate feelings.
5) Activity is concrete and assists in reality testing.
6) Teamwork facilitates cooperation.
7) Exercise is goal directed and facilitates self confidence and discipline.

The therapeutic properties of reflection were also discussed in a special issue of *The Journal of Experiential Education* devoted to this topic. Horwood defined the goal of reflection as assisting students in "constructing meaning out of their experiences." This meaning serves to link the past and the present and is critical to the growth experienced from outdoor programs. Again, Horwood captures the essence of reflection when he states: "The direct product of reflection is the discovery of new connections between the most recent experience and past ones, including past thoughts" (Horwood, 1989, p. 7). In much the same way, Stremba stresses the importance of reflection in experiential learning, and asserts that "The mountains do not speak for themselves" (Stremba, 1989, p. 7). He then suggests a few issues that should be considered when discussing the process of reflection. First, the participants must be told ahead of time that an integral part of their program is talking about their experiences and trying to fit them into a larger context. Second, the process of reflection should be encouraged, as it makes the entire outdoor experience more holistic, and finally, reflection aids the program participants by giving them "tools" to take "the experience back home with them" (Stremba, 1989, p. 7).

Continuing with a discussion of therapeutic issues, Kimball (1983) discusses the role of the wilderness as playing a part in the larger mental health system, rather than standing alone as a therapeutic device. He identifies one of the most therapeutic aspects of the wilderness as its ambiguity. In fact, he compares it to the ambiguity of the Rorschach, and suggests that the wilderness experience can be effectively used as a diagnostic tool. In this regard, the wilderness is the means, and treatment and evaluation is the end. Finally, he asserts that experience is inherently more therapeutic than analysis (Kimball, 1983).

Clearly, this recent literature is an improvement in that it attempts to identify therapeutic issues which form the foundation of wilderness programs. However, many of these discussions fail to provide the reader with any detailed description of the actual therapeutic processes. Nadler and Luckner (1992) are innovators in their discussion of the dynamics of processing adventure experiences. In this context, they explore growth at the edge of the familiar and the use of metaphor in processing experience.

Hughes and Dudley (1973, p. 49) are also unusual in that they attempt to discuss their therapeutic approach. As such, they present a set of psychological dynamics which form the foundation for their hospital based program. These include: (1) focus on activating the reality principle, and squelching the pleasure principle; (2) the provision of structured group therapy; (3) encouraging the expression of aggression and anger; (4) focus on the development of basic trust; (5) increasing the positive identification with adults; and (6) increasing self-esteem. These authors are innovative in that they present such a detailed description of their program. However, they do not offer any empirical evaluation of their program, leaving one with a description of an interesting, innovative approach to working with adolescents, with no notion of its actual effectiveness.

In much the same way, Barley (1972) presents an interesting description of his program which adds to the general literature on therapeutic camping, yet offers no real empirical demonstration of efficacy. One hundred boys aged 12 1/2 to 15 from the Horizons Youth Camp in Boston were evaluated. Instead of collecting objective data, the boys were observed.

Generally, the impressions gained suggested that the campers did better in school and seemed to be better adjusted following their camping experience. More specifically, Barley (1972, p. 18) presents a number of general impressions about the program including the following: (1) risk taking increased when the boys trusted the adults in the camp, (2) all of the campers must be treated as individuals, (3) the counselors must begin "where the kids are at", (4) rugged physical activities are the activities of choice in the outdoor setting, as they provide a sense of challenge, (5) the camp experience should not be shorter than 4 weeks, (6) the camp should include a plan for follow-up, and finally, (7) the counselors should be good role models.

Although many of these general impressions may seem to simply be common sense, they are important in that they give the reader a clearer sense of both the structure and function of the specific program. In the absence of any evaluation data, this program description becomes the only criterion on which to evaluate this program, and represents an initial attempt at process evaluation.

Research Reports

It is beyond the scope of this chapter, or this book, to discuss all of the research that has been done on wilderness programs. Rather than attempt such a feat, we will highlight some areas (such as self-concept and recidivism) where change has been demonstrated in the literature. The interested reader is referred to Ewert's (1983) work on self-concept change in wilderness programs for more comprehensive coverage of this topic.

As has been previously discussed, the lack of objective evaluation data seems to be problematic in many of the reports on recent programs. A few did, however, attempt to document their effectiveness. These reports range from subjective, rather sketchy evaluations to well designed research studies. Shniderman (1974) for example, examined the impact of a day camping program on boys aged 5-1/2 to 11-1/2. The social adjustment subtest of the California Test of Personality was used as the primary measurement instrument. This test was administered to the campers before and after their camp experience, and was given to a control group of boys at comparable times. Additionally, parents of the boys in both groups were asked to rate their son's level of general adjustment at post-test. Generally, the results suggested that no significant differences were found between the treatment and control groups on the California Test, or in the parent's ratings. Interestingly, however, the campers rated themselves as being better adjusted after their camp experience. Thus, this study seems to suggest no differences on objective measures, but the participants perceived themselves as benefiting from the experience.

Krieger (1973) reported on the outcomes associated with the J Bar Double C-Ranch Camp operated by the Denver Jewish Community Center. One hundred and ten campers who participated in a month long camping experience were compared with a control group of 71 young people. The following research questions guided this evaluation: (1) What is the effect of the program on self concept change? (2) Are younger campers (8-11) more apt to have self concept change than older campers (12-15)? (3) Will males change more than females? (4) Is there a relationship between self concept change and behavioral change? (Krieger, 1973, p. 16). In order to answer these research questions, the Lipsitt Self Concept Scale for children and the Bowers Behavior Rating Scale were administered at both pre-test and post-test. Basically, the results indicated that there was a significant increase in self concept in the campers group at post-test. This group also experienced a significant decrease in negative behaviors following their camping experience. No significant sex or age differences were found, nor was there any significant relationship between self concept change and behavioral change.

This study was interesting in that it utilized well designed research questions and standardized instruments. From examining these results, it appears that the camping experience was therapeutic for the participants. Importantly, the benefits of this program appeared to apply equally to males and females across the age groups. Finally, this study gives us more insight into the dynamics of affective change and behavioral change, as there was no relationship noted between self concept and behavioral change. It could be that intensive follow-up work is needed in these camping programs to demonstrate and solidify the linkages between changes in affective and attitudinal state and behavior change.

A more recent study examined the effects of camp on both self concept and behavior. Chenery (1981) studied 77 female campers ranging in age from

8-12, who were participants in a 7 1/2 week long summer camp in Union, Maine. These campers were supervised by 13 female counselors, representing a low camper/counselor ratio. Measurement instruments were administered at pre-test and post-test. All campers were given the following: The Piers-Harris Self Concept Scale, a Classroom Behavior Inventory (revised and renamed the Camper Behavior Inventory), a Camper Questionnaire, and a Children's Report of Parent Behavior Inventory. Basically, the results of this study indicated a significant increase in self concept at post-test. Interestingly, no significant increases in positive behaviors were noted, but negative behaviors decreased. Finally, the campers who had rated their counselors as "accepting" had more self concept change and positive behavior change.

Once again, we find the increase in self concept being associated with participation in an outdoor program. Another common therapeutic gain seems to be a decrease in negative behaviors among participants. This study is interesting in that it also points to the role of the counselor in facilitating this change. The reader will recall that the role and the qualifications of wilderness counselors were discussed briefly as an important issue in the early wilderness programs. Unfortunately, this issue has not been given the serious attention that it deserves, thus it remains a rather unexplored area of investigation.

This lack of focus on the "wilderness counselor" could be partially due to the fact that many of the outcome studies presented are evaluations of residential camps and are not programs specifically designed as wilderness therapy. A few studies have been done which examined the impact of specifically designed therapeutic programs.

Adams (1970) evaluated a 30-day wilderness program for 19 adolescent psychiatric inpatients, utilizing non-hospitalized adolescents as a control group. Data were collected up to 28 months following the program and indicated that the hospital patients experienced increases in self esteem, self reliance, and feelings of physical adequacy. Additionally, their rehospitalization rate at follow-up was only 15%. These results appear to be promising; however, the author does not provide baseline hospitalization rates for this group, thus interpretation of the rehospitalization rates is difficult.

Positive change in psychiatric patients was also demonstrated by Jerstad and Selzer (1973). Fifty-one patients, ranging in age from adolescents to the elderly participated in a wilderness trip as an adjunct to hospital treatment. Thirty-one of the patients experienced improvements of a sufficient nature to warrant their discharge from the hospital following the wilderness program. Once again, although encouraging, this study relies largely on clinical impressions rather than on objective measurement instruments. Additionally, in interpreting the results, no breakdown of the differential effects of the treatment on specific age groups was presented. Thus, it is difficult to draw conclusions regarding the efficacy of this program for adolescents.

The authors' own model of intervention, The Wilderness Therapy Program, has been applied and evaluated with adolescent inpatients. This program involves exposing adolescents to an intensive backpacking experience in a wilderness area. Prior to the trip, the male and female participants, with the assistance of their parents and therapist, develop a set of treatment goals. These individual goals form the basis for the group therapy sessions during the trip. All participants are required to attend and to contribute to the group therapy sessions which are held daily on the backpack trail, with individual therapy being provided as needed. Importantly, all therapeutic goals and counseling services are provided only by licensed mental health professionals (Berman & Davis-Berman, 1989).

Fourteen adolescent inpatients from two Midwestern psychiatric hospitals ranging in age from 13-17 went on the Wilderness Therapy trip. Five measures were given to all participants including: (1) Individual Treatment Plan Objectives (ITP), (2) The Rotter Internal-External Locus of Control Scale (Rotter, 1966), (3) The Wilderness Therapy Checklist; designed for the trip, this measure assessed peer interaction, affect, self-esteem, response initiation and conflict, (4) A frequency count of critical incidents, and (5) The Brief Symptom Inventory (BSI). All participants were given these measures at admission to the program, at pre-test, at post-test, and at discharge from the hospital (Berman & Anton, 1988).

The interpretation of the results of this study is made more difficult by the fact that some of the participants were deemed as inappropriate for inclusion on the trip. Since this time, the authors have developed exclusionary criteria for participant selection. Basically, however the results suggested that the participants changed an average of 3 points on a 7 point scale on meeting their treatment plan goals, and that they experienced significant change on the Wilderness Therapy Checklist in all areas except interaction with peers and conflict. Importantly, significant decreases in behavioral symptoms were reported at post-test.

Finally, on the locus of control measure, all of the participants displayed a trend toward becoming more internal (Berman & Anton, 1988). However, the small sample size, and the lack of a comparison group compromise the integrity of the study and limit our ability to draw conclusions.

Wilderness approaches to therapy have also been applied to outpatient settings. Kaplan (1974) examined the impact of an out-of-doors program on the self-esteem and self assessment of 10 young males, with a matched group of students serving as a comparison group. The results clearly suggested that self-esteem and self evaluation were more positive in the treatment group than in the comparison group. Additionally, six months after termination of the program, the changes appeared to be fairly stable. This study was interesting in that it did utilize a comparison group and did attempt to assess the stability of change over time. The results, however, appear to be based largely on clinical impressions, as the specific techniques used for measurement were not presented. Finally, the use of male subjects limits the generalizability of the study results.

The work done by Kaplan is indeed intriguing, and deserves further attention. In a recent book (Kaplan & Kaplan, 1989), these authors describe the development and evaluation of the Outdoor Challenge Program over the course of ten years. In short, over this time, 176 individuals participated in backpacking experiences ranging in length from 9 to 14 days. Through the years of the program, the majority of the participants were male and female adolescents, with 46 adults also participating (Kaplan & Kaplan, 1989).

Funded by the U.S. Forest Service, much of the research on this program focused on learning outdoor skills, and on measuring sources of confusion, worry and comfort among wilderness program participants. Interestingly, significant increases in self-confidence, responsibility, positive outlook, and being in touch with nature were found (Kaplan & Kaplan, 1989). These studies are rather unique in that they were conducted over such an extended period of time. Additionally, some subjective data was collected, especially when asking participants to reflect on their wilderness experience following their participation. On the other hand, this subjective data, and the relatively small samples employed, limit the generalizability of these results.

The use of clinical ratings of effectiveness can also be seen in a study reported by Burdsal and Force (1983). Ninety-nine male and 33 female adolescents were rated by counselors on six different personality dimensions following participation in each of three camping trips. The results suggested that following the trip, the male participants became less dependent and more self-reliant than the female participants. Unfortunately, these authors do not provide any information regarding specific measurement techniques.

More objective measurement techniques were reported by Marx (1988) in his evaluation of the Preble Chapel Teen Adventure Program. This program was developed in 1985, through the Maine State Child Welfare system. The majority of the clients were male, between the ages of 13 and 15, and had been abused and/or neglected.

This program is innovative in that it specifically defines itself as therapeutic. Additionally, the outdoor components of the program are only four days or less in duration. All of the participants engage in four months of the Outdoor Challenge, then are involved in eight months of community based follow-up programming. Prior to the Outdoor Challenge portion of the program, the counselor does a home visit. At this time, the counselor, parent, and teen develop a behavioral contract which stipulates three behavioral goals to work toward. Included in the contract are suggested rewards for compliance.

Unfortunately, no formal evaluation data has yet been generated from this program. However, the use of such behavioral contracting and rewards is conducive to objective evaluation. At this point, 20 youth have completed the program, with 95% rating the program positively, and 100% of their parents providing positive ratings (Marx, 1988). Although this program appears to have great potential for effective evaluation, to this point it relies again on subjective evaluations of effectiveness, rather than on objective measurement instruments.

In an attempt to minimize some of these methodological problems, Davis-Berman and Berman (1989) reported on the results of four Wilderness Therapy trips. Twenty-three adolescents, 15 boys and 8 girls aged 13 to 18, participated in one of the four trips. All of the youth were in outpatient counseling at the time of their entrance into the program. Generally, these adolescents were experiencing family problems, depressive symptoms, and problems with anger and impulse control.

Standardized measurement instruments were administered to the participants at pre-test and post-test. These instruments included: The Internal-External Locus of Control Scale (Rotter, 1966), a Self-Efficacy Inventory (Sherer et al., 1982), The Piers-Harris Self-Concept Scale (Piers & Harris, 1969), and The Brief Symptoms Inventory (Derogatis, 1975). This BSI was also administered at admission and discharge from the program.

In addition to these standardized instruments, the following were developed to be used to evaluate the program: The number of Critical Incidents per day was recorded for each participant; Individual Treatment Plan Goals (ITP) were developed for each adolescent prior to the departure of the trip; and The Wilderness Therapy Checklist. This instrument assessed peer interaction, affect, self-esteem, response initiation, and conflict on a 7 point scale, with higher numbers suggesting greater frequency of occurrence.

The results of this study indicated that self-efficacy and self esteem significantly improved at post-test. Significant changes were also seen on the Brief Symptoms Inventory (BSI). A significant decrease in reported symptoms was noted between admission, pre-test, post-test and discharge from the program. The participants tended to score more internally on the Locus of Control measure at post-test, however, this change was not statistically significant. Finally, change on all of the dimensions of the Wilderness Therapy Checklist was positive, with change in affect and cooperation being most prominent (Davis-Berman & Berman, 1989).

This study represents a more refined attempt at program evaluation. As such, it suggests that the Wilderness Therapy Program was indeed effective in producing positive change in its program participants. However, it is also plagued with some of the methodological difficulties discussed throughout this chapter. It appears that many of these difficulties are specific to wilderness programs, and that they will continue to surface in the study of outdoor program evaluation.

Although we like to think that we have made progress in the evaluation of these outcomes, the critique presented by Byers (1979) still seems relevant. He stated that there was very little empirical work done on the evaluation of outcome, especially in terms of short and long-term change. Importantly, he suggested that an evaluation of the process of the camping experience be included in the research reports. This type of evaluation would involve a detailed explication of the philosophy and objectives of the camp experience, a description of the program and the skills needed by the counselors, and finally, an account of the behaviors of both the program and the counselors (Byers, 1979).

Research on Outward Bound

Outward Bound is probably the best example of an outdoor program which offers such an evaluation of process. This section will present some of the philosophy behind this program and provide a sampling of the outcome and process research. Finally due to the large number of applications of Outward Bound to delinquents, studies of delinquency programs will be presented.

Outward Bound is the most thoroughly developed outdoor program for youth in existence today. The previous chapter mentioned the early Mountains Speak for Themselves perspective, and the debate in the field on the role of reflection. More recently, Outward Bound has utilized what has been called a Metaphoric Curriculum approach. As such, the outdoor experience is seen as a metaphor for real life activity. The emphasis is on "consciously framing course events so they become experiential metaphors for salient challenges in the students' daily lives" (Bacon, 1988, p. 13).

In extracting and examining such metaphors, a number of steps are taken. The problems and issues of participants are assessed, and the course challenges are developed. Throughout the course, the primacy of experience is stressed, as is the importance of succeeding in both the physical and metaphorical challenges (Bacon, 1988 pp. 13-47).

The structure of this approach attempts to confront the student with the physical, social, and natural environment with such interaction being central to Outward Bound (Richards, 1976, pp. 9-10). In fact, one of the foundations of the Outward Bound philosophy is that "to cope effectively with the unknown, an individual must first of all know himself and then have developed the ability and inclination to think into the unknown" (Richards, 1976, p. 20). This is accomplished through the "Discovery Learning" model, which involves providing students with arousing and novel stimuli, and encouraging them to discover ways to reduce the uncertainty of the situation and to cope effectively with it (Richards, 1976).

It is thought that Outward Bound is uniquely conducive to using this approach, as the outdoor environment, and the various tasks and exercises performed in this environment certainly represent the ultimate in uncertainty and ambiguity (Richards, 1976). Although the above comments are philosophical in nature, they do provide the reader with a feeling for the underlying rationale for the use of the outdoors in Outward Bound. The therapeutic component to Outward Bound is explained more concretely by Chase (1981). In speaking about the wilderness environment, he states: "coping behavior in the wilderness is positively reinforced, as are self-sufficiency, risk-taking, initiative, and cooperation" (Chase, 1981, p. 7). In addition to the wilderness environment facilitating coping, this environment is seen as encouraging interdependence and cooperation, and as imposing direct and very real consequences for behavior on the participants (Chase, 1981, p. 8). Finally, in addition to these general therapeutic qualities of the natural environment, the following goals are identified by Outward Bound for their participants (Chase, 1981, p. 6):

1) Increase in self-esteem
2) Movement toward a more internal locus of control
3) Cooperation, independence and compassion
4) Increased sense of responsibility for self, others and society
5) Greater awareness of dysfunctional behavior
6) Understand the value of risk-taking
7) Appropriate expression of human reactions
8) Increase in trust
9) Improvement in physical health and fitness
10) The development of new ways to recreate

Due to such a wide diversity of purpose and therapeutic goals, one should not be surprised to learn of the large number of Outward Bound Programs, or programs that incorporate Outward Bound into their curricula. Many of these programs will be presented in the next chapter on the varieties of outdoor programs available today. At this point, however, a few of the outcome studies pertaining to a variety of Outward Bound Programs will be presented to familiarize the reader with the current status of the effectiveness of the Outward Bound approach affecting change in the out-of-doors.

As with all of the previous outdoor programs, prior to reporting research studies, the critical issues relating to those studies must be presented. Although Outward Bound is certainly a well developed program, it also falls short in its efforts to evaluate its effectiveness. Shore (1977) speaks to this issue in a reference volume of Outward Bound outcome studies. Basically, Shore's (1977) critique of the program at that time is still valid today. He outlined a number of problem areas and concluded that the outcome literature for the program is weak and not linked to the actual details of the Outward Bound program itself. In detailing his objections, he suggests that the following issues are problematic: research designs are inadequate; attrition of participants; the implementation of many of the studies is flawed; and finally, there is a lack of theory related to the Outward Bound Program. Although more recent writings seem to incorporate a greater amount of theory, many of these areas remain quite troublesome.

Anecdotal reports of effectiveness were presented by Fletcher (1970) in his evaluation of the efficacy of Outward Bound Programs in Great Britain. Agencies which had sponsored these programs, as well as the participants themselves, were surveyed following the termination of the programs. Generally, 50% of the sponsoring agencies said that they felt that their programs were successful (Fletcher, 1970, p. 60). Even more glowing reports were given by the former students of Outward Bound. Eighty-six percent said that they felt that they had increased in self confidence as a result of their experience, and 78% felt that they had gained in maturity (Fletcher, 1970, pp. 60-61). Although interesting and supportive of Outward Bound, this study falls short in its lack of objective measurement, and its failure to connect the program with theory in any meaningful way.

A more objective attempt at evaluation was made through the Colorado Outward Bound School. Over 600 surveys were sent to former participants, with a return rate of 77%. Those responding answered questions about self-esteem, self awareness, self assertion, and acceptance of others. Participants were asked to rate the extent of their change as a result of the Outward Bound experience on these dimensions. Significant differences were found in self assertion, self-esteem, and acceptance of others. No significant differences were reported in self awareness (Smith, Gabriel, Schott, & Padia, 1975).

Although this study did make more of an attempt at rigorous evaluation, some shortcomings exist. For example, the reader is not told which instruments, if any, were used to assess the various psychological dimensions. Finally, to ask participants to rate their change on an item retrospectively is to possibly introduce bias into the study.

An evaluation of the Outward Bound Program at the VA hospital in White River Junction, Vermont utilized more objective measurement instruments. Males between the ages of 25 and 50, currently in a short-term psychiatric unit of the VA hospital, served as subjects. Six patients comprised the treatment group, while an additional seven patients were selected as a comparison group. The treatment consisted of a four-hour Outward Bound session once a week for three weeks, involving mainly ropes work and rock climbing experiences.

All of the subjects were administered the Hudson Generalized Contentment Scale and the Hudson Index of Self-Esteem at both pre-test and post-test (Stich & Sussman, 1981).

The treatment group increased in reported contentment at post-test. However, there were no significant differences between the treatment and comparison groups. No significant change or differences were found on the self-esteem measure. Participants were then surveyed four months after their participation in the program, were asked to give their subjective impressions of the Outward Bound experience, and were asked to rate its effect on their self-esteem. The majority of the respondents reported that Outward Bound had been a good experience for them, and that they had noticed small increases in their self-esteem (Stich & Sussman, 1981). Once again, although interesting, these results are plagued by problems in the study itself. For example, the small sample size in this study makes interpretation of the results difficult. Additionally, the follow-up portion of the study reported a 45% response rate, hindering the interpretation of the results.

A slightly larger sample incorporating both males and females was utilized in another evaluation of the Colorado Outward Bound School (Koepke, 1974). Thirty-three males and eleven females between the ages of 16 and 38 served as subjects. All were given the Gough Adjective Checklist, a real and ideal self-concept inventory, and a State-Trait Anxiety inventory at both pre-test and post-test.

The results suggested an increase in favorable adjectives and a decrease in unfavorable adjectives checked at post-test. Females reported more change on the real/ideal self-concept measure than did males, with males indicating more negative traits, and finally, the anxiety scores were significantly lower at post-test. There were no sex differences in the anxiety ratings.

In summarizing the results of this study, it can be suggested that the male and female participants were more similar than different. Also, self-concept was seen to increase, and the discrepancy between the real and ideal self decreased. Finally, anxiety was decreased at post-test (Koepke, 1974). The results of this study are more impressive, as a larger sample was used, as were objective measurement instruments. Unfortunately, the lack of a comparison group is problematic. Generally speaking, however, this study does suggest that Outward Bound inspired change in self-concept and anxiety in the participants. Improvements in self-esteem and coping were also reported in a study of the Dartmouth-Hitchcock Mental Health Center program (Stich & Gaylor, 1983). The unique aspect of this piece is that it relates Outward Bound to Bandura's (1977) self-efficacy theory. According to this theory, self-efficacy expectations are derived from the following sources: performance accomplishments; vicarious experience; verbal persuasion; emotional arousal; group support; and mastery (Bandura, 1977).

Stich and Gaylor (1983) argue that students learn performance accomplishments through direct experience, and the modeling of staff. They also gain vicarious experience through live and symbolic modeling through group discussion sessions. Verbal persuasion is experienced through interpretation and suggestions by the staff and peers, while emotional arousal is experienced by arousal around challenging activities. Group support is obviously experienced through the actual interaction with the group of leaders and peers. Finally, mastery is accomplished through generalizing these new skills and attitudes into performance (Stich & Gaylor, 1983, pp. 5-7).

Although not a report of an empirical study, this article is important in that it attempts to apply a theoretical framework to the structure and function of Outward Bound. The lack of such theoretical work was previously identified as a problem in the research on Outward Bound.

Another omission in the general Outward Bound literature, and most of the early literature on outdoor approaches to therapy, is research on the characteristics of the instructors and leaders involved in these programs. The reader will remember previous discussions of the importance of trained leaders, without any specification as to what kind of training should be secured, or what qualities in leaders are critical for the success of the program.

Riggins (1985) looked at the leadership qualities of 109 instructors and assistant instructors from the Colorado Outward Bound School. Biographical data were collected on all of the instructors. Then the research team classified each instructor as most effective, average, and least effective. These judgements were made rather subjectively, but did include many comments from students that had worked with these instructors on Outward Bound trips. Finally, the instructors were asked to complete a personality inventory which assessed their Interpersonal Relations orientation.

Interestingly, the results suggested that personality characteristics were not related to instructor effectiveness. Rather, age seemed to be a factor (older instructors were rated higher), as was gender (male instructors received higher ratings than females), and finally, those with Bachelor's degrees received higher ratings than those without degrees (Riggins, 1985, p. 8). This article is important in that it recognizes the need for research on instructor characteristics. If we are to finally determine what contributes to the success (or lack of success) of outdoor programs, we must engage in these types of research endeavors.

Clearly, Outward Bound has made many sound attempts to describe its process and to evaluate its outcome. In evaluating this research, we must remember the inherent difficulties with wilderness based studies. As such, Outward Bound distinguishes itself among programs. The final section in this chapter turns to delinquency programs, as they too, often represent exemplary evaluation attempts. Some of these programs are part of Outward Bound, others are similar to Outward Bound, while others are unique in their perspective.

Delinquency Programs

When examining the research literature on wilderness programs, one encounters a large proportion of studies done on delinquent groups. Some (e.g. Nold & Wilpers, 1975) have suggested that the use of wilderness programs is especially applicable to delinquents, as the intensity of the experience facilitates cooperation, trust and a redirection of "machismo" in these adolescents (Nold & Wilpers, 1975, pp. 167-168).

Wichmann (1983) provides a review of recent studies evaluating delinquency programs. Similarly, Roberts (1988) provides such a review and suggests that wilderness programs are effective interventions for delinquents (Roberts, 1989).

One of the earliest but best designed delinquency studies was done by Kelly and Baer (1968). One hundred and twenty delinquent boys were studied in the state of Massachusetts. Of the sample, 60 were involved in Outward Bound, while 60 comprised a matched comparison group. All of the subjects were administered the Jesness Inventory at pre-test and post-test. The results basically suggested that the Outward Bound group showed significant positive changes on autism, alienation, asocial behavior, manifest aggression, social maladjustment, and value orientation, changes not seen in the comparison group.

The treatment group also showed improvement on the "I am" and the "I would like to be" scales of the self concept measure. Finally, after 9 months, the Outward Bound group had a recidivism rate of 20%, while the comparison group had a rate of 34% (Kelly & Baer, 1968). This early study is impressive in that it suggests the efficacy of Outward Bound in dealing with a difficult client population. This success is suggested through objective measurement instruments, as well as reports of recidivism, suggesting stability of change over time. Additionally, the rather large sample utilized by this study adds strength to its findings.

Kelly and Baer (1971) also compared the treatment of delinquent boys through Outward bound with a control group in a traditional inpatient treatment program. Unfortunately, this study was not as well conceived or executed as their previous work, illustrated by the fact that no standardized measurement instruments were used. The only measure used in the study was recidivism rate, with the Outward Bound group reporting a significantly lower recidivism after one year than did the control group. The lack of objective measurement, and specification of the actual recidivism rates makes the interpretation of these results difficult. Finally, to utilize an institutionalized control group to compare with an Outward Bound group compounds the potential bias in the study.

Willman and Chun (1973) reported on a program associated with Outward Bound called the Homeward Bound Program. This program for delinquent youth lasted six weeks and was developed and implemented by the Massachusetts Division of Youth Services. Fourteen months after termination of the outdoor program, the Outward Bound group had a recidivism rate of 20.8%, while a control group had a rate of 42.7% (Willman & Chun, 1973). Similar to other studies, this evaluation has some problems with its measurement techniques. Additionally, no information is given about the control group, so the reader is unable to judge the appropriateness of this group, and the means with which it was selected.

Recidivism over a five year period of time was examined by Baer and associates (1975). Sixty male delinquents from the Massachusetts Division of Youth Services completed a 26 day Outward Bound course. Following completion of the course, certificates were awarded. Instructors also rated all of the participants on a rating scale which assessed attitude, physical traits, and personality characteristics.

At five years follow-up, 30% of those who had received the certificates of completion of the program had become recidivated, whereas 90% of those who failed to receive certificates reoffended. In addition, based on the instructor ratings, the following factors were found to predict future recidivism: effort, maturity, and leadership (Baer, Jacobs, & Carr, 1975).

An equally rigorous evaluation was conducted by Cyntrynbaum and Ken (1975). Forty-nine delinquents enrolled in the Connecticut Wilderness School were compared with 54 matched control subjects. All subjects were administered the Semantic Differential, and the Borgatta & Fanshel Behavior Rating Scale at pre-test and post-test. Subjects were also administered a subjective outcome questionnaire at post-test. Interestingly, no real significant differences were found between the groups on the objective measures. However, the Wilderness School participants rated themselves as more powerful, loyal, trusting and satisfied than the control group.

At six months follow-up, the wilderness group reported significantly fewer arrests, legal problems, and drug and alcohol abuse on the outcome questionnaire. Finally, at six months post-treatment, this group had only an 11.1% recidivism rate, compared to a rate of 30.2% in the control group (Cyntrynbaum & Ken, 1975). Increases in positive behavior, more positive perceptions of the self, and increases in self-concept were seen following participation in the Wilderness Experience Program (currently called the Santa Fe Mountain Center) (Kimball, 1979). Although these results are encouraging, the lack of a comparison group detracts from their impact.

A final example of a delinquency study can be seen in the evaluation of the WAY (Wilderness Alternatives for Youth) program conducted by the Pacific Crest Outward Bound School (Sakofs, 1992). One hundred and fifteen participants were randomly assigned to control and experimental groups, and all were given 33 scales at pre-test and post-test, and at 3 months and one year follow-up. The experimental group participated in a three week wilderness program. Significant differences between these groups were seen on a number of measures including locus of control depression, aggression and counselor and parent ratings (Sakofs, 1992).

In reflecting on this range of studies done on the effectiveness of wilderness programs with delinquents, a few observations can be made. Wichmann (1983) suggests that generally, these programs seem to note change following wilderness programs in the areas of personal and interpersonal growth, as well as in recidivism, a measure of the stability of change over time (Wichmann, 1983, 13-14).

Roberts (1988) criticizes this reliance on recidivism, as he asserts that it is a fairly subjective measure, and lacks consistency in its definition. Despite these rather promising comments, the problems in these studies have also been pointed out. If the evaluation of wilderness programs is to continue, certain research flaws must be attended to.

These include the use of small sample sizes, the more effective use of control groups, and random assignment to groups. Finally, it has been suggested that greater attention be paid to the theoretical perspective behind wilderness programs. As we measure outcome and comment on effectiveness, it is critical to have a solid appreciation of the theory behind these programs, as we attempt to explain their effectiveness as well as their shortcomings (Wichmann, 1983, pp. 15-16).

Hopefully, this chapter has aptly represented the strengths and weaknesses of various research studies performed on wilderness programs. Clearly, many of these programs claim to facilitate change in the participants, and many do actually document change. We applaud the programs who are committed to research and who have contributed to this literature. On the other hand, we feel a responsibility to illuminate some of the flaws in the research literature, with the intent of facilitating dialogue among those in the field. Chapter 8 in this book is devoted solely to the topic of research and program evaluation. Therein, the interested reader will find more detailed information and will be confronted with other issues.

At the present time, we are more interested in identifying the variety of program types that are currently being offered. This variety is one of the factors which makes research projects so difficult to design and implement. Chapter 5 provides a sampling of the different types of wilderness program offerings available today. It is our hope that this chapter will provide a framework for organizing and categorizing the vastly diverse outdoor programs operating today.

References

Adams, W.D. (1970). Survival training: Its effects on self-concept and selected personality factors of emotionally disturbed adolescents. (Doctoral dissertation, University of Utah, 1969). *Dissertation Abstracts International, 31,* 388B.

Bacon, S. (1988). Paradox and double-binds in adventure-based education. Eric Document Reproduction Service No. 296832, Greenwich, Conn.: Outward Bound, USA, 4-30.

Baer, D., Jacobs, P., & Carr, F. (1975). Instructors' ratings of delinquents after Outward Bound survival training and their subsequent recidivism. *Psychological Reports, 36,* 547-553.

Bandura, A. (1977). Self-efficacy: Toward a unifying theory of behavioral change. *Psychological Review,* (2), 191-215.

Barley, F. (1972). Camp can change campus attitudes. *Camping Magazine, 44* (7), 18.

Berman, D., & Anton, M. (1988). A wilderness therapy program as an alternative to adolescent psychiatric hospitalization. *Residential Treatment for Children and Youth, 5,* 39-52.

Berman, D., & Davis-Berman, J. (1989). Wilderness therapy: A therapeutic adventure for adolescents. *Journal of Independent Social Work, 3* (3), 65-77.

Broida, D., Proudman, B., & Magee, G. (1978). Gaining awareness through adventure. *Parks and Recreation,* 30-34.

Burdsal, C., & Force, R.C. (1983). An examination of counselor ratings of behavior problem youth in an early stage, community-based intervention program. *Journal of Clinical Psychology, 39,* 353-360.

Byers, E.S. (1979). Wilderness camping as a therapy for emotionally disturbed children: A critical review. *Exceptional Children, 45* (8), 628-635.

Chase, W. (1981). Outward Bound as an adjunct to therapy. (Report WORC 014601). Denver, Colo: Colorado Outward Bound School. (ERIC Document Reproduction Service No. ED 241204). (1-17).

Chenery, M. (1981). Effects of summer camp on child development and contributions of counselors to those effects. *Journal of Leisure Research,* third quarter, 195-207.

Clarke, G., & Eells, E. (1974). Early findings on values of camping now available. *Camping Magazine, 47* (2), 8-9.

Cyntrynbaum, S., & Ken, K. (1975). *The Connecticut wilderness program: A preliminary report.* Hartford, CT: State of Connecticut Council on Human Services.

Davis-Berman, J., & Berman, D. (1989). The Wilderness Therapy Program: An empirical study of its effects with adolescents in an outpatient setting. *Journal of Contemporary Psychotherapy, 19* (4), 271-281.

Derogatis, L. R. (1975). *Brief symptom inventory.* Riverwood, MD: Clinical Psychometric Research.

Ewert, A. (1983). *Outdoor adventure and self-concept: A research analysis.* Eugene, Oregon: University of Oregon.

Ewert, A. (1989). *Outdoor adventure pursuits: Foundations, models, and theories.* Columbus, OH: Publishing Horizons.

Fletcher, B. A. (1970). *Students of Outward Bound schools in Great Britain: A follow-up study.* University of Bristol, School of Education.

Gass, M. (Ed). (1993). *Adventure therapy: Therapeutic applications of adventure programming.* Dubuque, Iowa: Kendall/Hunt.

Hammerman, D., & Hammerman, W. (Eds.) (1973). *Outdoor education: A book of readings.* Minneapolis, MN: Burgess Publishing Co.

Horwood, B. (1989). Reflections on reflection. *Journal of Experiential Education, 12* (2), 7-8.

Hughes, A., & Dudley, H. (1973). An old idea for a new problem: Camping as a treatment for the emotionally disturbed in our state hospitals. *Adolescence, 8,* 43-50.

Jerstad, L., & Selzer, J. (1973). Adventure experiences as treatment for residential mental patients. *Therapeutic Recreation Journal, 7,* 8-11.

Kaplan, R. (1974). Some psychological benefits of an outdoor challenge program. *Environment and Behavior, 6,* 101-115.

Kaplan, R., & Kaplan, S. (1989). *The experience of nature: A psychological perspective.* New York: Cambridge University Press.

Kelly, F.J., & Baer, D. J. (1968). *Outward Bound schools as an alternative to institutionalization for adolescent delinquent boys.* Boston: Fandel Press.

Kelly, F. J., & Baer, D. J. (1971). Physical challenge as a treatment for delinquency. *Crime and Delinquency, 17,* 437-445.

Kimball, R. O. (1979). *Wilderness experience program: Final evaluation report.* Santa Fe: State of New Mexico Forensic System.

Kimball, R. O. (1983). The wilderness as therapy. *Journal of Experiential Education, 6* (3), 7-16.

Klocke, D., & Wichern, D. (1980). Mountain-bound: A test of counseling techniques. *The School Counselor,* November, 105-108.

Koepke, S. (1974). The effects of Outward Bound participation upon anxiety and self-concept. (Report No. RC 008 234) (ERIC Document Reproduction Service No. ED 099162), (1-7).

Krieger, W. (1973). Study on self-concept change in campers. *Camping Magazine, 45* (4), 16-17.

Lowry, T. (1974). (Ed.) *Camping therapy: Its uses in psychiatry and rehabilitation.* Springfield, IL: Charles C. Thomas.

Marx, E., (1988). Camping for crippled children. *Camping Magazine, 16,* 5.

Miles, J., & Priest, S. (1990). *Adventure education.* State College, PA: Venture Publishing.

Nadler, R., & Luckner, J. (1992). *Processing the adventure experience: Theory and practice.* Dubuque, Iowa: Kendall/Hunt.

Nold, J., & Wilpers, M. (1975). Wilderness training as an alternative to incarceration. In C. Dodge, (Ed.), *A nation without prisons* (pp. 155-169). Lexington, MA: Lexington Books.

Piers, E., & Harris, D. (1969). *Manual for the Piers-Harris children's self-concept scale.* Nashville: Counselor Recordings and Tests.

Richards, G. (1976). Some psychological bases and aspects of Outward Bound. (Report No. RC 013007). Sydney: Australian Outward Bound School. (ERIC Document Reproduction Service No. ED 209043).

Riggins, R. (1985). The Colorado Outward Bound School: Biographical and personality factors contributing to the leadership effectiveness of instructors. *Journal of Environmental Education, 16* (3), 6-11.

Roberts, A. (1988). Wilderness program for juvenile offenders: A challenging alternative. *Juvenile and Family Court Journal,* 1-12.

Roberts, A. (1989). Wilderness experiences: Camps and outdoor programs. In A. Roberts (Ed.), *Juvenile Justice: Policies, programs, and services* (pp. 194-218). Chicago: The Dorsey Press.

Rotter, J. (1966). Generalized expectancies for internal versus external control of reinforcement. *Psychological Monographs, 80* (1, Whole No. 609)

Sakofs, M. (1992). Assessing the impact of the wilderness alternative for youth programme. *Journal of Adventure Education and Outdoor Leadership, 9* (4), 16-21.

Schoel, J., Prouty, D., and Radcliffe, P. (1988). *Islands of healing: A guide to adventure-based counseling.* Hamilton, MA: Project Adventure, Inc.

Sherer, M., Maddux, J., Mercandante, B., Prentice-Dunn, S., Jacobs, B., and Rogers, R. (1982). The Self-efficacy Scale: Construction and Validation. *Psychological Reports, 51,* 663-671.

Shniderman, C. M. (1974). Impact of therapeutic camping. *Social Work, 19,* 354-357.

Shore, A. (1977). *Outward Bound: A reference volume.* Greenwich, CT: Outward Bound Inc.

Smith, M., Gabriel, R., Schott, J., and Padia, W. (1975). *Evaluation of the effects of Outward Bound.* University of Colorado: Bureau of Educational Field Services.

Stich, T. (1983). Experiential therapy. *Journal of Experiential Education, 6* (3), 22-30.

Stich, T., & Gaylor, M. (1983). Outward Bound: An innovative patient education program. (Report No. RC 014830). (ERIC Document Reproduction Service ED 247047), (1-18).

Stich, T., & Sussman, L. (1981). Outward Bound: An adjunctive psychiatric therapy: Preliminary research findings. (Report No. RC 014538). (ERIC Document Reproduction Service No. ED 239791), (1-7).

Stremba, B. (1989). Reflection: A process to learn about self through outdoor adventure. *Journal of Experiential Education, 12* (2), 7-9.

Teschner, D., & Wolter, J. (Eds.) (1984). *Wilderness Challenge: Outdoor education alternatives for youth in need.* Hadlyme, CT: The Institute of Experiential Studies.

Wichman, T. (1983). Evaluating Outward Bound for delinquent youth. *Journal of Experiential Education, 5* (3), 10-16.

Willman, H., & Chun, R. (1973). Homeward Bound: An alternative to the institutionalization of adjudicated juvenile offenders. *Federal Probation,* September, 52-58.

Chapter Five ▽

Varieties of Programs

The previous chapter provided the reader with only a small taste of the wide variety of programs utilizing the wilderness today. With the popularity of these types of programs, any comprehensive listing will soon become outdated. However, we will attempt to provide the reader with information on the more prominent programs in the appendix of the book.

This chapter does not cover outdoor programs in an inclusive and comprehensive way. Rather, it provides the reader with examples of a variety of different types of programs. In gathering this data, we decided to guide our search by referring to those programs identified as U.S. members of the Association for Experiential Education. We contacted all of the 1990-91 organizational members through the mail. Following this survey, we utilized the same procedure using the 1991-92 membership list. Thus, we felt that we were ensured of the most current compilation of programs across the nation. As a result, most of the programs discussed in this chapter and in the appendix are members of the Association for Experiential Education; however, some are not.

For the purposes of this chapter and the appendix to this book, we needed to categorize program types in order to present them in an orderly fashion. This was a very difficult task, as many programs fall into more than one category. We decided to group the programs into the following categories: Mental Health programs, Court programs, School programs, Health programs, and Enrichment programs. The predominant emphasis of each program was used in this classification scheme. There are certainly a number of programs in existence which do not fit into these categories, and there are a number of fine programs within these categories which were not included in this chapter.

It is the intent of this chapter to provide the reader with a taste of the available program types, and thus, to encourage more in-depth exploration of these wilderness programs. In the following classification of programs, we attempted to determine the primary emphasis of the program based on the materials given to us. We apologize if any program does not agree with its classification.

Mental Health Programs

A number of mental health programs utilizing the wilderness have been developed throughout the country, with the vast majority of these programs catering to troubled youth. The reader can refer to the previous chapter for a discussion of many of these programs, including the Wilderness Therapy Program developed by the present authors, and the Outward Bound Program for troubled youth. As was seen, the Outward Bound program is one of the most fully developed and prominent programs in the country today.

Generally, the mental health programs can be separated into those which are conducted on an outpatient basis, and those which are more residential or reflect an inpatient setting. Additionally, many of the programs that identify themselves as therapeutic in their orientation also focus on the problem of substance abuse, with some of the programs being solely identified as treating substance abuse.

Not surprisingly, many of the programs identified as residential or inpatient in their setting are privately sponsored, with some for-profit and some non-profit facilities. Many of the inpatient programs offer a rather restricted experiential therapy component to their program, with the most popular outdoor modality being ropes courses. Other programs do offer a more extensive outdoor component which even includes a wilderness residential experience. As was previously mentioned, these inpatient programs often serve clients experiencing substance abuse, with a few programs devoted solely to this clientele.

In terms of therapy, the approaches reported are as diverse as the clients served and the program designs. However, the substance abuse programs seemed to rely on the "12 step" approach or some variation of this model. Many of the programs mentioned "metaphor therapy," akin to the Outward Bound model, and finally, some programs mentioned individual and/or group therapy approaches, without providing specific information as to the implementation of this therapy. Finally, there is virtually no ongoing evaluation of the effectiveness of these inpatient programs.

Similar to the inpatient programs, the outpatient programs reflect a tremendous diversity of clients and problem focus. Most of the programs surveyed reported that they were private in their sponsorship, with some being for-profit and others non-profit. A few programs did identify themselves as public in their sponsorship. Fee schedules for these programs are very different, and reflect the vast diversity of structure and function of the programs. As such, the fees range from zero to almost $10,000 for a thirty-day program. The clients served in these outpatient programs are more functional than those enrolled in the inpatient programs. Often, the adolescents are aggressive, impulsive, depressed, and are experimenting with, or are addicted to a variety of substances. Unlike the inpatient programs, the outpatient programs tend to be lengthier and involve more intensive wilderness components. The majority of the programs involve extended camping and/or backpacking, with many programs spending up to a month in wilderness settings.

Although all of these outpatient programs are designed to be therapeutic, very few of them actually describe their approach to therapy in the wilderness. Thus, one is left with vague impressions, rather than explicit models and therapeutic techniques. Finally, the majority of the programs appear to collect evaluation data in a very informal fashion. Questionnaires are sent to families following completion of the program asking for their assessments of change. Very little formal, empirically sound research appears to have been done. In order to provide the reader with a more realistic feel for some of these programs, brief descriptions of some representative programs will be given.

An example of a privately sponsored outpatient program is the Wilderness Conquest program located in Idaho. Clients ranging in age from 13-26 are eligible to participate; however, those with a history of violence or sex offenses are excluded. Typically, those enrolled are depressed, have low self-esteem, and are withdrawn. This program seems to be rather rigorous and may be more physically demanding than some of the others. The outdoor experiences center around desert camping, rappelling and rock climbing. Participants are expected to use stone age skills in order to successfully negotiate the environment, and they are equipped with just the essentials.

Therapeutically, this program is less structured than those previously described. All of the staff have some kind of counseling experience, and many are familiar with a 12-step model. While in the wilderness, all of the participants are expected to participate in "circle processing." This involves processing experiences and feelings as they occur. No real formal therapy is required with the exception of using the 12-step model as a framework for living, and as a model for use in later therapy. In fact, the family is sent books and tapes on this model while the client is in the program, so that they may become familiar with it (Wilderness Conquest, 1991).

An interesting program called On Belay Youth and Family Services in Wisconsin is a private non-profit agency which provides service at no cost to the client, as the county Human Services Department pays for service. The clients, ranging in age from 11-14, are often referred by city agencies, including the juvenile court, although this is not a court-related program, nor does it focus on serving delinquents. Adolescents experiencing drug and/or family problems are also referred.

Basically, while in this program, the participants live at home and participate in year round outdoor activities, such as skiing, winter camping, summer camping, canoeing, and sailing. These outings may range from 3 days in length to one week. While at home, participants may also come to the center once a week where recreational events throughout the city are planned. During their time in the program, participants experience individual, group and family therapy. In addition, parenting training and therapy is provided for parents (On Belay Youth and Family Services, 1991).

Finally, an interesting program with both an inpatient and an outpatient component is the Interventions program. This program almost exclusively serves a chemically dependent population, which includes both adolescents and adults. Due to the federal/state sponsorship of the program, it has become very accessible, and has grown in size. Currently, there are 27 different programs in three states, with tentative expansion plans.

Utilizing a wide variety of outdoor experiences, this program offers 2-3 day trips, and some longer two week trips. A qualified social worker is present as a staff person on each trip, and participants experience group and individual therapy. In addition, a great deal of importance is attached to the peer group and to positive peer pressure (Interventions, 1991).

In addition to outpatient programs, many inpatient facilities have incorporated the therapeutic aspects of the wilderness into their treatment regimes for adolescents. Once again, the problem of substance abuse is often incorporated into the treatment model. Inner Harbour Hospital, formerly the Anneewakee Hospital, is a fairly prominent example of a hospital program which has incorporated wilderness programs into its treatment approach. This hospital distinguishes itself in that its outdoor component is more extensive, and involves the actual day-to-day living of the participants. Originally opened in 1960, this hospital has three campuses, two in Georgia and one in Florida, each of which are situated on acres of wilderness land. The program requires the adolescents to live in cabins, and to rely on wood stoves and lanterns for power. All participants are involved in outdoor "learning modules," which may include ropes courses or horsemanship, with each module lasting 10-12 weeks.

Capitalizing on the natural consequences bestowed by the environment, the Inner Harbour program focuses on utilizing the group as a vehicle for change, and the impact of positive group peer pressure. Facilitating this therapeutic focus is the therapy team consisting of a physician, psychologist, nurse, social worker, teacher, and an experiential therapist. In addition to the regular program, the hospital sponsors a special chemical dependency program. Finally, this program also has a fully developed educational component, including an accredited elementary, middle and high school. Clearly, the Inner Harbour program is quite comprehensive in its offerings, and seems to truly combine the structure of a residential program with the flexibility and creativity of a program based in the out-of-doors (Inner Harbour Hospital, 1991).

Less dependent on the hospital setting, the Beech Hill Hospital offers the Outward Bound Adolescent Chemical Dependency Program. Participants can be involved in a 22 day trip to either Maine or Florida. The program includes a learning component, which involves substance abuse education, and participation in rock climbing, ropes courses, and a solo experience. Individual counseling and group therapy is provided by professional counselors, and family members are involved in a two day family program. In an attempt to facilitate long term change, aftercare sessions are conducted for the first three months after the end of the program (Beech Hill Hospital, 1991).

Offering a more residential type program, the John De La Howe School distinguishes itself through its history and its present program. Founded in 1796, this school was previously an orphanage, while today it serves as a state boarding school. This program is unusual in that it is state supported, and is thus governed by the state of South Carolina, making it accessible to all state residents. Basically, those children assigned to the wilderness component of the program build and live in their own outdoor structures. The program requires the participants to take responsibility for their own dwellings, and to procure and fix their own food on the weekends.

In addition to experiencing the challenge of wilderness living, the participants are exposed to therapy, both alone and with their family. In fact, prior to being accepted into the program, the entire family must agree to participate in family counseling. Finally, this program is interesting in that it attempts to incorporate the notion of peer evaluation. In order to be released from the program, parents, counselors, the client, and the other participants must agree that the individual is ready to leave (The John De La Howe School, 1991).

A final example of a residentially based mental health program is the Salesmanship Club Youth and Family Center in Dallas. The reader will recall a discussion of this program in a previous chapter as one of the original mental health programs in the country. First developed in 1920, this program is still going strong today.

The Salesmanship Club is residential in nature, with 6-9 months being the average length of stay. Catering to adolescents aged 11 to 16 with behavioral difficulties, the following services are offered: year round residential placement, group counseling, special education classes, and family therapy. Participants are assigned to groups of 12 campers and they engage in wilderness experiences such as backpacking and canoeing. All of the adolescents also attend school for three hours every day while at camp.

The therapeutic nature of this camp experience is clearly shown through the group and family therapy requirements. Additionally, the staff administering these services all have graduate degrees in their respective fields. In support of the professional nature of this program, all of the staff at the camp, including those not even involved in the mental health aspects, have college degrees (The Salesmanship Club Youth and Family Center, 1991).

Court Programs

Although a number of the mental health programs included clients with court related issues, there are some wilderness programs devoted strictly to the treatment of delinquents. Obviously, however, many of those in these programs are suffering from addictions or psychological problems or more commonly, both. This section of this chapter will devote itself exclusively to mentioning programs serving delinquent populations.

Interestingly, there are far fewer programs for delinquent populations than there are for adolescents with mental health problems. The programs that do exist seem to have a few commonalities including the following: most programs are designed for male adolescents, the programs serve as a last resort attempt at rehabilitation, and many are residential in nature.

The severity of the difficulties experienced by the delinquent clients truly makes these court-related programs distinct from the mental health programs. The adolescents sent to these programs have often been in numerous outpatient and inpatient settings, and have failed to change in meaningful ways in these programs. Thus, wilderness programs for delinquents usually serve as an alternative to traditional incarceration, or as an adjunct to some kind of residential care. In this situation, the wilderness trips would be based and run out of a residential program to which the clients would return upon completion of the wilderness experience.

Similar to the mental health programs, there is a great diversity in the funding of court-related programs. However, some interesting public/private joint programs exist. There is also a tremendous variety in the extensiveness of the wilderness experience between programs, with offerings ranging from ropes courses to lengthy camping programs.

As with the mental health programs, we will try to give the reader a taste of some of the actual programs operating in the area. Once again, the following section does not attempt to describe all or even a representative number of court related wilderness programs. Rather, a select few will be mentioned, and the interested reader will be referred to the appendix for further information on programs. As was previously discussed, some methodologically sound evaluations of wilderness programs with delinquents do exist; thus, these programs have become more prominent than the mental health programs designed for adolescents. The reader will remember that the Outward Bound program has always been central to the wilderness treatment of delinquents, with their program being applied to delinquency programs in Massachusetts, for example (Kelly & Baer, 1968). Other prominent programs include the Santa Fe Mountain Center, formerly called the Wilderness Experience Center (Kimball, 1979). Discussion of the research supporting these programs can be found in Chapter 4.

One of the most controversial outdoor programs serving delinquents is the Vision Quest Program, based in Tucson, Arizona. This program was founded in 1973 by department of corrections workers who were frustrated with the lack of innovative programming for use with delinquent adolescents. Through the years, this program has grown in its popularity, and currently serves adolescents who are referred by the court system or by social service agencies.

Thus, the majority of Vision Quest participants are involved either directly or indirectly with the criminal justice system.

The Vision Quest program is quite extensive, and offers a number of alternative programs from which to choose. The adolescents usually begin the program by attending the Impact Camp. This is a base camp where participants work on various physical and psychological issues in a camp setting. Completion of this portion of the program qualifies the participants to move to other program options. One such option is the wagon train. This program involves the adolescents travelling in wagon trains during the day and sleeping in teepees at night. The goal of this program is to experience many of the trials and tribulations of the frontier, and work toward becoming self sufficient. Participants also attend school for four hours per day in the wagon train program. The wagon train is just one of many specialized programs offered by Vision Quest.

In addition to the short term therapeutic programs, Vision Quest also sponsors a residential component. Adolescents who have completed the other programs may choose to live in a group home setting. The goal of this placement is to eventually facilitate the adolescent's adjustment back to the home and the community. Finally, the HomeQuest program serves adolescents living in the community. Participants come to the Vision Quest facilities for their evening meal, and for activities and counseling. As was mentioned, those who enter the Vision Quest program may choose to participate in a number of different programs; however, all must be willing to commit for a period of at least one year. In this regard, Vision Quest is a more long term program than some of the other mental health or delinquency programs (Vision Quest, 1991).

The Santa Fe Mountain Center represents another program which has been a leader in the innovative treatment of delinquents. Wilderness adventure courses provide delinquent youth with empowering experiences which facilitate the development of long-term behavioral change. Unlike some other programs, the Santa Fe Mountain Center program is very sophisticated in its realization that the "high" that one might experience following a wilderness experience is not true long term change. Rather, they see the role of the wilderness adventure as being an aid to diagnosis, and a "projective psychological test" (Kimball, 1983, p. 8).

Another interesting feature of the Santa Fe Mountain Center program is that it operates within the criminal justice system, rather than as an alternative to traditional treatment. Finally, some of the best evaluation of wilderness programs comes out of this program, further enhancing its credibility. The program offerings are so diverse that it is not possible to describe a typical offering. Suffice it to say that the wilderness programs are developed to supplement more traditional treatment, and each program is designed to meet the needs of the specific client group (Kimball, 1983).

Another interesting example of programming for delinquent adolescents is the GIG (Group and Individual Growth) program conducted for the Department of Welfare in Pennsylvania. Although the course was run for the state of Pennsylvania, the sponsoring agency is Passages to Adventure, an organization based in West Virginia. Project GIG is a 28 day course for male delinquents, offered in the state of Pennsylvania throughout the year. All of the youths attend this program as a result of their court involvement. As with many other programs, Project GIG is a multi-element course, including backpacking, rock climbing, caving, and solo experiences.

As of this writing, Project GIG has been operating for two years and has run a total of 15 courses, with 161 youth finishing the course. Preliminary data suggests that this program is much less costly than incarceration, and it appears that recidivism is rather low among those who successfully completed the program. According to Passages to Adventure, the recidivism rate for the two year program was 18% (Passages to Adventure, 1991).

The Wilderness Challenge School in Virginia also offers a program for delinquent adolescents. This program is important in that it offers a more comprehensive approach than some of the other programs in this area. Utilizing a more long-term format, the program begins with the wilderness component, called the Wilderness Challenge Course. This course is 10 days long and is a multi-element course which includes backpacking, canoeing and rock climbing. Following completion of the wilderness challenge, participants attend six two hour classes on life skills, including the facilitation of communication and problem solving skills. The remainder of the program involves meetings to review progress toward meeting treatment goals, individual and family counseling, and adventure weekends.

Adventure weekends usually involve the wilderness, such as a canoeing weekend, and are attended only by the adolescents. Family are included in another program called the family outing weekend. During these weekends, group and family cohesion is focused on. Following the completion of three adventure weekends, and the previously described program, the adolescent receives a certificate of graduation.

The Wilderness Challenge School, like most delinquency programs, was developed in response to a lack of alternative programming for delinquent or at-risk adolescents. As with most programs of this type, an attempt is made to document the effectiveness and efficiency of the program in terms of recidivism and cost effectiveness. As of this writing, the recidivism rate had been decreased by one-half following participation in the program, and follow-up data five years later suggested that 70% of the graduates had stayed out of legal trouble. This data is strengthened by the fact that this program was also reported to be only one-tenth of the cost of traditional treatment or incarceration (Wilderness Challenge School, 1991).

Another example of a program for delinquents is the TresslerCare Wilderness School in Pennsylvania. Combining a wilderness component and a residential center, this program offers a comprehensive program for delinquent adolescents. Basically, participants first complete an intense, multi-element wilderness program. The first part of this trip occurs in Pennsylvania, with the remainder of the trip taking place in North Carolina. This trip includes a solo experience and marathon running. At the conclusion of this trip, some of the participants are ready to leave treatment. Others, however, are not, and are referred to the school program. In this program, students live in cabins, and move to more comfortable cabins based on their progress. In addition to wilderness type living, students attend school, participate in work crew projects, participate in counseling, and engage in community service (TresslerCare Wilderness School, 1991). This program, thus, represents a combination of wilderness and residential experience.

Finally, one cannot discuss court related wilderness programs without mentioning the Eckard Family Youth Alternative programs. Encompassing at least seven states at the time of this writing, this program was serving 1200 clients, and operating with 1000 staff.

It is impossible to fully describe this organization in this chapter; thus, we will only attempt a brief summary. Basically, this is a residentially based program that serves delinquents of a varying degree of severity, ranging from high risk youth, to those who are currently incarcerated. These youth are served through the following programs: The Eckard Wilderness Educational System, The Eckard Youth Development Center, The Eckard Youth Challenge Program, and The Florida Conservation Corps. These programs are designed to be "holistic, comprehensive, and directed toward success upon community re-entry" (Eckard Family Youth Alternatives, 1991, p. i).

The Eckard program is quite renowned, and includes challenge courses (for first time offenders), regular wilderness programs, and residential centers. In the midst of all of this activity, family meetings occur on a regular basis, as does follow-up for six months after completion of the program. Interestingly, the Eckard organization is rather unique in that it emphasizes the importance of outcome evaluation. Since a 1986 mandate to evaluate in the state of Florida, this program has been collecting data. Currently, they are in the midst of completing a five year outcome evaluation (Eckard Family Youth Alternatives, 1991).

School Programs

For purposes of the present chapter, school programs will refer to wilderness programs that are in some substantial way affiliated with the mainstream primary or secondary school system in the United States. These programs are interesting as a group because they all seem to be based on a value that states that for many children, experiential learning is superior to any other kind of learning, and that there are simply some things in this world that are better taught outside of the classroom. Despite this rather convincing position, there are not many well developed school-related wilderness programs currently in operation.

In addition to a focus on experiential learning, school programs seem to have accepted the challenge of trying to empower and facilitate the personal growth of their students. Thus, one will find that some of the school programs do teach things about nature and the wilderness in their programs, but that they also strive to teach lessons about self-esteem, responsibility, leadership, risk-taking, and respect for diversity. Some of these school programs are specifically geared to youth-at-risk. This population is often identified by teachers and other school personnel as students that have a strong potential to become delinquent. By targeting these students for school-related programs, an attempt is made at prevention of future problems. Finally, the school-related programs have served to open the wilderness to all of the youth in their areas of service. Many are funded at least partially by the school system, and thus are not very expensive for the students to access. This issue of cost is critical, as the cost of many of the outdoor programs is so prohibitive that it limits the access of the program to only a few.

Thus it can be suggested that the school programs might serve a preventative purpose. By applying the notions about the restorative and healing aspects of the wilderness to school children, we may serve to enhance their physical and/or mental coping skills. Additionally, by exposing children to wilderness programming, we offer them avenues of exploration which may be used for a lifetime.

Certainly, one of the most prominent school-related programs is the Project Adventure program. Project Adventure itself was begun in 1971 by a high school principal in Massachusetts. Interestingly, this founder, Jerry Pieh, was the son of the founder of the Minnesota Outward Bound School. Thus, it seems natural that he would see the value of bringing some of the therapeutic lessons of the out-of-doors to the school setting. During the 1970's, through various grants, a Project Adventure curriculum was developed and implemented in the Hamilton-Wenham high school (Schoel, Prouty, & Radcliffe, 1988).

Shortly after the successful development of the program, the Project Adventure staff began to focus on training others in this approach to experiential learning. By 1982, over 5,000 educators had attended a training seminar, and 500 schools had implemented at least part of the Project Adventure model. It was in 1982 that Project Adventure became a non-profit corporation, and they have been training educators and other human service professionals ever since (Schoel, Prouty, & Radcliffe, 1988, p. 7).

In addition to introducing the notion of experiential learning into the school, the Project Adventure program developed and continues to support a therapeutic modality called Adventure Based Counseling. This type of counseling approach was first implemented in an action seminar at the Hamilton-Wenham high school, and involved learning through adventure, group activity, and community service. This approach to counseling is still alive today and forms the basis for many therapeutic outdoor programs (Schoel, Prouty, & Radcliffe, 1988).

It is impossible to do justice to the Project Adventure program in this chapter. Suffice it to say that it is extremely well developed, and focuses on processing and giving meaning to the physical and wilderness experiences that one encounters. In this regard, one can clearly see the influence of the Outward Bound approach in using the wilderness and personal experiences as metaphors for real life situations.

It should also be noted that although Project Adventure clearly has been a leader in bringing the out-of-doors into the schools, their model has also been adopted in many health care settings, and with a variety of client types. Finally, in their capacity as educators, the staff of Project Adventure have written a number of books and articles on a variety of topics related to teaching through the use of the outdoors. Interested readers are referred to Project Adventure for a list of these publications. (Project Adventure, 1991).

Focusing on self awareness, self-esteem and building communication skills, the Project Pride program in New Haven, Connecticut brings adventure based learning to the school setting. This program does not utilize intensive wilderness excursions, but rather, focuses on games and other problem solving tasks performed in an outdoor setting. Weekend adventure components of the program allow participants to camp out, and to test themselves as they go through both low and high ropes initiatives (Project Pride, 1991).

Less growth oriented is the relatively new Discovery Program at Camp Allen in Texas. Focusing on experiential approaches to learning, this program exposes students to a variety of learning experiences related to ecology, pioneer living and wilderness education. In addition, this program includes a ropes challenge course. It is important to realize that this program is geared to supplement traditional classroom experiences, and is open to primary and secondary school children (Discovery Program Camp Allen, 1991).

An unusual program can be found operating within the Birmingham Public School system in Birmingham, Michigan. The Experiential Learning Center is funded by the school system itself, and introduces students to many of the rich aspects of both urban and wilderness environments. Woven throughout this program is the importance of processing the experience, and to learn and grow in self awareness and awareness of others while experiencing.

Not surprisingly, one can see elements of the Project Adventure model in this program, and the material distributed by the Experiential Learning Center suggests that the Project Adventure staff continues to do training sessions with the staff. At the time of this writing, the Center was sponsoring a number of exciting programs including: a spring wilderness project, an urban adventure project, a city issues project, and a multicultural communications weekend (Birmingham Public Schools, 1991).

Another innovative school program can be found in the New York City Outward Bound Center. Currently, six public high schools in New York City are participating in the program. Instructors in the classroom cover such areas as the development of character, service, and the lessons of the outdoors. There is also a focus on cooperation, risk taking and self-esteem. Coupled with this work in the classroom setting, students are taken on rock climbing, backpacking, and service activities after school and on weekends. The promoters of this program cite many positive consequences of this program, including: school becomes more interesting for the students; values are formed and character building occurs; self-esteem improves; students feel less isolated; literacy skills improve; caring and service increases; and racial barriers are broken down (New York City Outward Bound Center, 1991).

Similar in its philosophy and program offerings, the Thompson Island Outward Bound program serves the youth of the greater Boston area. This program was developed in 1988, from a cooperative union between Outward Bound, The Hurricane Island Outward Bound School, and the Thompson Island Education Center. Offerings are very diverse, and range from a few days to three years in length. Last year, over 7,000 youth took part in this program (Thompson Island Outward Bound, 1991).

A final example of a school program can be found in the Rocky Mountain Academy in Idaho. This school is a year round boarding school, with an enrollment of 150 in grades 7 through 12. Although not designed as a therapeutic camp, this school is often attended by students whose past school history was less than successful. What distinguishes this school from other boarding schools is its requirement that students participate in wilderness expeditions as part of their curriculum. The rationale behind this approach is that these experiences contribute to the development of problem solving skills, and enhance self knowledge and self-esteem in ways that traditional school programs fail (Rocky Mountain Academy, 1991).

Health Care Programs

A relatively recent innovation in the use of outdoor therapeutic methods is the application of this approach to those experiencing health problems or physical disability. Although these programs are not numerous, they are certainly growing in popularity. Basically, the use of the wilderness modality with these types of client groups is supported by the traditional arguments in favor of the effectiveness of treatment in the out-of-doors. Clients facing disease or disability are placed in an unfamiliar environment where they must develop new ways of responding and coping. Additionally, the consequences of this environment are immediate and often quite positive, enhancing the participant's sense of self-worth. These individuals, it is hoped, will gain a new sense of power and control over their lives through participation in an outdoor course. Succeeding at such a challenge serves to facilitate growth and build self-esteem. Finally, although not espoused as a cure for a physical condition, the challenge of physical activity and the intimate link that the physical body and the spirit and the mind share is critical to the rationale behind these programs.

One of the leaders in health services programs, not surprisingly, has been the Outward Bound Program, with the North Carolina and Colorado Schools having distinct offerings. The North Carolina School offers health services courses on a contractual basis with agencies. In this way, the program can be tailored to the specific needs of the agency and the clientele. According to the North Carolina School, in the health services courses, there is an attempt to work on self-esteem, confidence, trust, and coping with fear, to name a few therapeutic issues. Some of the courses that have been offered to clients with physical problems include: chemical dependency recovery, cancer survivors, and disabled veterans (The North Carolina Outward Bound School, 1991).

In much the same way, the Colorado Outward Bound School's health services courses focus on growth, risk-taking, and self-esteem. Each of the courses is again tailored to meet the needs of the specific client group, and thus, a variety of outdoor experiences may be included in different courses. The substance abuse program includes those 12 years of age and older, referred from inpatient, outpatient or self-referral sources. This program has become very popular, with more than 6,000 clients completing it since 1978. Another interesting program option is the eating disorders course. This offering is open to both men and women recovering from an eating disorder. Cancer patients and their families or support people may enroll in the

Challenging the Course of Cancer offering. This course is tailored to the physical needs of the clients, and focuses on empowerment, trust and risk.

These are but a few of the health services programs offered by Outward Bound. In addition, they provide training courses for health care professionals. Two interesting options are the Wilderness Therapy Practicum and the Professional Development Seminars. The Wilderness Therapy Practicum involves a 10-day course through the Colorado Outward Bound School. The purpose of this course is to provide an understanding of the Outward Bound approach as it fits with more traditional treatment models. More personal in nature, the Professional Development Seminars focus on the personal growth of professionals in the health care fields. One of the goals of this program is to increase the effectiveness of these professionals by reducing burnout, and fostering personal growth (The Colorado Outward Bound School, 1991).

A second general category in the health services wilderness course offerings is the application of the therapeutic properties of the out-of-doors to the physically handicapped. The Breckenridge Outdoor Education Center has been a leader in this type of programming. The Center was first opened in 1976, and since that time has been dedicated to offering outdoor adventure experiences to those with disabilities. As with other programs, the Center offers many of their services on a contractual basis, working with outside agencies and individuals. Types of clients participating on these contractually developed courses include: cancer patients, head and spinal cord injured patients, the hearing impaired, and the developmentally disabled. Despite the innovativeness of these programs, The Breckenridge Center is most renowned for its adaptive skiing program. Finally, professional training and consulting is an important function that the Center performs (Breckenridge Outdoor Education Center, 1991).

Working with individuals who are victims of automobile accidents, the Challenge Rehabilitation program teaches clients to trust, to take risks again, and to gain a sense of control over their world. The participants engage in activities which serve to enhance their self confidence, problem solving abilities and social interaction skills to name a few. This is accomplished through meeting once weekly for four weeks in the initial phase of the program, and then participating in the outdoor experiences in the second phase. Extensive recording of feelings and experiences and in-depth processing characterize this program. Due to the specific nature of this program's clientele, the program has developed a professional advisory team which includes physicians, psychologists, social workers, counselors, and registered nurses (Challenge Rehabilitation, 1991).

Yet another interesting example of a health related outdoor program is the Accessible Adventures program, based in Oregon. The major service of this program lies in the designing and actual building of challenge and ropes courses that are accessible to all, including the physically disabled. These services are provided for a fee on a consultancy basis. Included in the purchase of a ropes or challenge course is training of the staff and the leader who will be utilizing the equipment. In addition to these services, Accessible Adventures also leads trips which are accessible to all. Examples of such trip offerings include trips to Kenya and Sweden (Accessible Adventures, 1991).

Finally, the Environmental Traveling Companions program encourages those with a variety of disabilities to participate in wilderness activities. Founded in 1971, this program runs sea kayaking, skiing, and whitewater rafting trips. Individuals with hearing, visual, and a wide variety of physical impairments serve as participants. The rationale behind this program is that by stretching the limits and boundaries of the participants, they take risks and grow beyond their greatest expectations (Environmental Traveling Companions, 1991).

Enrichment Programs

The growth in the number and variety of outdoor enrichment programs in the past few years has indeed been dramatic. In fact, there is no question that the largest number of programs known to these authors fall into this category. Since many readers will be familiar with these types of programs, or may access them in the future for themselves or for their clients, we will provide the reader with an exposure to the diversity of program offerings in this category. However, due to the therapeutic focus of this book, and to the sheer volume of programs, detailed descriptions will not be given.

For more detailed information, the reader is encouraged to contact the program directly. Once again, in writing this chapter we chose programs which we thought were either particularly interesting, or that seemed representative of programs in this area. We realize that many fine programs are not discussed in this section.

For the purposes of this chapter, enrichment programs are defined as programs not specifically therapeutic in nature, although program goals may certainly include personal growth. Generally, these programs are geared toward high functioning physically and mentally healthy people. Examples of some of these program types include: Leadership and training programs, Executive programs, and University programs.

Leadership and Training Programs

As has been mentioned throughout this book, Outward Bound is probably the most renowned outdoor program currently operating, and can be considered to be the largest enrichment program operating today. The North Carolina, Voyager, Hurricane Island, Colorado, and Pacific Crest schools offer a wide range of courses, the majority of which are designed for the high functioning individual. Examples include their regular intensive courses, leadership courses, over 40 courses, women only courses, and couples courses. It is difficult to imagine a personal growth experience that Outward Bound could not provide. Inherent in all of their courses, as has been discussed, is the use of outdoor challenge, physical rigor, and risk-taking as metaphors for real life experiences. We encourage the interested reader to contact Outward Bound directly as complete description of their offerings is beyond the scope of this book (Outward Bound Schools, 1991).

Focusing more on the development of leadership skills, The National Outdoor Leadership School (NOLS), is clearly one of the premiere enrichment programs currently available. This school has been in operation since 1965, and has served more than 28,000 students. Courses range in length from two weeks to three months, and a number of different course options are available. The NOLS program distinguishes itself in that it focuses on the development of responsible leadership in wilderness settings. According to NOLS, their mission is "to be the best source and teacher of wilderness skills and leadership which protect user and the environment" (NOLS, 1991, p. 3). In accomplishing this mission, all of the courses include information and experience in the following areas: safety and judgment, leadership and teamwork, outdoor skills, and environmental studies (NOLS, 1991).

As mentioned, the NOLS program is not therapeutic in its approach and it does not cater to adolescents. Some examples of the types of courses that are offered include: wilderness courses, sea kayaking, mountaineering, an educators' course, winter courses, courses for adults aged 25 and older, and semester long courses for college credit. With a focus on wilderness skills, conservation and leadership, this program is truly unique.

Also focusing on the development of outdoor leaders, the Wilderness Education Association serves as an accrediting body for university programs, facilitates research and curriculum development related to wilderness education, and provides consulting services to universities. Programs which have earned affiliate status with this association offer the WEA's National Standard Program for outdoor leadership certification (Wilderness Education Association, 1991).

Less involved with wilderness leadership, the National Audubon Society Expedition Institute offers students the opportunity to earn a Bachelors or Masters degree. These unique programs involve extensive travel and experiential learning opportunities, and are based on the concept of expedition education (National Audubon Society, 1991).

Finally, the National Wildlife Federation offers a variety of enrichment programs for individuals of various ages. Wildlife Camp allows children to experience the beauty and challenge of the outdoor environment, while the leadership training program prepares teens for future leadership roles. The teen adventure program allows adolescents to participate in a more extended hiking experience. In addition to programs for children and adolescents, the Federation offers NatureQuest, a training program for those who work in outdoor settings, and conservation summits. The summits involve recreation and education in a selected outdoor location. Finally, the Federation leads expeditions throughout the world (National Wildlife Federation, 1991).

Executive Programs

The 1980s saw a proliferation of outdoor programs geared toward training for executives and other business personnel. As an adjunct to staff training, these approaches have begun to replace the team building and leadership training retreats so often seen in the business world. Generally, these executive programs focus around team building and/or leadership training. As with the other program categories, a tremendous number of executive programs currently exist. Our intent is to mention but a few.

Corporate Adventure was founded in 1982, and thus far has trained over 7500 executives. Based in Virginia, this program provides the following services to business clients: goal setting, assessment, intervention, and integration. The interventive component of this package involves the use of outdoor activities and challenges to facilitate team building and leadership development and enhancement (Corporate Adventure, 1991).

In much the same way, the Executive Expeditions program in Georgia provides assessment and intervention for the business community. Most of the clients are interested in assistance with team building and leadership development and enhancement. It is important to note that the needs of the specific client are identified and a program is then tailored to meet those needs. Thus, the outdoor modalities used may vary quite dramatically from company to company. Examples of outdoor activities used by Executive Expeditions include: camping in Alabama, rock climbing at Lake Placid, and river rescue in North Carolina (Executive Adventures, 1991).

The Catalyst Consulting Team is similar to the above executive programs in that it provides assessment, consultation, and the implementation of outdoor experiences to companies. Primarily utilizing ropes as their outdoor modality, this program focuses on team building and the strengthening of teams within organizations (Catalyst Consulting Team, 1991).

A final and interesting example of an executive enrichment program is the American Leadership Forum. Founded in 1980, the Forum is dedicated to training and facilitating the leadership abilities of a diverse group of men and women. Currently, there are programs in five American cities. Within these areas, 20 community leaders are selected to participate in a 22 day program spread throughout one year. Of interest to us is the initial part of the program, the Wilderness Challenge.

This wilderness component is the first part of the leadership program, and involves a 6 day experience in Colorado. Participants are exposed to rock climbing, hiking, and a peak climb. Throughout the wilderness program, risk-taking, cooperation, and vision are focused upon. This program is innovative in that it is a national approach to cultivating leaders which has incorporated the use of the wilderness in a central fashion in its program (American Leadership Forum, 1991).

University Programs

A number of universities have established programs which incorporate experience in the wilderness. Some of these programs are part of academic departments, and are given traditional academic credit, while others are student enrichment programs which carry no formal credit. Finally, other university programs are affiliated with the Wilderness Education Association and offer the National Standard Program. The WEA provides other course offerings as well, and maintains accreditation standards for member universities and agencies. The interested reader is encouraged to contact WEA for more complete information (Wilderness Education Association, 1991).

An interesting university-based program exists at the Northern Illinois University. Called Corporate Adventure, this program works with executives on team building and leadership in much the same way as the previously discussed executive programs. This program is unique, however, in that it is sponsored and executed by a university. The sessions are generally short-term and are facilitated by faculty at the university, as the program is administered through the College of Continuing Education. The predominant outdoor modalities in this program are ropes and outdoor games and exercises (Northern Illinois University, 1991).

Other university based programs involve the offering of outdoor classes, organized trips, and equipment rental for students. Examples of these types of programs can be found at Cornell University's Outdoor Education Center, The Outdoor Adventures program at the University of Nebraska, and at the Washington State University. These types of offerings are becoming increasingly popular as universities recognize more options than traditional physical education offerings for their students (Cornell University, 1991; University of Nebraska, 1991; Washington State University, 1991).

Committed even more to the notion of outdoor experience are the universities which incorporate the wilderness into their curricula. Again, the number of these innovative and interesting programs is steadily growing, so we are able to discuss but a few. Prescott College in Arizona requires that students spend half of their time in the field, experiencing and doing. Their

Outdoor Action program exposes students to wilderness skills training, wilderness exploration, and group and work experience. Within this program, students can focus on wilderness leadership, outdoor education, outdoor program administration, or outdoor education for special populations. Students attend classes during the 10-week-long Fall and Spring quarters. In addition, three one-month-long blocks in the Fall, Winter, and Spring are used for more intensive and experiential work. Students at this university actually earn a Bachelor of Arts degree through this unique curriculum (Prescott College, 1991).

Another university example can be found in the College of Dupage program in Illinois. Their Field Studies program offers courses for academic credit which often involve extensive travel and wilderness adventure. Examples of some of the courses include: Capture the Canadian Coast, Vision Quest (a week of backpacking in Canada), and Hike Hawaii (College of Dupage, 1991).

Finally, the George Williams College offers a variety of options for the pursuit of outdoor interests. This program offers structured internships in outdoor settings which may be taken for academic credit. They also offer a variety of programs including: the OWLS (Outdoor Wisconsin Leadership School), and programs instructing educators on incorporating aspects of the out-of-doors into their educational settings (George Williams College, 1991).

The intent of this chapter has been to represent some of the existing outdoor programs in the United States. We have attempted to focus most heavily on programs with at least a quasi-therapeutic emphasis in this chapter. Even some of the enrichment programs seem to work toward enhancing individual and/or family functioning.

When considering the range of programs offered today, a few comments are in order. First, the diversity of program types is almost overwhelming. We have seen programs which range from ropes courses and courses with minimal outdoor involvement to very intensive backpack experiences. In addition to the variety of program types, the clientele served are also extremely diverse. We have discussed programs targeting high-level executives, troubled adolescents, inner-city school children, and disabled individuals, to name a few.

Another interesting dimension to the outdoor programs is the sponsorship/cost of these programs. Many of the programs are private in their sponsorship, and are quite costly to participants. Others are totally subsidized by state or county funds, and are delivered at little or no charge. Finally, some programs have a combined private/public sponsorship.

It is important to note that this diverse group of program offerings does not seem to be governed or guided in any way by any external guidelines or standards. Thus, there are no accreditation processes which ensure the quality of the various programs with the exception of WEA's standards for their member universities. This is an issue that is at the forefront of wilderness programming. As of this writing, the Association for Experiential Education and the Council on Accreditation of Services for Families and Children have begun to develop a set of standards for the development and evaluation of residential wilderness programs.

One of the arguments for such increased professionalization of the field is that it enhances the reputation of such programs. We have argued elsewhere (Davis-Berman & Berman, 1992) that it is morally and scientifically necessary to document that program designs are solid, that staffing is appropriate, and that the program actually works. These issues will be discussed at greater length in the last chapter of this book. However, at this point, we would assert that a critical part of increased respectability involves greater attention to program design, and to the actual therapeutic elements of the program.

The following chapter discusses the importance of theory to the design and implementation of wilderness programs. Although some readers may be intimidated by the notion of theory, we suggest its fundamental importance. Finally, our discussion of theory includes numerous examples relating wilderness programming to a variety of theoretical approaches.

References

Accessible Adventures. (1991). Published program materials. Portland, Oregon.

American Leadership Forum. (1991). Published program materials. Houston, Texas.

Beech Hill Hospital. (1991). Published program materials. Dublin, New Hampshire.

Birmingham Public Schools. (1991). Published program materials. Birmingham, Alabama.

Breckenridge Outdoor Education Center. (1991). Published program materials. Breckenridge, Colorado.

Camp Allen. (1991). Published program materials. Navasota, Texas.

Catalyst Consulting Team. (1991). Published program materials. Soquel, California.

Challenge Rehabilitation. (1991). Published program materials. Colorado Springs, Colorado.

College of Du Page. (1991). Published program materials. Glen Ellyn, Illinois.

Colorado Outward Bound School. (1991). Published program materials. Denver, Colorado.

Cornell University. (1991). Published program materials. Ithaca, New York.

Corporate Adventure. (1991). Published program materials. Reston, Virginia.

Davis-Berman, J., & Berman, D. (1992). Program evaluation: A model for wilderness therapeutic programs. Unpublished manuscript.

Eckard Family Youth Alternative (1991). Annual Descriptive Summary and published program materials. Exeter, Rhode Island.

Environmental Traveling Companions. (1991). Published program materials. San Francisco, California.

Executive Adventure. (1991). Published program materials. Atlanta, Georgia.

Executive Expeditions. (1991). Published program materials. Marietta, Georgia.

George Williams College. (1991). Published program materials. Williams Bay, Wisconsin.

Inner Harbour Hospital. (1991). Published program materials. Douglasville, Georgia.

Interventions. (1991). Published program materials. Chicago, Illinois.

John de la Howe School. (1991). Published program materials. McCormick, South Carolina.

Kelly, F. J., & Baer, D. J. (1968). *Outward Bound schools as an alternative to institutionalization for adolescent delinquent boys.* Boston: Fandel Press.

Kimball, R. O. (1983). The wilderness as therapy. *Journal of Experiential Education, 6* (3), 7-16.

Kimball, R. O. (1979). *Wilderness experience program: Final evaluation report.* Santa Fe: State of New Mexico Forensic System.

National Audubon Society. (1991). Published program materials. Mt. Vernon, Maine.

National Wildlife Federation. (1991). Published program materials. Vienna, Virginia.

National Outdoor Leadership School. (1991). Published program materials. Lander, Wyoming.

New York City Outward Bound. (1991). Published program materials. New York, New York.

North Carolina Outward Bound. (1991). Published program materials. Morgantown, North Carolina.

Northern Illinois University. (1991). Published program materials. Dekalb, Illinois.

On Belay Youth and Family Services Inc. (1991). Published program materials. Madison, Wisconsin.

Passages to Adventure. (1991). Published program materials. Fayetteville, West Virginia.

Prescott College. (1991). Published program materials. Prescott, Arizona.

Project Adventure. (1991). Published program materials. Hamilton, Massachusetts.

Project Pride. (1991). Published program materials. Hamden, Connecticut.

Rocky Mountain Academy. (1991). Published program materials. Bonners Ferry, Idaho.

Salesmanship Club Youth and Family Centers. (1991). Published program materials. Dallas, Texas.

Santa Fe Mountain Center. (1991). Published program materials. Santa Fe, New Mexico.

Schoel, J., Prouty, D., & Radcliffe, P. (1988). *Islands of healing: A guide to adventure-based counseling.* Hamilton, MA: Project Adventure, Inc.

Thompson Island Outward Bound. (1991). Published program materials. Boston, Massachusetts.

Tressler Care School. (1991). Published program materials. Boiling Springs, Pennsylvania.

University of Nebraska. (1991). Published program materials. Lincoln, Nebraska.

Vision Quest. (1991). Published program materials. Tucson, Arizona.

Washington State University. (1991). Published program materials. Pullman, Washington.

Wilderness Challenge School. (1991). Published program materials. Chesapeake, Virginia.

Wilderness Conquest. (1991). Published Program materials. Monticello, Utah.

Wilderness Education Association. (1991). Published program materials. Saranac Lake, New York.

Chapter Six ▽

Theoretical Understanding of Wilderness Experiences

Anecdotal reports of the success of outdoor adventure programs are manifold; some are even inspiring. For example, Godfrey (1980), who joined trips from Outward Bound programs all over the country, shared his impressions in a captivating combination of dialogue among participants and a more dispassionate didactic presentation of the inner workings of such programs. Presumably, he was attempting to answer the question of why these programs work. From his view and based on his reading of related material, much of the success of the program depends on a leader who moves "from a highly involved, directive role in the early stages of a program and progressively withdraws to the point where the students are making all the decisions themselves" (p. 258). Elsewhere in his book, Godfrey captures the essence of the issue of directive versus nondirective leadership styles when he quotes an instructor reflecting on this topic (p. 151). Initially, that instructor endorsed a directive style when he said: "There are times when the only thing they understand is getting their asses kicked." Only shortly afterwards, however, he endorsed a nondirective approach, noting that the balance between these approaches is difficult.

There have been very few comprehensive attempts to theoretically account for the changes posited as a result of wilderness therapy. The reader will remember our previous discussion of the lack of theoretical basis for these programs. The wide variety of program offerings presented in Chapter 5 also attests to the lack of theoretical grounding in the field. In this chapter, we will discuss the importance and nature of theories, and then summarize previous attempts to theoretically explain wilderness therapy. Finally, we will present systems theory as an explanatory model that we believe has much to offer this field.

The Importance of Theories

Theories allow for the organization of knowledge in such as way as to render it more useful. By useful, reference is made to the ability to enhance our communication, increase our understanding of a phenomenon, make predictions about behavior and influence behavior.

Communication

The terms of a theory allow one to parsimoniously summarize behavior. The more the terms are operationally defined in the language of observable events or behaviors, the easier this is to do. For example, Ewert (1989) makes reference to "outdoor adventure pursuits" as including outdoor activities involving risk and uncertain outcome. Ewert lists 21 of these activities, as diverse as backpacking, SCUBA, hot-air ballooning and kayaking. By accepting this definition of outdoor adventure, we not only have an understanding of the salient aspects of the above mentioned activities, but could also name other activities within this category that are not on Ewert's list, like wind-surfing. Theory, then, allows one to organize observations in a way that enables understanding and increases effective communication.

Understanding

It is easier to discuss definitions in terms of how we observe them than it is to discuss a vaguer concept: understanding. When reference is made to understanding a concept, one often means that it makes sense out of past events that heretofore were either not understood in their relations to each other or were only partially understood. In dealing with troubled adolescents, for example, we are always looking to theory to help explain why certain behaviors occurred and how they fit in with other aspects of that individual's personality. So, while it is not too difficult to define aggressive behavior in terms of hitting, shouting, or swearing (i.e., an operational definition), it is more difficult to understand that behavior in the context of the individual's personality. Gaining insight into the personality may be accomplished with reference to theory, perhaps in this case by reference to role models and ways of dealing with conflicts learned growing up in an abusive family.

It is appropriate to note that theories are akin to models. They provide us with abstract, and in the best cases, logically consistent, statements that allow for the deduction of facts. That is, theories are representations of reality rather than reality, per se. Theories are neither true nor false; they are models that may be useful because of their explanatory or predictive capacities. Theories are more or less useful to the extent that they permit the deduction of hypotheses that can be tested. And as will be seen, some of the theories to be presented are clearly more useful than are others for understanding changes that occur as a result of wilderness therapeutic experiences.

Prediction

When theories are said to facilitate prediction, it is meant that logical deductions will lead to the prediction or anticipation that certain behaviors will occur in certain situations. Predictions about the occurrence of specific events are referred to as hypotheses or theoretical assertions. There are two types of hypotheses or theoretical assertions that allow for theoretical predictions (Levy, 1970).

First, there are empirical generalizations. Empirical generalizations begin with the observation of numerous instances of a relationship among two or more classes of behaviors or events. This process begins with the observation of specific events, like noting that a person, Sue, who has been through a high ropes course, is making good eye contact with her peers when talking about her experience, or that Mark, who was reluctant to enter a kayak, now smiles as he eagerly puts on his life jacket, or that Jeff walks a little taller and straighter after a week of wilderness canoeing.

From these observations, it is possible to make an abstraction about classes of events; in this case, outdoor adventure pursuits and a sense of personal accomplishment. It is then possible to assert, based on our specific observations, that is reasonable to assume that the classes of events are related in a similar way. We would then predict that if A occurs, B will result. Again using this example, we would hypothesize that outdoor adventure pursuits result in a positive feeling of accomplishment.

In addition to empirical generalizations, there is a second type of theoretical assertion—the theoretical proposition. Theoretical propositions begin with empirical generalizations and try to account for the observed relationship by formulating a logical construct or intervening variable between the events. To stay with this same example, we could talk about how outdoor adventure pursuits theoretically alter self-esteem in a positive way, and how people with positive self-esteem exhibit adaptive types of behavior. We would then hypothesize that the changes observed in positive feelings of accomplishment are a function of increased self-esteem. This hypothesis is testable and falsifiable (which makes hypotheses different from theories).

It would be possible to give participants a measure of self-esteem, perhaps before and after an adventure activity, and predict that participants with the largest increases in self-esteem will exhibit more characteristics of positive feelings of accomplishment.

Having theories about the therapeutic aspects of wilderness experiences will allow us to make predictions about changes in participants' behavior. The better our theories, the more they should allow us to make predictions about what kind of activities will be most effective for what kinds of problems, in what kinds of settings, and for which people. Equally important, they should allow us to make predictions about those people who cannot be helped by participating in wilderness therapy programs. This latter point is often lost by some in this field who either explicitly or implicitly suggest that everyone benefits from adventure activities.

Influence Behavior

The final goal we will discuss concerns the application of theory in order to influence behavior. This concept is related to the notion of prediction, but whereas prediction pertains to testing a theory, influencing or "controlling" behavior involves the goal of behavior change (Liebert & Spiegler, 1987). In order to exemplify the notion of behavioral influence, imagine that our theory used to account for change as a result of wilderness experience also contains a postulate (or theoretical assertion) suggesting that the gains made during a wilderness experience will generalize to change in everyday behavior for those individuals most reflective and introspective. If we have been able to test this notion through observation and experimentation, then we are ready to use the theory for behavioral change.

Thus, we could reasonably assume that individuals who are reflective would maintain gains made during a wilderness adventure while those who are impulsive would not. This might lead us to alter our program for impulsive individuals or even by finding an alternate experience for them that might be more therapeutic. These efforts would be aimed at finding effective ways of altering behavior.

Evaluating Theories

There are a variety of conceptions regarding the nature of therapeutic change as a result of wilderness experiences. As we discussed in the previous section, we are not able to judge theories on the basis of truth, because theories are abstractions that represent views of reality; they are not reality, per se. That being the case, how are we to evaluate the theoretical accounts presented in this chapter? E. Jerry Phares (1984) has summarized a number of dimensions upon which theories of personality can be compared, and while we are not directly interested in personality, many of the dimensions he mentions are relevant to wilderness theories of behavior and personality change. As such, we will briefly examine theory's focus of convenience, breadth and significance, systematic nature, operationalization, parsimony, and utility.

Focus of Convenience

All theories tend to account for a differing set of situations or events. A theory's focus of convenience is said to be set of events or situations best explained by a given theory. Some theories will help us understand the nature of group interaction on effective change in wilderness therapy settings, while others may help explain behavior change as a result of the directness of feedback and resulting reinforcements in the natural environment. No theory will be able to explain all of the aspects of wilderness therapy. It may be helpful, however, to note each theory's focus.

Breadth and Significance

Although each theory will explain a different set of phenomena, broader theories tend to be valued over theories that deal with a restricted range of events. Of course, one must also take into account the significance of the phenomena explained. A broader theory that explains little of importance is certainly less valuable than a narrow theory that explains critical events.

Systematic vs. Unsystematic

A theory is systematic if it presents assumptions, conceptions, and postulates in such a way that they are clearly stated and interrelated. This is certainly to be preferred over theories that are loosely structured, ambiguous, or contain internal contradictions.

Operational vs. Nonoperational

Theories that operationally define the terms of the theory in ways that indicate how they are measured allow for hypotheses to be tested. When these terms are not operationally defined, it is difficult, if not impossible, to conduct research on wilderness theories of change. Imagine how difficult it would be to verify that wilderness experiences lead to increases in self-esteem if we had no observable ways of defining self-esteem.

Parsimony

Given two theories that explain the same events, that theory with the fewest and simplest constructs is most desirable. Stated otherwise, one should strive to explain an event in the simplest and yet comprehensive terms possible.

Utility

The ultimate goal of theories of wilderness change is that they have utility in terms of allowing for increased understanding, prediction and behavior change. Theories that have the most applicability are said to have utility. In that we are not looking for our theories to be true or false, what we can look for is the extent to which they offer utility.

With this background information on theories in mind, we now turn to an examination of theoretical perspectives which may be applied to the understanding of wilderness programs. Although there are certainly appropriate theories that we have not covered, the approaches discussed in this chapter seem especially applicable in outdoor settings.

The Restorative Environment

Kaplan and Kaplan, in *The Experience of Nature* (1989), present a model for understanding how the wilderness appears to restore people to a state in which they are more fully functioning. An intriguing aspect of their work is that they posit that this restorative function of the natural environment can occur not only from an extended wilderness trek, but also from working in a garden.

The Kaplans suggest that many of us feel emotionally "worn out, ready for a break or respite" (p. 178). This can happen as the result of stress, which they view as the anticipation of threat. Used in this way, the Kaplans' notion of stress appears related to Selye's (1976) general adaptation syndrome, in which he described the reactions of organisms to prolonged stress. Stress can certainly tax an organism's system, to the point, as described by Selye, that it can lead to exhaustion (or even death). The Kaplans also point out that we can become worn out, not only by the anticipation of threat, but just by prolonged work. This is what may be referred to as mental fatigue, a general concept that they refine with reference to William James's notion of attention.

William James made a distinction between two types of attention, based on the amount of energy it takes for a person to focus on an object or thought. Involuntary attention is effortless; for example, when we focus on something that is unique, novel or interesting. It may even give us a rest from more draining activities in which we have been engaged. Directed or voluntary attention, on the other hand, involves putting forth effort in order to focus on something. This latter state is achieved by inhibiting other, distracting stimuli, which results in fatigue because energy must be invested in this inhibitory process. The point being made is that some kinds of attentional processes involve the investment of emotional energy and may cause fatigue (directed attention), while others involve no effort and may even be relaxing and rejuvenating (involuntary attention).

Following the Kaplans, it is interesting to note that modern civilization required that people spend long periods of time directing their attention to focused activities. This requires the inhibition of competing foci that are irrelevant to the tasks at hand. Thus, mental fatigue sets in. Add to this the stress of anticipated threat—from illnesses, hard economic times, crime, etc.—and it is easy to see why we have increasing needs for rest and relaxation.

People often talk of the need to "get away from it all" when they are in such a state. When fatigued from stress or directed attention, escape may be better than staying in an emotionally draining situation. But escape alone is not enough, for if the new situation is confining, boring, or involves prolonged periods of directed attention, few benefits may accrue as a result of this experience. Environments that are restorative have a quality of "being in a whole other world." Kaplan and Kaplan (1989, p. 184) attempt to define what this means in the following quote:

> The sense of being in a whole other world implies extent—either physically or perceptually. To achieve the feeling of extent it is necessary to have interrelatedness of the immediately perceived elements, so that they constitute a portion of some larger whole. Thus there must be sufficient connectedness to make it possible to build a mental map and sufficient scope to make building the map worthwhile.

Two other elements are critical in order for an environment to be restorative, according to the Kaplans. One is that there must be some element of interest or fascination. This is important so that one is not bored and so that effortless, involuntary attention is used, as mentioned previously. The second critical element is that there needs to be compatibility between the environment and the individual. Without this compatibility, a person's abilities might not match environmental demands. In such a situation, a person would have a hard time coping; hardly a scenario for renewal.

In addition, Kaplan and Kaplan discuss the context in which these activities occur. Nature, in and of itself, seems to have a restorative function. There are unique aspects of the out-of-doors, in general, and wilderness, specifically, that lend to the fulfillment of the four essential components cited by the Kaplans. Perhaps we can briefly address these four components with specific reference to outdoor pursuits. Being in the natural environment does involve getting away (escape), even if it means leaving one's office or home to walk in a park, although there is a clearer break from the everyday world when one thinks of activities like canoeing down a wilderness river. With respect to the concept of extent, the wilderness, on many levels, provides a feeling that one's immediate experiences are part of a larger whole.

This can occur on many levels. For example, while hiking a wilderness trail, one may feel the presence of one's group of hikers, a sense of a "wilderness spirit," an idea about the trail one is travelling in compared to the greater wilderness area, a sense that one is mastering a set of skills that forms a body of knowledge, or even that there is continuity with other people who traveled this same land in a similar fashion.

There is so much about the natural world to find interesting. There may be elements of physical activity, risk-taking, flora and fauna, aspects of history, the development of specific skills like orienteering, beautiful vistas, etc. At first glance, it might seem that there is little in the wilderness with which most people would find compatibility. However, even if the environment is threatening or the activities involve risk-taking, compatibility is usually found with the group, for everyone has set of common goals (e.g., having fun, learning new skills, creating a supportive environment in which change is facilitated).

Of course, there may be incompatibility with specific modalities of outdoor pursuits that do not fit a given individual, even if there are common group goals, as just mentioned. For this reason, there should be a range of possible modalities in order to enhance the compatibility between individuals and the environment. One only needs to browse through a catalogue of offerings from Outward Bound or the National Outdoor Leadership School to appreciate the many forms of outdoor adventure that are available. The

Kaplans maintain that these restorative qualities can be found in simple natural environments, including gardens.

This final point about the apparent healing qualities of nature is similar to much of the discussion in Chapter 2 in which we discussed the view that the wilderness has been viewed by many, from varied fields and over many years, to have almost magical abilities to enable us to be more fully functioning. This somewhat mystical explanation is explored more deeply by those espousing transpersonal theories, and will be discussed in greater depth later in this chapter. At this point, we turn our discussion to a more recognizable theoretical approach: social learning theory.

Social Learning Theory

Social learning theories can be traced back to the seminal work of Miller and Dollard (1941), *Social Learning and Imitation.* It was this work that launched much of the later investigations on imitative behavior. For our purposes, we will look at three components of social learning theory. First, we will briefly summarize the work by early theorists on observational learning. Then, consideration will be given to Rotter's work on locus of control. Finally, we will discuss Bandura's theory of self-efficacy.

Modeling

Miller and Dollard (1941) presented two types of learning that can occur by watching others. In copying, the learner matches the responses of the model. For example, one might teach a group of adolescents on a backpacking trip how to set up their tents by modeling that behavior and having the adolescents copy the essential steps of laying out the body of the tent, putting the poles together, etc. The second type of imitative behavior is matched-dependent learning. This type of learning through observation involves an older, more experienced or more skilled model who does things in order to get reinforcement, and a younger or less experienced learner who follows the leader because following has led to reinforcement for the novice.

This model of imitation is based on a drive reduction model, with key concepts being drive, cue, response and reinforcement. To exemplify this model, imagine a leader who has a need for comfort (drive) and searches the area for a level campsite near water (cue), the leader then sets up camp (response), and then stretches out to relax (reward).

Bandura and his colleagues (for a general review, see Bandura, 1971) took issue with the Dollard and Miller notion of drive reduction, arguing that a behavior could be acquired through observation without being demonstrated. Bandura suggests that three types of learning can occur as a result of observing a model. Observational learning occurs when one acquires a new behavior as a result of observing another. Modeling can also inhibit or disinhibit what has been previously learned, as may be the case when adolescents inhibit comments that are aggressive, demeaning or irrelevant while in group therapy. Response facilitation is when the responses of others are imitated and closely resembles Dollard and Miller's matched-dependent learning.

Bandura (1971) has suggested four processes that are critical in the observational process. The first phase involves attentional processes that govern who is observed and what is observed. Wilderness therapy leaders have many of the qualities that lead to participants modeling them: likability, distinctiveness, and the motivation of the learner are all factors. The next phase involves retention processes to insure that what was learned is remembered. Among other factors influencing this phase, rehearsal is important and is a critical aspect to most outdoor adventure activities. The third phase, motor reproduction processes, pertains to the ability to perform what was learned. This is governed by one's ability, self-observation and feedback. Adventure activities are geared at such a level that all the participants should be able to perform the behaviors. Self-observation can occur through the use of videotaping activities, a common occurrence for some activities like white-water kayaking or rafting, and feedback is a critical phase of learning all outdoor skills. The fourth phase, motivational processes, has to do with the extent to which the modeled behaviors are rewarded. This is determined by reinforcements for the behaviors and can be internal, external or vicarious as a result of watching others being rewarded (or punished) for performing a certain behavior.

Locus of Control

Julian Rotter formulated his social learning theory (1954) in a systematic way, with 7 postulates and 12 corollaries. The interested reader is referred to the primary source for a comprehensive understanding of the theory. For our purposes, an abbreviated look at this theory will suffice. One of the most often discussed changes participants experience as a result of outdoor adventure pursuits is an increased feeling of responsibility for the events in their lives. This is akin to Rotter's notion of internal vs. external locus of control.

Many of the adolescents who are participants on a wilderness therapy trip might be described as having an external locus of control in that they feel they are not responsible for the outcomes of their actions; that is, whether or not they get rewards is a function of luck, fate or powerful others. Hopefully, participation in wilderness therapy changes their locus of control so they come to believe that the outcome of their actions is a function of effort, skill, personality or other internal factors (internal locus of control). To more fully understand Rotter's theory, let's take a look at how locus of control fits broader theoretical statements about behavior. To predict a person's behavior, Rotter uses the following formula:

$$BPx,s1,Ra = f(Ex,Ra,s1 \& RVa,s1)$$

Essentially what this formula says is that the probability that a given behavior (BPx) will occur in a specific situation (s1), in order to obtain a specific reinforcement (Ra) is a function of ones expectancy (E) that the behavior (x) in that situation (s1) will lead to the reinforcement (Ra) and the reinforcement value (RV) of that reinforcement (a) in this situation (s1). Stated otherwise, a specific, goal directed behavior will occur if the individual believes that the behavior will lead to a specific reinforcement and if that reinforcement is desirable.

While the above formula refers to specific behaviors in specific situations, he also has a general formula for looking at more global behavior. Locus of control is a general expectation about the outcome of one's behavior. Another generalized expectancy is interpersonal trust. Many of the participants of wilderness therapy programs lack trust, and for good reasons.

These general expectancies combine with specific expectancies. When entering a new situation, there are few if any expectancies because one has little or no experience in this or related situations. In this case, one has to rely on trust and locus of control to determine whether or not a given behavior will lead to reinforcement. It may be for this reason that new participants are often tentative and overly cautious. As they observe others, modeling takes place and one sees vicarious reinforcement, providing specific expectancies that increase as one engages in the activity and is reinforced.

As an example, consider the participant whose parents have told her innumerable times to clean her room and to keep her personal items organized, all to no avail. From Rotter's perspective, she has not cleaned her room because either she does not believe that doing so will lead to reinforcement, or the reinforcements for cleaning her room are not desirable.

In base camp, wilderness leaders also suggest that participants organize their belongings in their backpacks so that, for example, your rain poncho, toilet paper, snacks and water are easily accessible. Reinforcement is immediate and direct the first time it rains, you have to go to the bathroom, need a snack or are thirsty. In this situation our participant quickly learns that only she controls her pack and doing so is highly reinforcing. Additionally, participants in this situation also learn that the leaders are trustworthy and that listening to and modeling them results in an easier time on the trail—factors that increase one's general expectancies about interpersonal trust (you can rely on the word of the leaders) and locus of control (you control much of what happens to you).

Self-Efficacy

Self-efficacy is a term used by Bandura (1977; 1982) to describe the belief that one can perform a given behavior. Self-efficacy differs from locus of control in that the former concerns the probability that one can successfully execute a behavior while the latter pertains to the belief that a given behavior will result in a specific reinforcement.

Our judgments of self-efficacy do not have do be accurate. That is, some people may believe they have the ability to accomplish something without actually being able to do it. Our percept of self-efficacy depends on four sources of information. According to Bandura (1982, p. 126): "These include performance attainments; vicarious experiences of observing the performance of others; verbal persuasion and allied types of social influences that one posses certain capabilities; and physiological states from which people partly judge their capability, strength, and vulnerability." Of these four types of information, performance attainments are the most powerful because they involve actual attempts to master the environment. If one is successful, self-efficacy is enhanced. If a person tries to perform a behavior under at least moderately favorable circumstances and fails, however, feelings of self-efficacy are lowered. But one does not have to try to perform directly, one's percepts of self-efficacy can be altered vicariously by observing others. In this way, one's own self-efficacy can be heightened or lessened by observing the efforts of others whom we feel are similar.

Verbal persuasion is the technique most used by therapists, but may be of limited value. Bandura suggests that trying to convince someone to do something (persuasive efficacy) has the "greatest impact on people who have some reason to believe that they can produce effects through their actions" (1982, p. 127). That is, it may get people to try harder so that they succeed.

People's physiological states give them feedback about their capability to perform. If, for example, one approaches a rapid in a canoe and feels an increase in heart rate, respiration, and notices sweating, one's estimation of being capable of negotiating the rapid may be diminished. These physiological cues, like the cues we get from actual or vicarious performance or from persuasion, are cognitively processed in our appraisal of self-efficacy.

McGowan (1986) has applied self-efficacy theory to experiential education by considering implications for each of the four methods of change discussed by Bandura. In doing so, he presents examples of ways in which personal change in outdoor settings is a function of performance accomplishments, modeling, verbal persuasion and heightened arousal. He is particularly interested in using self-efficacy to increase participants' responsibility for themselves and concludes that applications of Bandura's theory are effective ways of accomplishing this change.

The inability to change one's life can lead to feelings of depression and sometimes, anxiety. This is related to the concept of learned helplessness (Seligman, 1975) in which an individual's behavior is found to be independent of the outcome of those actions. Bandura suggests the need to determine the source for the feelings of inefficacy. Feelings of futility can arise from the feeling that one is not capable (low self-efficacy judgment) or that the environment is unresponsive or hostile to one's efforts (low outcome judgment).

Many of the adolescents with whom we have worked on wilderness therapy trips have a sense of helplessness that they attribute to their own inability, but which is actually the result of a nonsupportive, hostile or abusive environment. Performance may also be hindered by focusing on what is unfamiliar or uncomfortable in a situation rather than what is comfortable and within one's range of abilities. Bandura also mentions that self-efficacy can be undermined by being in an inferior role or bearing negative labels.

A combination of strategies for increasing self-efficacy is suggested by Bandura's theory. These strategies range from the acquisition of skill, to observing others, verbal persuasion, or even altering cognitive appraisals. Another strategy is to alter the environment to make it more conducive to, and supportive of, change. In wilderness therapy programs, participants are given a variety of tools. Some are internal (e.g., learning how to ford a river) and some are external (e.g., wearing specialized hiking boots on the trail), some are solitary (e.g., writing feelings in a journal when one misses home) and some are collective (e.g., making a z-drag to get your kayak off a rock).

Following this consideration of self-efficacy, we now turn to the more global concepts of self-esteem, effectance motivation, self-actualization, and self theory.

Self-Esteem

Notions of self-concept have a central role in modern personality theory that can be traced back to William James one hundred years ago. Since that time, numerous theorists have included the notion of self in their theories, including psychoanalysts' use of the term "ego." It is since the time of the Second World War, however, that self-concept has been theoretically connected to the notion of self-esteem. While many theorists have discussed self-esteem and self-concept, three of the most notable theorists in this area are White, Rogers and Maslow. In discussing this concept, we use the terms self-esteem, self-worth and self-concept interchangeably.

Bandura (1990) makes a distinction between perceived competence (self-efficacy) and self-esteem, while acknowledging that they are often referred to interchangeably in the psychological literature. He refers to the former in terms of one's view of personal capabilities and the later, to how well on likes oneself. He goes on however, to suggest that they can be linked in that self-esteem can come from personal estimations of competence.

Harter (1990), however, sees self-esteem as a global, overall estimation of one's value, in seeming contrast to self-efficacy, which she views with more domain specific. At various life stages, she presents self-concept as being related to differing domains of competence. For example, in adolescence, she depicts self-concept as being related to competence in terms of school, job, athletics, physical appearance, relationships with others (peers, close friends, boy- or girlfriends), as well as one's conduct or morality (p. 73).

Our interests are more directed toward how one feels about oneself as well as one's estimation of abilities. We see the two as being interrelated and treat them as such. Thus, in this section, we present both theories of competence motivation (White) and self-worth (Rogers) in that they both relate to the striving for growth and personal enhancement.

As we have mentioned in Chapters 4, 5, and 9, gains in self-esteem as a result of participation in wilderness therapy have been well documented. Ewert (1983) summarizes the research in the field of outdoor adventure pertaining to self-concept prior to 1982. He also briefly discusses many of the theories not presented in the current chapter, including psychoanalytic, existential, trait and social psychological theories.

Effectance Motivation

Robert White (1959) wrote a now classic piece on positive strivings entitled Competence Reconsidered. In it, he convincingly argued that psychoanalysis's emphasis on drive reduction as the source of human motivation was, at best, incomplete. A more complete portrayal of human motivation must consider people's drive to gain mastery over their environments. It must explain why people do things even when their basic biological (idinal) urges are seemingly satisfied.

White brought in evidence from physiology and neurology, but his description of infants at play perhaps best exemplifies his notion of positive strivings (1959, p. 326). Infants at play learn by manipulating toys—shaking them, looking at them, dropping things—all in preparation for more advanced activities later learned. He called this motivation to explore and master the environment, competence motivation or effectance motivation. This motivation is based on ego urges toward mastery rather than idinal urges for drive reduction.

Later, White (1960) went on to describe how competence motivation can co-exist with idinal urges and how each of Freud's psychosexual stages of development also involves mastery. For example, in the oral stage of development, White sees feeding as the precursor for self-mastery and mastery of the environment. He views the negativism ("terrible twos") and locomotion of the anal stage as critical to the development of autonomy. More direct connections may be seen between wilderness therapy and White's postulated motivational issues in the phallic, latency and genital stages. The locomotion, verbal and abstract skills gained in the phallic stage are suggested by White to foster a sense of personal competence. Many of the adventure activities are directly aimed at getting youngsters to exercise and develop physical, verbal and abstract aspects of functioning and have noted resulting gains in self-esteem. Another phallic stage task related to what one might learn on a wilderness trip is the imitation of adults (leaders). Similarly, White suggests that tasks gained in the latency stage concerned with competence include peer relationships, learning to compromise and learning to protect oneself. Again these tasks are either taught directly or indirectly in wilderness programs. Finally, wilderness therapy can directly help foster the genital stage task of bringing together the person's sense of competence and sense of identity.

In addition to White's theoretical conceptions involving motivation to master the environment and the expansion of the psychosexual stages to include competence, he also discussed the individual's sense of effectance. This sense of being able to master the environment is a concept clearly related to self-esteem and can also be compared to Bandura's previously discussed notion of self-efficacy. Summarizing this latter component of White's competence model, Monte (1980, p. 203) stated: "The sense of efficacy, fueled by the inherent effectance ego energy, can only develop in an interpersonal milieu, through interactions with people who reflect in their responses to the child's efforts their own competencies, and who model the rewards of personal mastery in their healthy and joyous living." From this quote, there are clear recommendations about how wilderness programs should use the power of the group, create positive interactions among participants and staff, and use positive role models for staff.

Self-Actualization

Abraham Maslow began his career in psychology studying the dominance behavior of monkeys. He noted that dominance was rarely based on physical aggression; rather, it was a resulting manifestation of an inner "dominance-feeling." Early in his career he lost his enthusiasm for monkeys and turned his focus to well functioning people, while maintaining an interest in dominance-feeling. His definition of dominance-feeling parallels definitions of self-esteem and self-worth, as may be evident in the following quote by Maslow (as cited in Monte 1980, p. 552):

> High dominance-feeling empirically involves good self-confidence, self-assurance, high evaluation of the self, feelings of general

capability or superiority, and lack of shyness, timidity, self-consciousness or embarrassment.

These interests led to the study of self-actualization, the inherent motivation to be fully functioning. Maslow (1954; 1962) developed a theory of psychological needs based on the concept of self-actualization. In this theory, there is a hierarchy of needs such that the more basic needs are preeminent. That is, given a state of deprivation, the more basic needs will emerge before the higher needs.

Only when a hierarchically lower need is relatively satisfied will a higher need emerge. The lower needs are also referred to as basic needs or deficiency needs. They are satisfied primarily by external sources, as opposed to growth needs, which are satisfied from within. The most basic needs are physiological and are basic for survival. They include food, water, sleep, shelter from the elements and a host of other needs. Maslow felt that it was not necessary to enumerate all of these needs (Goble, 1976). Once these needs are relatively sated, the needs for safety emerge. Whereas a basic need may be for warmth, a safety need may be for comfort and security. These needs may also include the freedom from threat, a certain amount of orderliness and predictability, and the absence of pain and anxiety.

If these needs are met, the next needs to dominate are those for belongingness and love. Maslow's (1954) characterization of these needs could aptly be used to describe some of the participants in the Wilderness Therapy Program who have been severely abused. After a few days in the program, when physiological needs have been cared for and the routine of the program is established, a participant:

> will hunger for affectionate relations with people in general, namely for a place in his group, and he will strive with great intensity to achieve this goal. He will want to attain such a place more than anything else in the world and maybe even forget that once, when he was hungry, he sneered at love as unreal or unnecessary or unimportant (cited by Goble, 1976, p. 40).

To this, and consistent with Maslow, we would add that our hypothetical participant "sneered at love" not only when he was hungry, but also, tired, hurt, scared, or in other ways deprived of his physiological or safety needs. When not deprived of these basic needs, people seek out affection and connectedness with others. This implies receiving caring and giving it, as well.

Esteem needs are next to emerge. Again, these needs only emerge when the more basic needs have been largely satisfied. Thus, Maslow theorizes that an individual will be concerned with an inner sense of value only when there are no threats to physiological and safety needs and when there is a sense of love and belongingness. Esteem needs take two forms, the first of which is for self-esteem. At this stage, people want to feel good about themselves because of a sense of mastery or achievement. Note that it is this part of Maslow's theory that meshes with other theories' concept of self-esteem. The second form of esteem needs is in terms of recognition from others in which one feels respect, recognition, appreciation or even status.

The next need is the need for self-actualization. This is the need to achieve one's fullest potential, to become fully functioning, to grow to capacity in one's own unique way. Malsow discussed this need as being the motivating force for growth in the personality, although he thought of this force as being easily thwarted. Thus, he believed that few individuals were self-actualized. Many of us, however, experience moments in which we are fully functioning. These, Maslow referred to as peak experiences, moments when you become what you are doing, in which there is no sense of self-consciousness. Instead, there is spontaneity, expressiveness, a sense of freedom, control and happiness.

Many people find that they are able to have peak experiences hiking down a trail. In such instances, they are not aware of the trail beneath their feet or the pack on their backs; instead, they are a part of the environment, moving with it, in harmony and bliss.

In what kind of environment can the basic needs be satisfied? A variety of preconditions must exist in the surrounding circumstances (Maslow, 1954). The environment must allow for people to express their feelings verbally or behaviorally (as long as no harm is done to others). People must also have the right to defend themselves against threat. There also must be fairness, honesty, justice and orderliness. Goble (1976) mentions another aspect that is needed for growth to occur. It is one that captures the spirit of adventure pursuits—challenge.

Self Theory

In consonance with Maslow, Rogers believes that people are motivated toward self-actualization. Their actions are directed by the desire for self-actualization, based on their own perceptions of their needs. Rogers' most definitive statement of his theory of the development of self was outlined in his work, "A theory of personality" (1973).

According to Rogers, the actualizing tendency begins in infancy as the baby differentiates experiences into those that occur in the outside world versus those that are internal. This internal awareness constitutes the formation of self-concept. As this self-concept develops, so does the infant's need for positive regard, a need that is universal. As an outgrowth of this need for positive regard, we develop a regard for ourselves (self-regard) that is learned in relationship to our experiences with others.

When we receive positive regard from others only when we think, feel or act in certain ways, Rogers refers to this as conditional positive regard. Under these circumstances, we learn that certain of our experiences lead to love and acceptance, while others do not. When that happens, some of our experiences become unacceptable. Acceptable experiences are not threatening to us and are perceived accurately. Unacceptable experiences threaten us because they have been associated with conditional regard and are distorted or denied from consciousness (the basic defense mechanisms). When this happens, a state of incongruence exists between self and experience. In other words, there becomes a psychic conflict between self and one's experiences. This is Roger's basic statement about the nature of maladjustment (Rogers, 1959, p. 220):

> From this point on his concept of self includes distorted perceptions which do not accurately represent his experience, and his experience includes elements which are not included in the picture he has of himself. Thus, he can no longer live as a unified whole person...

This is in contrast with what happens when an infant grows up with unconditional positive regard. Then, the child's need for positive regard is satisfied regardless of what she experiences. This is not to say that the parent likes and approves of everything the child does, for it is possible to love and value the child without liking all of her thoughts, feelings and actions. Stated otherwise, the child here knows that she is loved regardless of her experiences, resulting in congruity between self and experiences. There is no threat to her feelings of positive regard or her self-image. All of her experiences are therefore equally acceptable and she is free to chose those experiences that lead to self-actualization and reject the others.

According to Rogers, those people who grow up with conditional positive regard sometimes behave in accord with their need for self-actualization (when their experiences are acceptable), and sometimes behave in response to the conditional positive regard they have received from others (when their experiences are unacceptable). A person in this situation, states Rogers (1973, p. 220):

> has not been true to himself, to his own natural organismic valuing of experience, but for the sake of preserving the positive regard of others has now come to falsify some of the values he experiences and to perceive them only in terms based on their value to others. Yet this has not been a conscious choice, but a natural—and tragic—development in infancy.

Therapy from this perspective is geared toward undoing this process so that a person can accept all experiences, using the organismic valuing process, making the self congruent with one's experiences. It should be clear that this person will then see reality clearly, with no need for denial or distortion. Therapy proceeds by increasing unconditional positive regard from significant others, "in a context of empathic understanding," leading to an increase in the person's positive self-regard.

Since the participants of wilderness therapy programs have emotional conflicts and difficulties, from Rogers' perspective, they are in a state of incongruity with their experiences. Our role as therapist leaders is to provide a warm, accepting environment, with group support in order to lessen feelings of personal threat so the person can lower defenses, leading to more congruence between self and experiences. As a result, self-regard should increase, adjustment should increase, and the person can use the organismic valuing process in order to regulate behavior. This is the process by which, from this theoretical perspective, the person becomes more fully functioning.

Transpersonal Theories

The theoretical accounts of self-actualization and self-esteem have more recently been included in an area referred to as Transpersonal Psychology. In fact, Maslow was the first president of the Association for Transpersonal Psychology. This area of study is intended to expand upon other movements in psychology.

The first movement is usually referred to as psychoanalytic, the second, behaviorist, and the third force is the humanistic movement (Goble, 1976). In contrast to these forces, "[t]ranspersonal approaches draw upon the first three forces while going beyond to see humans as intuitive, mystical, psychic and spiritual. Above all, humans are viewed as unifiable, having the potential for harmonious and holistic development of all their potentials" (Hendricks & Weinhold, 1982, p. 8).

Tart (1975) defines Transpersonal Psychology as dealing with higher human processes that include spirituality and the development of human potential. Finally, Sutich (as cited in Tart, 1975, p. 2) defines this field as being "concerned with the empirical, scientific study of, and responsible implementation of the findings relevant to becoming, and individual and spiritual meta-needs, ultimate values, unitive consciousness, peak experiences, B-values, ecstasy, mystical experience, awe, being, self-actualization...."

Brown (1989) has approached outdoor adventure pursuits from the perspective of Transpersonal Psychology in an attempt to account for personal growth that occurs in nature. As others have before him, Brown refers to increases in our sense of awe, inner calm and other spiritual needs as a process of transformation. He goes so far as to present specific techniques that can be employed to enhance personal growth. These range from meditation and relaxation to the use of symbols and myths to enhance transformation. The entirety of Transpersonal Psychology encompasses concepts from many of the eastern religions and is beyond the scope of our theoretical concerns. Our discussion is necessarily narrower and will focus on the use of symbols and myths.

Carl Jung's theory of personality bears some striking similarity to Freud's. And well it should, for the two collaborated for at least a few years, with Freud trying to encourage and yet, control Jung's theoretical ideas. Jung, sponsored by Freud, became president of the Association of Psycho-Analysis. It is not surprising, therefore, that many of Jung's theoretical concepts are similar to Freud's. Jung's conceptualization of the psyche is that it is comprised of three levels (for a more complete summary, see Hall & Nordby, 1973). The first, the consciousness, contains aspects of the mind of which the individual has direct awareness. The ego, following Freud, is that part of the consciousness that organizes one's experiences, memories and feelings.

The second level of the mind for Jung is the personal unconscious. This area is the repository for those experiences that are not recognized by the consciousness. These experiences may have been conscious and were then forgotten. They may also have been threatening to the person and were repressed or denied by way of defense mechanisms. These contents can become conscious when they are needed, making Jung's unconscious more like Freud's preconscious mind. The contents of the personal unconscious can cluster together to form complexes. Complexes can exert great force in terms of one's personality, as might be expected from someone who has a "guilt complex." That individual's life could largely be ruled by trying to be perfect, overjudging when one transgressed, etc. In this way, many of one's thoughts, feelings, sensations and behaviors can be related to the complex.

Complexes need not be negative, and in fact, they can be ruling passions. Jung gives Van Gogh's passion for art as an example of a complex. Jung speculated that complexes came from at least two sources. One was from the traumas of childhood. Thus, an abused child may grow up to make sure never to be vulnerable to others, could take up martial arts, become a spokesperson for the downtrodden, become a victim again, or even victimize others. A second source for a complex originates from a much deeper place in the psyche—from archetypes in the collective unconscious, as will be discussed below.

Freud and Jung fell out in 1912. This may have been the result of the publication of Jung's book, *Symbols of Transformation*. According to Campbell (1971), this book presented ideas that Freud could not tolerate. While Freud was working on sexual impulses as expressed in the Oedipus myth, Jung was developing concepts related to the collective unconscious, which Freud likened to "occultism."

The collective unconscious contains archetypes or prototypes of experience that are inherited as images from our ancestral past. They are not images, per se, but, rather, the predisposition to have certain experiences. In this way, we may find a campfire to be a source of security because our ancestors gathered around fires to ward off harm, provide warmth and cook food. Campbell (1971) addresses the characteristics of archetypes: these archetypes are expressions of "common human needs, instincts, and potentials" and they are reflected in cultural traditions and myths. Individuals who are psychologically unbalanced have fantasies and dreams that contain fragments of myths. These dreams are best interpreted by comparing them to myths that will allow the person to reestablish balance and direction. "The posture of the unconscious is compensatory to consciousness, and its productions, dreams, and fantasies, consequently, are not only corrective but also prospective, giving clues, if properly read, to those functions and archetypes of the psyche pressing, at the moment, for recognition" (Campbell, 1971, xxii-xxiii).

Two archetypes in particular facilitate transformation in that they help organize, balance and unify the psyche (Rychlak, 1973). These archetypes are quaternity and mandala. There is a similarity between these two symbols in that they represent unifying forces within the psyche. Quaternity refers to the quality of being divisible by four. Quaternity is reflected in things composed of four, as a compass is composed of four directions or a map has four sides and directions. The floor of a tent is rectangular. These symbolize completeness.

Mandala, a Sanskrit word for circle, refers to wholeness as reflected in circles. They represent the centering of one's personality. According to Jung, common mandalas are flowers, wheels—in them, a round structure surrounds a central point. Consider the symbol that we use to represent our Wilderness Therapy Program. Although it was not designed with Jung in mind, it's use as a healing symbol is certainly consistent with the mandala. Brown (1989) even has participants in his program draw mandalas as a mechanism for positive change.

For Jung, therapeutic change occurs by helping the client unify polarized aspects of the psyche. The primary way of doing this is by getting in touch with the unconscious part of the psyche, then integrating it with the conscious side. In that archetypes reside in the unconscious, the use of symbols of transformation, like circles or four-sided symbols, aid in reaching the collective unconscious. Besides symbol creation, the other main strategy for creating change is through verbal means, such as in more traditional psychotherapy. Health is achieved when the two halves of the personality are

Figure 6-1. Wilderness Therapy Program Symbol

balanced in such a way that the midpoint of the personality resides somewhere between the conscious and unconscious realms.

In an article directed at analyzing camping from a Jungian perspective, Tally (1974) cites that Jung built a living structure out of stone on the banks of Lake Zurich in the midst of trees and forest. He cooked his meals over the fire and drew his water from a well. These actions are consistent with the theoretical notions outlined above, in which the expected result would be increased balance of the psyche, and more effective patterns of overt behavior. He also spent extensive amounts of time studying more primitive peoples from other parts of the world, with an apparent understanding of the constructive value of living closer to nature.

From this, one can extrapolate applications to wilderness programs, not only in terms of the value of specific symbols, like having group meetings in a circle around a fire, but also in terms of more global inner changes, as Tally points out would be expected from taking an "over-educated, one-sided intellectual" into an environment in which there is a "sense of the mystery of nature" (p. 6).

Systems Theory

Systems theory has roots in the biological sciences (Von Bertalanffy, 1950), with applications of this theory being made to the social sciences a few years later (Miller, 1955; 1965). More recently, work in the social sciences has included more developed definitions of systems and their components, as well as implications for applications of systems theory (e.g., Compton & Galaway, 1989).

A promising recent approach to working with troubled adolescents has been through the application of systems theory. In this vein, adolescent problems are seen to occur within the family. While the family may or may not be responsible for the onset of problems (that is, some problems may be a function of biological processes or peer pressures), the family does have a role in maintaining, exacerbating, and alleviating problems. Some of the principles of systems theory as they apply to change within families have been discussed by Koman and Stechler (1985, p. 11) in the *Handbook of Adolescents and Family Therapy.* (1) The family system in which the adolescent lives is an open system to the extent that exchange is possible with the outside environment (the larger system), but relatively closed to the extent that the family attempts to maintain its integrity in the midst of certain outside forces identified as "destructive." (2) The system attempts to maintain stability by dampening forces that would create disequilibrium. (3) In order for change to occur, there must be disequilibrium. (4) When there are problems in the family, the problems must be experienced as dysfunctional before they can willingly be changed; otherwise, the family will attempt to resist change and maintain homeostasis. (5) Certain therapeutic situations make it easier for change to be made by families.

Stated otherwise, because of the interdependence of family members and the tendency for systems to maintain stability, it is often difficult to change individuals' behaviors—without the assistance of the family system. Wilderness therapy programs provide a different system for the adolescent's behavior. Many problem behaviors are not consistent with wilderness therapy. For example, for the wilderness program to work smoothly, thereby producing reinforcements to the participants and staff alike, participants need to cooperate, communicate well, take responsibility for oneself and the group, etc. Individuals who are withdrawn, have trouble communicating, or are verbally aggressive often have trouble and quickly learn that their behavior is not rewarded.

Conceptually, wilderness programs can be seen as an alternative to the family, school and community system. Prosocial and more adaptive behaviors that were not directly reinforced in these other systems are reinforced in wilderness groups. Thus, it is often easier to change behaviors in the wilderness than it is at home. Of course, the wilderness program must be tied into the family and community in order to generalize from behavior changes in the wilderness. It would be of little benefit to change behaviors in the wilderness if they could not be maintained when back in the community.

Unfortunately, all too often the link between the wilderness program and the community is weak or nonexistent.

Systems theory can also be used to conceptualize the planning and development of wilderness programs. In an article we wrote on this topic (Berman & Davis-Berman, 1991), consideration was given to planning, implementing and evaluating wilderness programs from a systems theory framework. From this framework, we stressed that the adolescent targeted for change is connected to various systems: family, community, social service organization, school, etc. Equally important are administrative issues, including marketing to gain recognition and participants, funding of the program, and networking to benefit the participant, family, community and involved social service agencies.

Applying the Criteria for Evaluating Theories

We began this chapter with consideration of a number of criteria for evaluating theories. Let us return to a discussion of those criteria. The first we considered pertained to the range of convenience. Each of the theories considered in this chapter has a different focus. While some theories dealt only with self-esteem, others with learning through observation, and still others, with unconscious psychological processes. We also noted that broader theories tended to be preferred over narrower theories. In this regard, some theories—notably, those pertaining to locus of control, self-efficacy and self-esteem—were narrower in scope, while others—transpersonal and self-actualization theories—were broader. Balancing this issue of breadth, one needs to consider the importance of the constructs each theory deals with. Thus, while self-efficacy may be a relatively narrow concept, its significance makes this an important theory to consider.

All of the theories considered are systematic in that they are more than a collection of unconnected concepts. Some, however, are more systematic than others. Rotter's social learning theory is often pointed out as an example of a systematic theory, and one can readily see the interconnected of the basic terms of the theory. Other theoretical accounts, like the notion of the "restorative environment" appear less systematic. One should not conclude, however, that unsystematic theories are to be discarded, for they often make important contributions to our knowledge.

Some theories are notable for their ability to operationally define key concepts. Locus of control, for example, is easily measured by a number of instruments. Other concepts, like those stemming from Jung's theory, are quite difficult to operationally define. These latter concepts are more abstract and less rooted to observable events. There are so few theories that have been applied to this area of growth and change that comparisons are difficult.

Moreover, rather than eliminating theoretical explanations, we are really interested in expanding the breadth, depth and range of theoretical explanations. Nevertheless, parsimony is still an issue when two theories explain the same events. Take the issue of why participants model the behavior of the wilderness leaders. Social learning theory seems to have a much simpler explanatory model for why this occurs than does Bly's (1990) account as related in *Iron John*.

Finally, we discussed the criterion of utility. On this count, systems theory has much to offer in terms of understanding the need for taking the adolescent out of the family setting, employing an alternative to traditional models of treatment, and coordinating what happens in the wilderness with community institutions. Systems theory can be used in conjunction with other theoretical models and thus, can add to our understanding of wilderness therapy. It should still be recognized that no theory adequately explains the range and depth of events, making it crucial for there to be continued attempts to apply theories to wilderness therapy.

Having established the need for theory, and the importance of a theoretical basis for wilderness therapy programs, we now turn to the actual concrete steps in designing such a program.

References

Bandura, A. (1971). *Social learning theory.* Morristown, NJ: General Learning Press.

Bandura, A. (1977). Self-efficacy: Toward a unifying theory of behavioral change. *Psychological Review, 84,* 191-215.

Bandura, A. (1982). Self-efficacy mechanism in human agency. *American Psychologist, 31,* 122-147.

Bandura, A. (1990). Conclusion: Reflections on nonability determinants of competence. In R. Sternberg & J. Kolligen, (Eds.), *Competence considered* (pp. 315-362). New Haven: Yale University Press.

Berman, D. & Davis-Berman, J. (1991). Wilderness therapy and adolescent mental health: Administrative and clinical issues. *Administration and Policy in Mental Health, 18,* 373-379.

Bly, R. (1990). *Iron John: A book about men.* Reading, MA: Addison-Wesley.

Brown, M. (1989). Transpersonal psychology: Facilitating transformation in outdoor experiential education. *Journal of Experiential Education, 12,* 47-56.

Campbell, J. (Ed.). (1971). *The portable Jung.* New York: Penguin Books.

Compton, B. & Galaway, B. (1989). *Social work processes.* Belmont, CA: Wadsworth.

Ewert, A. W. (1983). *Outdoor adventure and self-concept: A research analysis.* Eugene, OR: University of Oregon Center of Leisure Studies.

Ewert, A. W. (1989). *Outdoor adventure pursuits: Foundations, models, and theories.* Columbus, Ohio: Publishing Horizons.

Goble, F. (1976). *The third force.* New York: Pocket Books.

Godfrey, R. (1980). *Outward Bound: Schools of the possible.* Garden City, NY: Anchor Press.

Hall, C. & Nordby, V. (1973). *A primer of Jungian psychology.* NY: Mentor.

Harter, S. (1990). Causes, correlates, and the functional role of global self-worth: A life span perspective. In R. Sternberg & J. Kolligen, (Eds.), *Competence considered* (pp. 67-97). New Haven: Yale University Press.

Hendricks, G. & Weinhold, B. (1982). *Transpersonal approaches to counseling and psychotherapy.* Denver: Love Publishing.

Kaplan, R. & Kaplan, S. (1984). *The experience of nature: A psychological perspective.* Cambridge, England: Cambridge University.

Koman, S. & Stechler, G. (1985). Making the jump to systems. In M. Mirkin & S. Koman, (Eds.), *Handbook of adolescents and family therapy* (pp. 3-20). New York: Gardner.

Levy, L. (1970). *Conceptions of personality: Theories and research.* New York: Random House.

Liebert, R. M. & Spiegler, M. D. (1987). *Personality: Strategies and issues.* Chicago: Dorsey.

Maslow, A. (1962). *Toward a psychology of being.* New York: Van Nostrand.

Maslow, A. (1984). *Motivation and personality.* New York: Harper and Row.

McGowan, M. (1986). Self efficacy: Operationalizing challenge education. *The Bradford Papers Annual,* 1, 65-69.

Miller, J. G. (1955). Toward a general theory for the behavioral sciences. *American Psychologist\,* 10, 513-531.

Miller, J. G. (1965). Living systems: Basic concepts. *Behavioral Studies,* 10, 193-237.

Miller, N. & Dollard, J. (1941). *Social learning and imitation.* New Haven: Yale University Press.

Monte, C. F. (1980). *Beneath the mask: An introduction to theories of personality.* New York: Holt, Rinehart and Winston.

Phares, E. J. (1984). *Introduction to personality.* Columbus, Ohio: Charles E. Merrill.

Rogers, C. (1959). A theory of therapy, personality, and interpersonal relationships as developed in the client-centered framework. In S. Koch (Ed.), *Psychology: A study of a science* (Vol 3). New York: McGraw Hill. (Reprinted as "A theory of personality." In T. Millon, (Ed.), *Theories of psychopathology and personality* (pp. 217-230). Philadelphia: W. B. Saunders, 1973.)

Rotter, J. B. (1954). *Social learning and clinical psychology.* Englewood Cliffs, NJ: Prentice-Hall.

Rotter, J. B. (1971). Generalized expectancies of interpersonal trust. *American Psychologist,* 26, 443-452.

Rychlak, J. (1973). *Introduction to personality and psychotherapy: A theory-construction approach.* Boston: Houghton Mifflin.

Seligman, M. (1975). *Helplessness: On depression, development, and death.* San Francisco: Freeman.

Selye, H. (1976). *The stress of life.* New York: McGraw Hill.

Talley, J. (1974). Camping experience and the unconscious. In T. Lowry, (Ed.), *Camping therapy: Its uses in psychiatry and rehabilitation* (pp. 3-7). Springfield, IL: Charles Thomas.

Tart, C. (1975). *Transpersonal psychologies.* New York: Harper and Row.

Von Bertalanffy, L. (1950). An overview of general system theory. *British Journal of Philosophical Science,* 1, 134-165.

White, R. W. (1959). Motivation reconsidered: The concept of competence. *Psychological Review,* 66, 297-333.

White, R. W. (1960). Competence and the psychosexual stages of development. In M. R. Jones (Ed.), *Nebraska symposium on motivation, 8* (pp. 97-141). Lincoln: University of Nebraska Press.

Chapter Seven ▽

Designing a Program

By this point, we hope that you are intrigued by the notion of incorporating wilderness counseling into your own programs or have already done so. This is equally possible for the therapist who finds limitations in traditional practice settings as it is for the outdoor educator who works with special populations and would like to do more in terms of integrating counseling with experience. From our perspective, the key to successful integration of outdoor and counseling approaches is in planning. In general terms, this planning consists of three phases: program design, implementation, and evaluation. In this chapter we will give consideration to all three phases, with examples of ways in which this process can materialize.

As was established in the preceding chapter, good practice develops out of theory. Having a theoretical model allows one to plan for services in a way that is logically consistent and which allows for the interrelatedness of program components. As discussed, systems theory has much to offer in the way of providing a framework for wilderness therapy; thus systems theory will be used as the theoretical model in this chapter as well.

Wilderness therapy is more than tacking aspects of one practice field on to another. That is, having a ropes course does not transform a psychiatric hospital into an adventure based program, in the same way that asking participants to talk about their experiences does not make an outdoor program therapy. Instead, with proper planning and consideration, adventure-based activities, when combined with elements of counseling, may be utilized to meet specific goals of the program and needs of the participants. What follows is a model for the design, implementation and evaluation of wilderness therapy programs.

Program Design

Needs

The first step in planning a program involves determining the needs of the program or the participants. In other words, one might begin by asking the question, "do we or our clients have needs that are not being met because of limitations in our programs?" or "are there alternate ways of helping our clients meet their needs?"

In a paper written a few years ago, we (Berman & Davis-Berman, 1991) suggested some goals for wilderness therapy that are consistent with many mental health agency ideals. These included the concepts of the provision of a continuum of services, in the least restrictive environment, where there is an opportunity to grow and experience immediate and naturally occurring consequences for one's behavior. And while these may be principles that most mental health practitioners endorse, they are rarely provided. For example, there are very few alternatives open to most adolescents in need of counseling besides outpatient therapy and confinement (in the form of residential treatment). The notion of the least restrictive environment implies that a person should not be restricted more than is necessary, but when the alternatives are outpatient counseling and confinement, there is truly little choice in settings.   Parenthetically, this lack of options is partly due to the structure of most insurance policies, in that they will only cover outpatient counseling or psychiatric hospitalization. When we think of wilderness therapy as a growth-enhancing experience, we mean that in two ways. First, it is growthful in that it ideally helps people overcome and then transcend some of their problems. It also provides a setting and a way of approaching personal change that is novel for most clients, allows them to see new vistas, facilitates meeting new people, and encourages them to relate to others in unique ways. This, and the personal challenge of adventure-based programs, gives one an opportunity for personal growth in a way that is usually thought of as enrichment rather than therapy.

The final idea expressed above, regarding consequences of behavior, pertains to the fact that most counseling opportunities involve change through verbal/cognitive mediation. This methodology works for many, but not all, participants in counseling. For others, especially teens, parental admonitions about the harsh realities to be experienced in the outside world represent boring harangues rather than sage advice.

For others, information is processed through actions and feelings, not intellect. Thus, counseling in an office often fails to reach many in need. Wilderness therapy overcomes many of these obstacles to counseling. It is an alternative to traditional modes of therapy that involve constraints with regard to the structure and confinement of many programs. It also involves experiences that offer immediate consequences with less emphasis on cognitively mediated change. Finally, it is also a more intensive counseling experience than will be found in most outpatient settings, but certainly less restrictive than residential programs that involve long stays or in locked facilities.

Expansion of adventure-based programs to include wilderness therapy can be approached in a manner that is similar to that just taken for counseling programs. Adventure-based programs involve perceived risk, group interactions and reinforcement for cooperation. That is, they provide an environment in which, ideally, change is fostered. Perhaps this is why programs of this sort have such appeal for use with special populations. There is a big difference, however, between presenting people with an enriching setting and maximizing their ability to use that setting beneficially. This is where more counseling becomes critical. Moreover, there are, by definition, special challenges one encounters when working with people who are emotionally needy that are often surmountable through the application of therapy skills.

Another consideration that should be taken into account when contemplating transforming adventure education into wilderness therapy relates to the generalizability of changes created through outdoor adventure-based learning experiences. Most of us who have been in these settings find ourselves thinking, feeling and acting in ways that are different from our everyday experiences. Using these new-found changes when one returns to "normal" life is often difficult, and many find that they quickly return to their old patterns of living. This potential shortcoming can be dealt with as a therapy issue.

These identified program goals should then be considered in the context of other services or programs rendered. This systems' analysis will help ensure that wilderness programs do not unwittingly conflict with other programming in terms of such factors as budget, staffing patterns, treatment planning and alternative services that are available.

Early in the planning process, consideration should be given to the selection of participants, both in terms of staff and clients. The participants can be considered as a subsystem, upon whom much of the responsibility for the success of the programs rests. Therefore, care must go into the selection process.

Staff

One wishes that staff could be equally qualified to provide counseling and outdoor adventure programs, but this goal is probably both unrealistic and unnecessary. At a minimum, we believe that all staff should be comfortable enough with their wilderness skills so that they can focus on the needs of the clients. They may also need to take over the physical aspects of the program in the event of an emergency. First aid and CPR training, and preferably certification, seem appropriate for minimal standards. For those staff who coordinate the physical, "hard skills" components of the program, there are certification programs for outdoor leaders, like those offered by the Wilderness Education Association (WEA; Cockrell & Lupton, 1991). Other programs, such as National Outdoor Leadership School (NOLS) and Outward Bound, also offer outdoor leadership courses.

It should be acknowledged that many outdoor leaders lack these more formal methods for acquiring outdoor skills. In recognition of this fact, the Council on Accreditation of Services for Families and Children (COA) Therapeutic Wilderness Task Force has recommended that programs be coordinated by a person who has: "at least three years progressively responsible experience in an outdoor education program for at-risk or troubled youth; demonstrated technical competence and safety skills; problem-solving and leadership skills, sound judgement, and capabilities in interpersonal communication and group facilitation; and skills in the use of outdoor and camping experiences for therapeutic purposes" (COA, 1992 p. 2).

Our assessment of these differing levels of competence is that while it may be desirable to have certified wilderness leaders, they are few and far between, not many programs offer such training (although the number of WEA programs is increasing every year), and there are many well qualified, experienced staff who have not gone that route in developing their competencies.

On the other hand, we feel that the COA standards are too lax for those in supervisory positions, since it means that courses can be supervised and coordinated by individuals who have little or no formal training in any field related to at-risk or troubled youth. Instead, we suggest that the COA standards might be acceptable for supervisees; supervisors should have higher levels of training.

In addition, outdoor leaders should have specific skills in the outdoor activities utilized. If, for example, canoeing is employed in the wilderness program, the outdoor leaders should be certified (by the Red Cross, American Canoe Association, etc.). For other areas, where there may not be certification, outdoor leaders should have demonstrable skills. *Safety Practices in Adventure Programming* (Priest & Dixon, 1990) is an excellent source for equipment, instructional, participant, environmental and ethical standards for a number of technical activities.

Staff who provide for the mental health needs of the clients should meet the same rigorous standards that would apply in other settings. Thus counseling and/or psychotherapy (we use the terms synonymously) should be provided by professional mental health staff who are trained and licensed in accordance with state statutes and national standards. By making this recommendation, we are suggesting, at a minimum, a bifurcated staff in which there are different criteria for those coordinating the physical components of the program and those coordinating the counseling components.

If there is easy access to the group and a way of communicating with the program base camp or office, the counseling aspects of the program can perhaps be carried out by a mental health aide. Otherwise, we recommend that only fully trained mental health professionals provide these services.

There are at least four reasons for suggesting this high level of standards. First, we believe that clients in wilderness programs deserve the same level of care that they would find in non-wilderness settings. When wilderness programs make claims about psychological growth and/or treatment and have at-risk or emotionally troubled clients, services should be provided by highly qualified professionals. This is an important standard in order to weed out those programs that view themselves as alternative psychiatric treatments, but run their programs like boot camps. Programs like these have been noted for the harm they can do (Matthews, 1991).

Second, our experiences with wilderness trips for emotionally troubled adolescents have involved psychiatric emergencies requiring the skill and training of a highly qualified mental health professional. In these situations, we believe that there is an unacceptable level of risk by having psychiatric emergencies handled by a paraprofessional who is supervised by a professional in a distant location. Brief synopses of two of these emergency situations are summarized in Figure 7-1. We have changed the names and some of the specifics about these participants in order to protect their identities.

The third reason for having highly trained professionals provide for the mental health needs of clients is to capitalize on "therapeutic moments." By therapeutic moments, we refer to those times when an adroit intervention can greatly help someone deal with an unresolved conflict. An example of such a moment on the trail was when "Thomas," who was trying to deal with the deaths of many loved ones over a short period of time, lost a medallion given to him by his deceased uncle.

The fourth reason for having professionals pertains to insurance reimbursement for wilderness therapy. Many programs are striving to obtain third party payments for these services. If this is to be obtained, wilderness programs certainly must adhere to the high standards set by mental health clinics, private practices, hospitals and other psychiatric residential treatment facilities.

Clients

Most wilderness programs that are concerned with helping clients change behavioral, affective or personality variables work with adolescents from juvenile court, psychiatric hospitals or outpatient mental health settings. It should be acknowledged that there is often overlap among these populations in that the boundary between inpatients and outpatients is often indistinct. The same is also true for juvenile offenders and clients in counseling.

Even though some clients from each of these populations resemble clients from the other populations, at the other extreme, there are also vast differences among these populations. Consequently, an adolescent in an inpatient psychiatric unit with psychotic symptoms has markedly different problems than does an individual who is in a detention center for repeated burglaries or someone seeing a therapist once a week to deal with low self-esteem. It has been our experience that trips are most successful when they are planned around the needs of one population, either one of the populations mentioned or another population, such as individuals with specific physically challenging

Figure 7-1. Psychiatric Emergencies in the Field

Case 1.

Joey was a 17-year-old male resident of an acute-care adolescent psychiatric inpatient unit who was participating in a two-week backpacking wilderness therapy trip. He was admitted to the hospital unit for depression, accompanied by suicidal ideation, that began shortly after a beloved uncle died. Joey had been reluctant to discuss his sense of loss, or even, more generally, his depression. Almost halfway through the trip, however, he lost a medallion given to him by his uncle. Joey became quite agitated, wanted to retrace our steps over the past three days of travel, and tried to seclude himself from the group.

While our general approach to counseling is to bring problems back to the group for processing and resolution, we counseled Joey individually because of the personal nature of his issue. During this counseling, the rest of the group gathered to express their concern for Joey and to express their support for him. After much agony and many tears, Joey was able to come to his own resolution of this issue in individual therapy. His loss of the medallion was symbolic of his loss of his uncle. The medallion was now somewhere along a beautiful trail in the same way that he hoped his uncle was resting in a peaceful place. Joey, with help, was then able to share his resolution with the group. The group was supportive and most all of us shared tears as Joey said good-bye to his uncle.

Case 2.

Sixteen-year-old Tracy was referred from a partial hospitalization program. She was diagnosed as experiencing a post traumatic stress disorder as a result of alleged sexual abuse when she was a child. Three days out of base camp, Tracy began asking if someone was following us. Our attempts to assure her that we were alone on this isolated trail did little to alleviate her anxiety. On successive days, a story unravelled about a man from the Mafia following her to kill her for a crime she said she witnessed. She even drew a picture of this man. At this point, we wondered whether this was a flash-back to a time when she ran away from a treatment center where she was a resident, and therefore based on some truth, or whether this represented a paranoid delusion.

Three days before the trip was to end, Tracy ran into the woods and then back to camp, screaming. She said that she had been mortally wounded by the Mafia-man, who shot her in the leg. She pointed to a place on her calf where she said she had been shot by a poisonous bullet, although we were not able to see anything there. She then went into a catatonic-like state that lasted for hours. Finally, she opened her eyes and said, "I'm Tanya, Tracy is dead."

Following our established emergency procedures, one of us took charge of the larger group while the other, the mental health professional, focused on Tracy, who, by this time, was mute and shaking in what appeared to be abject fear. The therapist was able to calm Tracy, but was not able to help her regain contact with reality. Since it was dark and the situation was somewhat stabilized, we decided to stay the night at our campsite. Tracy stayed in a tent with the leaders, but was unable to get much rest.

In the morning, she was still disoriented and mute. We decided to lead the group out of the woods and to an organized Forest Service campground. There, we arranged for transportation to a community hospital. The therapist was able to share information with the physicians at the hospital, provide counseling while she was there, and arrange for her admission to a hospital near her home. Tracy stayed at that hospital for two days, until she could be transferred to the other hospital, where our diagnostic impressions of multiple personality were confirmed.

conditions. Then planning can focus on the needs of the population participating rather than trying to have one methodology that is intended to fit all needs. This relates to the concept of individual treatment planning, a topic to be addressed later in this chapter.

It is important for programs to define the population of clients for whom their programs are designed. This allows for the establishment of both inclusionary and exclusionary criteria. Clients should then be individually evaluated with consideration given to the needs of the individual and the design of the program.

Our experiences running wilderness therapy trips with inpatients, outpatients, residents from juvenile detention and child protective services homes has affirmed the need to have homogeneous populations in programs. It has also led us to the conclusion that wilderness therapy is perhaps most effective for withdrawn adolescents who have trouble sharing and being close to others, as well as more acting-out adolescents—although not necessarily on the same trip. One must consider how the group needs will best be served given individual participants' needs and problems. This is an extension of the systems-based approach.

Each program should establish its own set of exclusionary criteria for potential participants, based on the design of the program, the qualifications of staff, etc. For illustrative purposes, let us share some of the exclusionary criteria for our programs. It has been important to us to ensure that participants can actively understand the components of our program so that they can incorporate the experiences into a framework that will allow for change on the trip and the ability to reflect on the trip once they have returned home, to increase the generalizability of change.

Toward this end, we have excluded individuals whose cognitive ability is limited by psychosis, severe attention deficit disorder or retardation. This is not to say that programs cannot be designed for these individuals, only that ours has not been so designed. We have also attempted to exclude those individuals who are a threat to harm themselves or others. There may be other psychiatric disturbances that are so severe that the individual may have little to gain from our program or may interfere with others' ability to focus on their own needs (e.g., multiple personality). Finally, we do not accept participants who could achieve rapid change in a less intensive counseling setting.

Great exception is taken to those programs that allow clients (or their parents) to self-select for wilderness therapy programs. When this is the case, there is no opportunity to exclude individuals whose needs are not met by the program. Unfortunately, for many of these less than reputable programs, the criteria for inclusion is often the ability to pay tuition costs rather than the fit between the needs of the participant and the strengths of the program.

Other factors involved in the selection criteria for well designed programs are the age, and physical and medical status of applicants. Age may be an important factor so that applicants are physically and emotionally mature enough to benefit from the program. In addition, the mix of participants' ages is important in that it is difficult to attain group cohesiveness if participants are of very different ages and are confronting different developmental issues. Regarding physical status, consideration should be given to the physical challenges inherent to the program and the ability of each participant to master these challenges. For our backpacking trips, we know that a loaded pack at the beginning of a trip may weigh 30 pounds and fit a person who is at least five feet tall. This means that the fitness, height and weight of an applicant are important considerations for selection. Similarly, programs that are water oriented will require participants to have certain requisite swimming abilities.

When it comes to the medical status of applicants, it is important to know that an individual does not have any conditions that would impede one's ability to participate in the program. It is also necessary to know about allergies or medications. Most programs require applicants to have a physical examination by a physician and to complete a form attesting to the applicant's physical ability to participate in the program. The AEE has a variety of sample forms, including a medical form in an appendix to *Safety Practices in Adventure Programming* (Priest & Dixon, 1990). Having this information is not enough to be well prepared for medical emergencies. Staff should be knowledgeable about wilderness emergencies, should be trained in the use of first aid and CPR, and should be forewarned about potential medical problems of participants.

One of the cornerstones to dealing with wilderness emergencies is to prevent them. In this vein, participants who are allergic to bee stings should carry a "bee sting kit" prescribed by their physician. There are excellent sources of information on wilderness medicine (e.g., Forgey, 1987) and organizations that specialize in wilderness medical training for staff (e.g., Wilderness Medical Associates, RFD 2 Box 890, Bryant Pond, ME 04219).

Individual Treatment Planning

To the extent that wilderness therapy is a method of change for behavioral, affective or personality variables, as are other forms of mental health treatment, treatment goals should be tailored to meet the needs of the individual engaged in the program. While there are some benefits of participating in wilderness programs that are common to most participants, such as increases in self-esteem (Ewert, 1983), individual needs must also be addressed. This concept of individual treatment plans (ITPs) is one that is familiar to most mental health professionals, but may be unfamiliar to many outdoor leaders. ITPs help organize a team effort to help clients achieve agreed upon goals.

The components to an ITP include a global statement of the individual's problems or a diagnosis. If it is the latter, it is often expected to conform to a DSM-IIIR multiaxial diagnosis that includes a primary diagnosis, specific learning disabilities (for children and adolescents), medical problems and ratings of the severity of psychosocial stressors and an assessment of the global level of functioning (American Psychiatric Association, 1987).

This is usually followed by statements of general goals for this person and objectively defined measures of those goals (referred to as "objectives"). The method for arriving at each of these goals is then presented for each objective. As mentioned above, ITPs are a team effort, and involve the cooperation of those providing counseling and the individual receiving it. In this way, the client is an active participant in a process that involves consensus building and cooperation in order to reach a desired outcome. There may be deviations from this process if the participant is court-ordered or otherwise unable to consent, but in these circumstances, proxy consent may be obtained by parents, guardians or the court.

To provide more insight into this process, consider Ted, a depressed 17-year-old high school junior whose problems began two years ago when his parents divorced. He has poor grades, does not complete his assigned chores, spends time isolated in his room, and is rather cruel toward his younger brother. Ted has been in counseling with a psychologist, who reports that Ted is passive in therapy sessions and generally fails to follow through with recommendations. The treatment plan for Ted might include a brief description, like the one provided above, and a DSM-IIIR diagnosis on each of the five axes: Primary Diagnosis: 300.40 Dysthymic Disorder; Secondary Diagnosis: V71.09 None; Medical Problems: None; Severity of Psychosocial Stressors: 4-Severe (Divorce of Parents); Global Assessment of Functioning: 50-Serious.

One of the ways that we have found treatment planning to be a useful tool in planning change has been to develop a treatment plan for our wilderness trips with the participants in a group meeting prior to embarking. While this process of sharing problems and their solutions is often difficult for some participants, it sets the tone for our trips as a form of treatment.

ITPs can also be used as an evaluative methodology. More will be discussed about evaluation, but let us now introduce the concept of treatment plans as a way of measuring goal attainment. Participants can be asked to specify objectives to be worked on and then to rate the extent to which they feel they have attained each of these objectives on a 7-point scale from 1 (minimal) to 7 (complete). At the end of the trip, these ratings can again be obtained, with the difference averaged over the number of goals or objectives. This gives a objective measure of the mean amount of change per ITP item.

Figure 7-2. Treatment Planning

An integral part of the counseling process involves setting goals. These goals are often expressed in terms of an Individual Treatment Plan (ITP). Treatment plans should be established with the client, who signs off on the form. This helps ensure client participation in the counseling process. If the participant has been in counseling, that therapist should also have input into the process of formulating the ITP.

Not all ITP forms have the same items. However, commonly found components of an ITP are: (1) the presenting problem, summarizing the clients problems at the time of the initial assessment; (2) the diagnoses in terms of DSM-IIIR ; (3) Medications, both being prescribed for the disorders listed above, or that could have mood, cognitive or behavior altering properties; (4) critical problems about which the clinician should be aware; and (5) specific treatment goals, treatment designed to achieve these goals and the dates by which the goals should be achieved.

An important element of an ITP is that it is individualized to meet each client's needs. Some ITP forms make a distinction between goals and objectives, where the former are more global descriptions of the problem to be addressed and the latter are operationally defined in terms of how progress will be measured. For example, a goal might be to "decrease withdrawal" and the objective would be to "increase the frequency and duration of activities." On our form, a copy of which we have included, we only use the word "goal," but word it in such a way that the way it is to be measured is indicated. Thus, we might have a goal of "will try to get along better with parents by outlining a plan of conflict resolution that can be used with her family."

By "interventions" reference is made to the therapeutic modalities to be used to achieve the goal. In the case of the goal above, the intervention could be "discuss in daily group and write plan in journal." Since most wilderness programs are closed ended and have a termination date, all goals should be targeted for change on or before that date. Of course, all of the ITP goals should be related to the participant's psychological problems. To help participants keep these goals in mind, they can be given a copy of the ITP or be urged to write the goals in their journals.

Trip Planning

Planning the actual outdoor excursion can take months to complete. Points to be considered in the planning process include the nature of the outdoor

Figure 7-2. *Continued*

Wilderness Therapy Program
Individual Treatment Plan

Client Name: _____

Age:_____Sex:_____Referred by:_____

Dates and Location of WTP:_____

Presenting Problems:

_____

_____

_____

_____

DSM-IIIR Codes: Axis I:_____Axis II:_____Axis III:_____

                         Axis IV:_____Axis V:_____

Medications (Drug, dosage, reason):

_____

_____

Critical Problems (e.g., suicidal, combative, abuse, serious allergies)

GOALS	INTERVENTIONS	TARGET DATES
1.		
2.		
3.		
4.		

Client Signature:_____Date:_____

Clinician Signature:_____Date:_____

---

experience, the location of the experience, transportation, equipment needs, staffing issues, food, first aid and emergency procedures. The discussion that follows should not be considered to be an exhaustive discourse on all of the points that should be covered; rather, it is intended to present some of the more salient issues. Outdoor leadership training programs provide comprehensive coverage of these, and other, aspects of trip planning.

Most programs we have encountered utilize backpacking as their primary outdoor modality. This is not to say that other experiences would not be equally valuable, as suggested by Ewert's (1989) theoretical model of adventure activities. Our concern when working with people with emotional problems who are using this experience in order to change is that if the activities are exhausting, frightening, or otherwise draining, the individual may be preoccupied with coping with the physical aspects of the program rather than using them as a vehicle for change.

Thus it is recommended that the activity present a challenge, but one that does not detract from the therapeutic purpose of the program. In that backpacking is the most common modality, we will use it as the exemplar with the understanding that other activities can be used as adjuncts or alternatives.

Trip Length

The length of the trip is an important consideration. It should be long enough so that participants can work through the discomforts associated with being away from one's usual routines. Once this is accomplished, there is a sense of pace and comfort with the new activity. We have experimented with backpacking trips of various lengths. It is our experience that it is difficult to be on the trail for more than 8 or 9 days without reprovisioning, and once there is contact with the outside world, there is a certain period of readjusting to wilderness settings.

We have also found that it takes at least 5 days on the trail to work through the initial period of learning, followed by feelings of discomfort and breaking through to a period of ease on the trail. If we add two to three days in base camp teach essential skills and two days in base camp after the trip to debrief, the minimum program length would seem to be 9 days. To this, it is recommended that there be pre- and post-trip meetings to prepare participants for the trip and help them integrate their experiences into more stable changes when they return home. To lengthen trips, it is possible to add other activities, such as climbing or canoeing, or to reprovision, perhaps change sites, and then hit the trail again.

We have not seen any experimental literature that has investigated the effects of length of trip, type of activities, or combination of activities on measures of change for troubled participants. Ultimately, evidence of this sort will accrue and will allow program planning to be based on more than anecdotal findings.

Trip Location

Wherever the planned activities take place, staff should be well acquainted with the area. If this is on a river, there should be knowledge of rapids, hazards, ratings of difficulty, etc. Fortunately, there are books available that provide maps and narratives on many rivers. These do not take the place of experience, however, and staff should be skilled with the activity and knowledgeable about the area. If there any doubts about these skills, more qualified staff should be utilized or guides should be retained.

For backpacking, a similar procedure of considering different locations, checking out maps, talking to local officials (e.g., park or forest rangers), and personally scouting out trails is essential. Trails selected should be familiar to key staff, with adequate consideration given to the location of potable water, camping sites and evacuation routes.

We have discovered that when backpacking in some areas (e.g., National Parks or Lakeshores), there are designated sites where registered groups must stay. This policy makes good sense in terms of environmental impact and control of the trails, but is restrictive in terms of the needs of wilderness therapy trips because it forces the group to travel a certain distance from one site to another.

The alternative is to use trails in National Forests and other areas where there is more flexibility in selecting sites. In this way, the distance traveled in any given day may be largely determined by the needs of the group. Less distance can be covered if more time is spent in group therapy, and suitable alternative campsites are available. All trips should be coordinated with officials whose responsibility it is to oversee the area traveled. Of course, all necessary permits should be obtained, regardless of whether government or private individuals have jurisdiction.

An alternative strategy is to hire the services of others who can coordinate the trip for your participants. Some outfitters run programs for a variety of populations, especially for activities like white water rafting.

Staffing Patterns

The number and qualifications of staff is dependent on the size and characteristics of the participants. Both the COA (1992) and AEE (Priest & Dixon, 1990) have published standards in this area. The COA standards include at least two staff for any activity, one of which must have specialized training in the activity. When there are 12 or more participants, one staff must be added for every six additional participants, resulting in a staffing pattern of 1:4.

AEE standards make a distinction between required, recommended and suggested in terms of increasing standards of practice. These standards for staffing require at least one staff person, but recommend a minimum of two staff, so that one person can lead the group if the other is incapacitated. These standards go on to suggest that there should be increasing staff-to-participant ratios for more difficult activities. The following staff-to-participant ratios are excerpted from *Safety Practices* (Priest & Dixon, 1990, p. 18):

▽   1:12 for backpacking, ropes courses or bicycle touring;
▽   1:8 for canoe camping, rappelling, cross-country skiing;

∇   1:5 for whitewater canoeing, remote wilderness travel or sailing;
∇   1:3 for sea kayaking or glacier travel;
∇   1:2 for lead climbing or summit mountaineering.

Consideration should also be given to maximum group sizes. While 12 participants and one or two staff may be the suggested group size for bicycle touring, this would constitute an overly unwieldy size if group counseling were to be an integral part of the program. The size of the group should be considered in terms of the ecosystem expected to support the group and the group dynamics.

We are reminded of the backpacking trip we led a few years ago in Allegheny National Forest for adolescents who were in counseling. Our group consisted of two staff and eight participants. We came across another group, from a nationally known organization, consisting of three staff and 18 adjudicated adolescents. Their group was much too large for the trail system to handle them adequately. Where they camped, one could see numerous violations of the ethic of "low impact camping," not to mention the impossibility of conducting therapy with a group of that size.

In addition to staff-to-participant ratios needing to be altered for various types of activities, the ratios also should be determined on the basis of participant characteristics. With more high risk populations, 1:4 ratios may be needed instead of the usual 1:6 ratio. And if there are both high risk participants and high risk activities, the ratio may need to be reduced even further.

Menus

The importance of food cannot be stressed enough. Surely, food must be nutritious. In planning, consideration must be given to the fact that most adventure-based programs involve the expenditure of large amounts of energy. Winter activities burn more calories than do summer programs (it takes energy to keep your body warm) and vigorous activities burn more calories than do those that are more sedentary. Participants in severe weather expeditions may need as many as 6500 calories per day (Drury, Bonney & Cockrell, 1991). But food on a trip must be more than nutritious; you must be able to transport it, lack of refrigeration must be taken into account (except for winter trips), it must be prepared, and life will be much more pleasant on a trip if it is tasty. Add to this the fact that cost is a factor to feeding a group of people for an extended trip. Let us elaborate some of these points.

Meals should be well balanced so that participants' nutritional needs are met. This may involve consultation with a nutritional expert, or by consulting books on the topic. A good introductory chapter on this topic is by Drury,

Bonney & Cockrell (1991). Other requirements for an acceptable menu include lightweight, compact ingredients that can stand the jostling of a pack. Chocolate cookies may seem like the perfect dessert, but you may end up with only cookie crumbs by the time you get to eat them.

The time involved and the difficulty in preparing a meal are critical variables, given the nature of many programs. Unfortunately, we have learned through trial and error that meals that take a lot of preparation can seem like more trouble than they are worth if you are camping in the winter when the sun goes down early. Similarly, if you are camping in the rainy season, even under a tarp, lengthy food preparation can be a chore. Consider also the amount of fuel that is required to prepare meals.

We have chosen to use foods that require little preparation. The reason for this is twofold. First, our experience with adolescents has led us to believe that most teens will go hungry before they will cook elaborate meals. Many times we have seen teens eat raw oatmeal rather than take the time to cook it. Second, we take between one and two hours to conduct group therapy, usually after lunch, and if meal preparation is lengthy, there is little time for hiking or other activities. We would rather have more time for those other activities.

We offer a number of tips to those who are planning menus:

▽ If you are not experienced in planning menus, consult with someone who is. You do not want to find out that you've goofed when you are miles away from the nearest grocery.

▽ Don't try out new recipes on the trail. Try them at home first. If they are not good, don't include them.

▽ When packaging meals, remember that trash must be packed out. Keep packaging to a minimum, but make sure it is durable enough to be packed.

▽ Label the contents of packages and put instructions for preparation with those packages.

▽ Pack extra food. Food sometimes gets ruined or eaten by animals despite your best plans otherwise.

▽ At the end of a trip, discuss menu selections with participants. Find out what they liked least and most. Look at the contents of food sacks to see how much and which types of food are left. This can facilitate planning for the next trip.

Let us end this section with a few notes about water. Recent years have led to increasing awareness of giardia, and other water-borne sources of disease, discomfort and pollution. Water must be treated before consumed by being filtered, treated with chemicals (e.g., iodine), or boiled. Filtration is the only method that will remove pesticides and most other pollutants.

We suggest that participants be urged to drink water frequently and in large quantities. Physical activity leads to perspiration and water loss. Waiting until you are thirsty is generally accepted as waiting too long before drinking. A better test (Forgey, 1991) is if your urine is clear or light yellow. If it is cloudy or dark yellow, drink more water.

Assessment

Assessment takes place on may different levels and in numerous ways. Certainly, an assessment of potential applicants is a necessary part of the admission process of any program. In this way, it is critical to determine who is, and who is not, likely to benefit from the program being offered.

It is also important to assess individual changes in participants, as it would be for anybody engaged in a therapeutic program. Earlier in this chapter, we discussed the use of ITPs, one of the tools used to assess change. Another method involves therapists' impressions, as reflected in progress notes. We have charted participants' progress notes by bringing a small tape recorder and dictating notes each day.

Objective measures of participant change can involve the use of standardized psychometric tools. Changes can be documented by administering pre- and post-tests on the Child Behavior Checklist - Youth Self-Report (Achenbach & Edelbrock, 1983), the Piers-Harris Self-Concept Scale (Piers & Harris, 1969), or other instruments.

It is also possible to assess change in terms of behavioral measures of problems (or the lack thereof). A measure we have utilized is the frequency of critical incidents. This includes 11 behaviors that are considered to be critical in the sense that they jeopardize the health and safety of participants and/or the integrity of the program. These critical incidents and ITP ratings are contained in the Wilderness Therapy Checklist (WTC; Berman & Anton, 1985). Another set of behavioral measures contained in the WTC utilizes pre- post- ratings on 28 items that are related to interactions with peers, affect, self-esteem, conflict, response initiation and cooperation. For example, item 3) reads as follows: is abrasive/demeaning in comments towards and interactions with peers. This item is in the area of interactions with peers and, as with the other items, is scored on a 7-point scale ranging from 1 (never) to 7 (always). The WTC is displayed in Figure 7-3.

Assessment occurs not only in terms of selection of participants and measuring participant change; it also can involve assessing the efficacy of the program. This latter form of assessment is referred to as program evaluation and is discussed in depth in the next chapter.

Figure 7-3. Wilderness Therapy Checklist

The Wilderness Therapy Checklist (WTC) is an instrument designed with the assistance of Michael Anton to help identify a number of behaviors that we found to be important indicators of progress on therapeutic wilderness trips. The WTC lists 28 behavioral statements that are rated from 1 (Never) to 7 (Always). Not all behaviors are worded in the positive direction. That is, sometimes a score of 7 is positive and, other times, negative. For example, a score of 7 on item 1 ("Responds withour prompting when addressed by another.") is positive, while a score of 7 on item 10 ("Talks negatively about self and abilities.") is negative.

We have used this instrument to chart pre- and post- change by circling the ratings for each item before and after the trip, and looking at the difference. This instrument is used only as a measure of the behaviors listed; it is not intended to supplant standardized tests. A discussion of standardized tests and their use is discussed in more detail in Chapter 8.

Another facet of the WTC is a listing of nine "behavior incidents."These incidents reflect behaviors on the part of residents that threaten the viability of the program and include physical and verbal aggression, placing someone in danger, hurting self or others, refusing to participate and running away. Each incident is checked off on the WTC and is charted in more detail in daily notes. These incidents can be used with information about medical or environmental emergencies to give a complete record of major problems on a trip.

Our use of the behavior incidents is consistent with the categories used by the WEA Safety Committee (Myers, 1993). This committee advocates the use of four categories for incidents in order to track problems and then eliminate problems. This system includes illnesses, injuries, near misses ("close calls"that could have been dangerous) and motivational/behavioral incidents. All four types of incidents should be documented.

Conducting Therapy

In that counseling based outdoor adventure programs are intended to be therapeutic, designing a program of this sort necessitates plans for therapeutic intervention. While many of the activities may be intended to produce change, even without group or individual counseling, more verbal, traditional techniques may be needed to prepare participants for the physical challenges at hand or to promote internalization of these experiences.

We have already discussed how wilderness therapy may be especially well suited for adolescents who are not responsive to traditional modes of therapy. For this reason, duplicating in the out-of-doors what happens in a hospital or outpatient setting is equally unlikely to be successful. A different approach is needed.

Our experiences as therapists conducting wilderness therapy have led us to formulate an approach that works, at least for us and with our clients. This

Figure 7-3. *Continued*

Wilderness Therapy Program
Adolescent Behavior Checklist

Participant's Name_____ Sex_____

Age_____ Completed by_____ Date_____

The following items are to be rated before (pre=○) and after (post=▢) the trip for each participant. The behaviors are to be rated on a scale from 1 to 7 with 1 representing nonoccurence of the behavior in question and 7 representing a very high frequency of occurence. Accordingly, a 4 would be an average or expected level of occurence, with the range of numbers covering the continuum of possible diversity. Please circle only one number for each behavior on each administration of the checklist.

INTERACTIONS WITH PEERS

1) Responds without prompting when addressed   NEVER   ALWAYS
by another.   1   2   3   4   5   6   7

2) Is friendly and interested in peers; seeks them   NEVER   ALWAYS
out for interactions.   1   2   3   4   5   6   7

3) Is abrasive or demeaning in comments towards   NEVER   ALWAYS
and interactions with peers.   1   2   3   4   5   6   7

4) Is manipulative (friendly for secondary gain)   NEVER   ALWAYS
rather than genuine in interactions with peers.   1   2   3   4   5   6   7

5) Threatens others when does not get own way.   NEVER   ALWAYS
                                                  1   2   3   4   5   6   7

AFFECT

6) Depressed: remains withdrawn, minimizes   NEVER   ALWAYS
iteractions with others, moody or sad.   1   2   3   4   5   6   7

7) Tense or anxious: responds too quickly,   NEVER   ALWAYS
speech pressured, too "sharp.   1   2   3   4   5   6   7

8) Suspicious: lacks trust, wants information   NEVER   ALWAYS
repeated, believes only self, does not self-disclose.   1   2   3   4   5   6   7

9) Happy: smiles easily, laughs appropriately,   NEVER   ALWAYS
enjoys the company of others and daily activities.   1   2   3   4   5   6   7

SELF-ESTEEM

10) Talks negatively about self and abilities.   NEVER   ALWAYS
                                                  1   2   3   4   5   6   7

11) Criticizes accomplishments and performances   NEVER   ALWAYS
excessively even when adequate.   1   2   3   4   5   6   7

12) Displays poor posture, slouches, holds head   NEVER   ALWAYS
down, makes poor eye contact.   1   2   3   4   5   6   7

13) Says positive things about self when asked.   NEVER   ALWAYS
                                                  1   2   3   4   5   6   7

Figure 7-3. *Continued*

14) Talks openly about self and achivements. Takes pride in personal belongings and appearance.	NEVER 1	2	3	4	5	ALWAYS 6	7

CONFLICT

15) Downgrades others to make self look better.	NEVER 1	2	3	4	5	ALWAYS 6	7
16) Engages in malicious teasing and horseplay.	NEVER 1	2	3	4	5	ALWAYS 6	7
17) Argues over minor issues.	NEVER 1	2	3	4	5	ALWAYS 6	7
18) Becomes abusive when criticized or gives negative feedback.	NEVER 1	2	3	4	5	ALWAYS 6	7
Focuses externally when confronted with own issues.	NEVER 1	2	3	4	5	ALWAYS 6	7

RESPONSE INITIATION
(spontaneous behaviors)

20) Asks to read maps or literature about the trip.	NEVER 1	2	3	4	5	ALWAYS 6	7
21) Asks others about wldlife, terrain, etc.	NEVER 1	2	3	4	5	ALWAYS 6	7
22) Asks others about their feelings, perceptions and experiences.	NEVER 1	2	3	4	5	ALWAYS 6	7
23) Volunteers own feelings, thoughts and internal experiences.	NEVER 1	2	3	4	5	ALWAYS 6	7
24) Asks others for feedback about self.	NEVER 1	2	3	4	5	ALWAYS 6	7

COOPERATION

25) Offers help to peers.	NEVER 1	2	3	4	5	ALWAYS 6	7
26) Offers help to staff.	NEVER 1	2	3	4	5	ALWAYS 6	7
27) Complies with requests from staff.	NEVER 1	2	3	4	5	ALWAYS 6	7
28) Completes assigned tasks without additinal prompting.	NEVER 1	2	3	4	5	ALWAYS 6	7

BEHAVIOR INCIDENTS (Chart in daily notes)

29) Threatens others verbally._____
30) Threatens others physically._____
31) Hits others with hand._____
32) Hits others with weapon._____
33) Endangers self or others inadvertently._____
34) Endangers self or others intentionally._____
35) Attempts to or runs away._____
36) Hurts self or others intentionally._____
37) Refuses to participate._____

approach involves a focus on the here-and-now of immediate experiences, and relates those experiences to past problems and future goals. That approach is outlined below, as it evolves over the course of a trip.

We begin the group process by having meetings before the trip begins, usually over the course of a few weeks. These meetings involve both the participants and their parents or guardians. The first meeting involves setting the stage for group process. This takes place by getting everyone in a circle, introducing ourselves and asking everyone to talk about their interests in the program. By beginning this way, we want participants to understand that we are interested in them, their backgrounds, interests and feelings. It also becomes clear that we will be doing things as a group. Of course, these pre-trip meetings also involve sharing information, filling out forms, and other necessities, but even these tasks are completed within the group.

Successive meetings also involve sharing counseling experiences and each participant's goals for the trip. In this process of goal setting, parents are encouraged to contribute and input has been solicited from the participants' former counselors. Goal setting is conducted in a positive way by asking not just for the alleviation or elimination of undesirable behaviors or feelings, but more importantly, in terms of positive strivings—those things that the participant would like to improve, develop or increase. Thus, a withdrawn, depressed adolescent may be able to set goals of developing close friendships, become more active and have a good time. An acting out, aggressive adolescent may be able to set the goal of expressing anger in an appropriately assertive, nonviolent manner.

This goal setting is a therapeutic process in that it involves self-disclosure in a group setting where the therapist may help encourage and use counseling techniques like mirroring, reflection, and restatement. At times, it means dealing with resistance in participants, an aspect of counseling that should pose few problems to the seasoned therapist.

We strive for each participant to generate four or five goals achievable during the trip. Since it would be unrealistic for a participant to change her relationship with her parents, this would not be an appropriate goal; instead, she might be encouraged to develop a plan that would enhance her relationship with her parents and share that plan with her parents, perhaps in a letter. Participants are then asked to rate their pre-trip standing on each of these goals on a 7-point scale. These goals are then written as treatment plan objectives on the WTC. After the trip, participants are again asked to rate themselves on each objective.

By the time the trip begins, participants should have an introduction to each other and the leaders, should have experience sharing in the group setting, and should have established goals to work on during the trip. This is in addition to learning about the program, filling out forms and getting all their gear together.

Group therapy is an integral part of our program even after the trip begins. We find it most convenient to convene group after lunch, but other times might be just as suitable, as long as participants are not too tired to actively participate. The first group meeting after the trip begins usually begins with an open-ended question concerning how people are feeling. Nervousness, excitement, upset, relief, anger and sadness are all frequent feelings that are expressed. This sets the tone for dealing with feelings, as a group, and in the spirit of cooperation and caring. The therapist often has to work with the group to achieve these ends. It is also worth noting at this point that we find it best when all the leaders participate in group, with a therapist as the primary facilitator. Otherwise, group cohesiveness falters and the sense that we are all working together is difficult to achieve.

Periodically, in group, participants are asked how they are progressing toward their treatment goals and if the group can be of help in sorting things out, formulating plans, role playing a parent's reaction to a plan, or whatever.

The group is the central place where problems are directed. That is, if there is a problem among tent-mates, they are encouraged to address the issues with each other in group. Similarly, if a cooking team feels that one of its members is not pulling his or her weight, those people who are upset are urged to bring up the issue with the laggard in the group meeting. Again, this focuses on the group (analogous to the family) as the backdrop for the resolution of problems. Participants can then be coached and receive feedback when trying to resolve conflicts.

We have found it helpful to allow anyone in the group to call for an impromptu group if there is an important issue to be resolved. We are reminded of one of the times when participants have asked for groups. One morning, two boys from a four-person tent team approached the two leaders, expressing their upset with Tom, who had been urinating in his sleeping bag since the beginning of the trip. We urged them to ask for a meeting, and with some coaching they were able to tell Tom that they did not want to embarrass him, but that the tent (and Tom) was wet and smelled of urine. Tom was able to tearfully tell the group that he was embarrassed. The group was able to accept him and help him find a suitable solution (washing himself well each morning, putting his sleeping bag in a plastic sack while in the tent, hanging the sleeping bag out to dry each day).

As the trip progresses and participants are beginning to feel good about themselves and the group, they are asked to compare how they are feeling as compared to when they began the trip. A few days later, they are asked how they can keep these good feelings even after they return home. Strategies can be developed as part of the group process for distilling some of the more salient aspects of the program that contributes to feeling better and attempts can be made to make changes in their lives at home.

Leaders can also convene the group. Sometimes these group sessions need only meet for a short time. This might be the case when the group becomes fragmented on the trail and the leaders want to enhance a sense of *esprit de corps*.

Emphasizing group therapy does not negate the need for individual counseling. This seems especially appropriate when an individual needs help to deal with painful, conflictual or otherwise troubling issues. A scene of a staff counseling a participant comes to mind. At the end of a trip along Pictured Rocks National Lakeshore in the Upper Peninsula of Michigan, we were setting up camp in a wooded area on the back side of a sand dune. One of the staff, Frank, had taken Ann, a participant, on a walk to help her deal with some family issues. The two could be seen sitting in the sand, with Ann obviously listening to Frank. What is so striking about this image is not the fact that a therapist and an adolescent were communicating nor the setting, but the seeming contradiction in the two images fitting so well together. Ann was resistant to counseling during most of the trip and had avoided "one-on-one" interactions with staff and yet here she was sitting next to a psychiatrist, sharing and listening. It was dusk and the sand was bathed in rose-colored light. Grass on the side of the dune was moving in waves with the wind. Just below Frank and Ann was a set of bear prints in the sand, still looking distinct and fresh. While the concepts of counseling and wilderness seem antithetical, they can fit so well.

Used in this way, individual counseling can help participants confront inner issues in order to facilitate better functioning, not only on the trail, but at home, as well. We have found it constructive for individuals who have one-on-one sessions to share with the group the general nature of the topic. This helps the group feel connected to that individual and vice versa.

Another therapeutic tool we have found helpful involves the use of personal journals. To facilitate participants' self-disclosure in these journals, we stress their confidential nature. While many participants want to share the contents of the journals with staff and, sometimes, other participants, such disclosure is voluntary. The use of journals is also encouraged through the process of staff modeling. The therapist uses journal writing time to take notes of the days' therapeutic events (with the same contents as one would find in a patient chart). And the outdoor leader takes notes on physical aspects of the trip (camp sites, equipment failures, group activities, etc.). We have found it useful to make journal entries after group and before hitting the trail again after lunch.

To facilitate consistency among a variety of different therapeutic agendas—treatment plan goals, group therapy themes, feelings on the trip, group cohesiveness—an effort is made to suggest journal entry topics to participants. By suggesting these topics, one hopes that participants will gain an overview of the program, in the context of participants on the trip, family at home, friends, school, and other aspects germane to a systems theory approach. Topics that we have suggested to participants include the following:

▽ What are your goals for the trip? You may want to look at the treatment plans we filled out.

▽ How are you feeling about leaving home? How are you feeling about your tent-mates and cooking partners? Other participants?

▽ Have you surprised yourself in terms of being able to do, say or feel things that have been unexpected?

▽ Write a letter telling your parents how you would like to make things different when you return home.

▽ Write about some of the help you need from the group, parents or friends in order to make the changes you desire.

▽ How has this program helped you change?

▽ How can you keep the good feelings and the positive changes you've made on the trail after you return home?

▽ What have been the best parts of this program? The worst?

▽ What would you like to tell your therapist about this program?

Maintaining Change

The generalization of change from the trail to the home setting has been cited as one of the most difficult challenges for many programs (see Chapter 8 for a more extensive discussion of this topic). Perhaps those of us working in this area for a number of years were initially naive in believing that changes on the trail would lead to changes in the community. Were we wiser and more theoretically oriented, perhaps we would have known that behavior changes are short lived unless the program works to change the person's system that maintains behavior.

To effect long-term change, it is important to share with others in the participant's system what changes are likely to take place and how to prepare for the participant's return. This can be accomplished by including parents, teachers and/or therapists with information both before and after the program. Beforehand, knowledge can be shared about the nature of the program, changes that can be expected, and the participant's goals. Afterwards, these same people can be included in debriefings and suggestions can be made about supporting change.

These debriefings can include pictures and descriptions of the trip, factual data on behavior changes, progress notes from the counselors on the trip and letters the participants may want to share with parents. Since the experience of a trip is not a panacea, it should be viewed as a component of ongoing therapy. For this reason, we share progress notes, test data, and change on treatment goals with participants' therapists back in the community. This may be the best way of helping participants with ongoing mental health needs to continue working on issues explored while on the trip.

We have also experimented with having ongoing group therapy for participants who have been on our trips. There have been advantages and disadvantages to this type of group. The advantages include the fact that the therapists and participants already have an established therapeutic relationship from having worked together. Participants are well acquainted with the group process and all of the participants have a set of shared experiences. However, the group necessitates that participants live in the same geographic area. Further, unless the wilderness program has trips all year long, it is difficult to have a steady population of potential group members. As a result, we have found that groups dwindle in size and energy during those seasons when groups are not run. This presents a problem that is difficult to overcome.

There are many other ways of trying to maintain changes. Efforts can be made to keep in touch with past participants through personal letters or newsletters. Trips for alumni of previous trips can be organized, even if they are abbreviated. Reunions in which alumni and their families are invited to picnics have proven to be popular for our programs. These alternatives are, in all likelihood, not as effective as ongoing individual or group counseling, but they may enhance maintenance of gains better than no follow-up. This issue presents an empirical question best answered by further research.

Funding and Marketing

Funding and marketing may seem like issues to be dealt with by people other than outdoor leaders and therapists; however, without these concerns being addressed, a program cannot survive. Finances often force programs to close or greatly restrict their range of activities. They may also prohibit the offering of scholarships to needy applicants who, without financial support, would be unable to participate. Similarly, successful marketing assures that there is an adequate pool of appropriate referrals to the program. Adhering to a systems theory approach to wilderness therapy, marketing and funding are necessary components of well designed programs. Let us look at each of these issues.

Funding

While the facilities costs of establishing wilderness therapy programs may be relatively small compared to hospitals or clinics, other costs can be prohibitively high for many programs. Clearly, one major source of the cost of wilderness programs goes into having highly skilled professionals run programs with low staff-to-participant ratios.

For some types of wilderness programs, there are initial start-up costs of technical and expensive equipment. These costs are obviously more during the initial purchase period, but adolescents are hard on gear, reducing the life span of equipment. There are also costs for food, which can also be high if freeze dried, packable food is utilized. Not to be forgotten are transportation costs and the cost of insurance for the program.

There are a variety of sources of funding for wilderness therapy programs. Families usually provide some, if not all, of the tuition costs for many programs. But these costs can exclude some of those adolescents who can most benefit from wilderness-based counseling programs. We have recently completed an article (Davis-Berman, Berman & Capone, 1992) in which we surveyed all of the mental health wilderness programs that are affiliated with AEE. This study includes information about staff, clients, theoretical orientation, and costs.

Many insurance programs will reimburse policy holders for wilderness therapy as a mental health expense. To qualify, there must be a diagnosed psychiatric disorder and standard forms of treatment (e.g., group therapy) must be provided by mental health professionals who are eligible for third-party payments (e.g., psychologists, psychiatrists and, in some states, social workers). Each insurance company has its own set of rules and exclusions, but our experience with this source of funding has been very positive.

A second way in which insurance companies may pay for wilderness therapy is as a special type of residential treatment center for troubled youth. Those organizations that seek certification as residential programs through credentialling bodies such at the COA will seek insurance reimbursement. The difference between these two types of reimbursement is that the former seeks reimbursement for specific treatments rendered, while the second charges a daily rate for facility.

Finally, there are some hospital-based programs for adolescents who have been admitted to their inpatient programs. These programs receive reimbursement from insurance companies for daily room charges as well as any specific outdoor education activities that are therapeutic in nature (e.g., a ropes course).

Besides these three insurance-based funding sources, there are numerous grants that are available. Small grants may be obtainable from local service or charitable organizations to help defray these costs of the program. The United Way and the Jaycees have contributed to our programs in the past, the United Way with funds for a demonstration project and the Jaycees with partial scholarships for local youth. Funding can also be found at the city, county or state level to work with adolescents who are involved with the juvenile justice system, children's protective services, or who are otherwise at-risk. Larger scale grants may be obtained from national sources like the federal government, but these are usually for demonstration and research projects.

Finding a steady flow of adequate funding is often the critical task confronting wilderness therapy programs. We have yet to talk with staff from any program who have the money but no participants; it has always been the other way around. Often, finding funds involves creative financing based on all of the above mentioned sources.

Marketing

Obtaining funds is inherently related to establishing a good reputation and letting people know of the needs that are addressed by your program. There are specialists who can and will market your program or help you establish a viable plan for marketing. But this approach is costly and contrary to the "grass-roots" development style that typifies most programs.

Program brochures and mailings to professionals are ways of providing potential referral sources with information about your program. So, too, is the presentation of your program at professional conferences.

We have found that presenting research on our program at conferences and in published articles helps publicize our program, but rarely leads to referrals. Local and regional professional meetings are more effective in generating referrals. Other media exposure through newspaper articles, radio talk-shows, and television news programs are not only effective ways of reaching the public, but they are without cost.

Funding and marketing are necessary evils for outdoor therapy programs. They must be taken seriously and become an integral part of the program, for these components allow all the others to function.

In this chapter we have tried to outline many of the critical issues in establishing and maintaining a viable wilderness therapy program. From our discussion, it should be clear that most of the effort goes into planning. If the planning process is done well, running the trip can almost be anticlimactic in that it will go smoothly and with few surprises. A component of this planning which was alluded to in this chapter involves the evaluation of the impact and effectiveness of the program. We believe that evaluation is so important in planning and implementation that we have devoted the following chapter to this topic.

References

Achenbach, T. M. & Edelbrock, C. (1983). *Manual for the Child Behavior Checklist and Revised Child Behavior Profile.* Burlington, VT: University of Vermont.

American Psychiatric Association. (1987). *Diagnostic and statistical manual of mental disorders,* Third edition revised. Washington, DC: American Psychiatric Association.

Berman, D. S. & Davis-Berman, J. L. (1991). Wilderness therapy and adolescent mental health: Administrative and clinical issues. *Administration and Policy in Mental Health, 18,* 373-379.

Cockrell, D. & Lupton, F. (1991). An introduction to the Wilderness Education Association. In D. Cockrell (Ed.), *The wilderness educator: The Wilderness Education Association Curriculum Guide* (pp. 1-11). Merrillville, IN: ICS Books.

Council on Accreditation for Services to Families and Youth (1992). Draft of standards for therapeutic wilderness programming/experiential outdoor adventure education programs for at-risk youth. Unpublished document. NY: COA.

Davis-Berman, J. L., Berman, D. S. & Capone, L. (October 1992). Therapeutic wilderness programs: A survey of mental health offerings. Paper presented at the meeting of the Association for Experiential Education, Banff.

Drury, J., Bonney, B, & Cockrell, D. (1991). Rations planning and food preparation. In D. Cockrell (Ed.), *The wilderness educator: The Wilderness Education Association Curriculum Guide* (pp. 105-127). Merrillville, IN: ICS Books.

Ewert, A. W. (1983). *Outdoor adventure and self-concept: A research analysis.* Eugene, OR: University of Oregon.

Ewert, A. W. (1989). *Outdoor adventure pursuits: Foundations, models, and theories.* Columbus, OH: Publishing Horizons.

Forgey, W. W. (1991). Wilderness emergency procedures and treatment. In D. Cockrell, (Ed.), *The wilderness educator: The Wilderness Education Association Curriculum Guide* (pp. 149-167). Merrillville, IN: ICS Books.

Forgey, W. W. (1987). *Wilderness medicine,* Third Edition. Merrillville, IN: ICS Books.

Matthews, M. (1991). Wilderness programs offer promising alternative for some youth: More regulation likely. *Youth Law News, 12,* 12-15.

Myers, W. (1993 Spring). Incident Reports: Implications for Safety and Personal Development. *WEA Legend,* 7-8.

Piers, E. V. & Harris, D. B. (1969). *Manual for the Piers-Harris self concept scale*. Nashville, TN: Counselor Recordings and Tests.

Priest, S. & Dixon, T. (1990). *Safety practices in adventure programming*. Boulder, CO: Association for Experiential Education.

Chapter Eight

Program Evaluation

Throughout this book, we have raised the issue of program evaluation. Often, it has been discussed as an activity that is lacking in outdoor programs. At other times, we have challenged those in the field to conduct program evaluations in order to demonstrate the efficacy of their approaches, and thus to increase the professionalism of our field. Program evaluation has also been identified as an essential element in the process of program design. In fact, due to the importance of evaluation, we decided to consider and discuss it in this separate chapter rather than to include it in discussions of program design.

In this chapter we will build a general rationale for the use of program evaluation, then suggest how it might be used to evaluate wilderness programs. This first section focuses on the traditional quantitative approach to evaluation research. In an attempt to address some of the problems in the literature identified with this approach, we then suggest ideas for evaluation, including some underlying assumptions and ideas about research design and instrumentation.

The final section of this chapter introduces the use of qualitative research approaches in examining the process of outdoor programs. An argument is established for the combination of both quantitative and qualitative approaches in the evaluation of wilderness programs.

Program Evaluation

When reviewing the literature on program evaluation, one is immediately struck by the lack of consensus on just what program evaluation is and how it is done. Suchman (1967, p. 7), a prominent thinker in this area, defined evaluation research as "the utilization of scientific research methods and techniques for the purpose of making an evaluation." Greater specificity is offered by Rossi and Freeman (1982, p. 20) when they suggest that "evaluation research involves the use of social research methodologies to judge and improve the planning, monitoring, effectiveness, and efficiency of health, education, welfare, and other human service programs". Finally, Dooley (1990, p. 316) presents a more restricted view, "social research applied to the judgment of a program's success".

Obviously, there is no clear agreement as to the definition or general purpose of program evaluation. In fact, Patton (1982) suggests that there is no true definition of program evaluation. Despite such lack of consensus in the field, program evaluation has been widely utilized as a legitimate research method since the 1960s in this country, and in fact, its usage has increased steadily since this time. During the 1960s, three societal trends were identified which contributed to the increased attention to evaluation research: changes in the nature of social problems, changes in the structure and function of public agencies, and changes in the needs and expectations of the public (Suchman, 1967).

At this time, there was also a well documented shift from an individual model of poverty to a more social-structural approach. Society was seen as the culprit and cause of many of the major problems experienced by the individual. In other words, we as a society could no longer ignore the impact of various social problems on the larger community.

With this new awareness came a recognition of the need to effectively plan and evaluate programs which would affect the larger public. Additionally, during this time, the structure and function of many public agencies changed, necessitating an expansion of the scope of problems and the range of people served by various agencies. Thus, new and innovative programs were needed to deal with this enormous growth. Along with these new programs came the common sense idea that they should be planned in a systematic way, and that their results should be evaluated. Finally, changes in the needs and expectations of the public have been suggested as factors which contribute to the increase in program evaluation. This tendency for greater public awareness and involvement has also been referred to as the consumer movement (Suchman, 1967, pp. 3-5).

In addition to these themes, other writers on the history of evaluation research point to the use of research in the development of many of the social programs of the 1960s, to the proliferation of published research studies in the decade of the 1970s, and finally, to the budgetary cuts in the 1980s which prompted a greater reliance on the utilization of evaluation research in the development of social welfare programs (Hornick & Burrows, 1988).

The topic of evaluation research is made even more confusing by the fact that not only are there no real definitions of what evaluation is, there are no cut and dried evaluation methods. Rather, a number of different research designs, data collection, and data analysis procedures are used. Some have suggested typologies for program evaluation, or give guidelines for proceeding. An example of such a typology is presented by Dooley (1990, p. 320-321) and includes the following five stages: (1) needs assessment, (2) program monitoring, (3) program impact, (4) efficiency and (5) utilization. Other writers in the field have stated that programs be evaluated at a number of different levels including: innovative, established programs, and for the purpose of fine tuning established programs (Rossi & Freeman, 1982).

Given the lack of clarity in the field of program evaluation, one may wonder if it is beneficial to develop typologies for use with all program evaluations. Patton, an influential voice in the field, argues that this is impractical. He advocates that the program evaluator play a consultive role with the agency he/she plans to evaluate, and that the specifics of each evaluation be tailored to the particular evaluation situation (Patton, 1982). Despite the lack of consensus in the field of evaluation, there are general methods which are commonly utilized in evaluation research, the most predominant of these being the quantitative and qualitative approaches to research.

The quantitative method of inquiry still remains the most commonly used in the field of program evaluation, with its hypothetico-deductive focus, and its reliance on empirical data and statistical analysis (Patton, 1978). Since this approach reflects the generally acceptable scientific method, one might deduce that this is the only model to apply to program evaluation, and that it is well suited for such an application.

However, back in the 1950s, the potential problems with applying this approach to program evaluation were being discussed. C. Wright Mills (1959) highlighted this issue in his writing on the abstracted empiricists. First, he suggested that those espousing this quantitative perspective are generally not even aware that they are utilizing an empirical base, and that "abstracted empiricists often seem more concerned with the philosophy of science than with social study itself. Additionally, utilizing this method serves to determine or define the problems examined" (Mills, 1959, p. 57). Mills seems to be suggesting that the use of the quantitative method may become an end in itself, and that the original problem or program under investigation may become lost. He intimates that using empirical approaches may dictate what is studied, rather than tailoring the research method to appropriately address the research problem.

In much the same way, Patton (1978) calls the quantitative approach limited, and suggests that it not only limits the social problems and programs which are studied, but that it prevents investigators from being open to alternative approaches. This perception of the quantitative approach as superior is supported by Bernstein and Freeman (1975). They analyzed 236 evaluation studies, and attempted to identify indicators of research quality. Their conclusions suggested that items like sampling, statistical methods, and other aspects of traditional quantitative research were indicative of high quality research.

A holistic-inductive paradigm represents an alternative to this traditional model and forms the underlying rationale for the qualitative approach to research. It also assumes that some phenomena are not amenable to numerical mediation, and that different kinds of problems require different types of research methodologies (Patton, 1978, p. 212).

Not surprisingly, the research literature is rather sparse on the topic of qualitative approaches, with much of this work being done within the discipline of Anthropology. In more specific terms, qualitative approaches to research are characterized by the following: (1) Naturalistic emphasis—the researcher examines naturally occurring processes. These projects tend to take place in their natural environments, rather than in laboratory settings. (2) Inductive approach—these studies do not begin with a framework or a theoretical perspective on the problem. Rather, they take an exploratory, flexible approach to the problem. (3) Active participation—qualitative research approaches involve actually going into the field and immersing oneself in the activity that is being evaluated, and, (4) Holistic orientation—given the fact that qualitative research approaches are not confined by the strict principles of science, they are more flexible and holistic in their orientation (Patton, 1987, p. 9-17).

Clearly, the quantitative and qualitative approaches to research are fundamentally different. One could argue that they both have value and can be applied to a number of research settings. Traditionally, as well as currently, the majority of evaluation studies utilize quantitative approaches. The next section of this chapter will examine some of the approaches that have been used to evaluate wilderness programs. From the literature presented in an earlier chapter, it generally appears that a combination of quantitative and qualitative methods have been used. However, due to the challenges of the outdoor environment, attaining scientific rigor has been difficult.

Current Research

As has been discussed in previous chapters, a number of research reports on the effectiveness of various types of wilderness programs have appeared in the literature. Many of these studies are hindered by methodological difficulties, or have relied heavily on clinical and other subjective reports of change or satisfaction with the program.

However, despite criticisms of the current and recent literature, it is clear that the evaluation of wilderness programs is a timely topic. Fairly recent writings (Ewert, 1989; 1983; Teschner & Wolter, 1984) have focused on developing evaluation strategies. Central to this dialogue is the controversy over quantitative versus qualitative research methods. In fact, these research issues have become so prominent that the *Journal of Experiential Education* recently devoted an entire issue to them.

It is difficult to categorize and make generalizations from the widely diverse literature presented in this book. The present attempt at such an analysis restricts itself to a discussion of the studies previously reported herein. While we recognize that other studies exist, especially as related to the Outward Bound literature, it was impossible to include all of them in the present discussion.

When examining the literature, it is critical to determine which instruments if any appear to be widely used and which are valid and reliable measures of the outcome of wilderness programs. It has been previously established that the quantitative approach to research requires the use of standardized and vali-dated research instruments. The measurement of self-esteem or some measure of self-concept appears repeatedly in these studies. (The interested reader is referred to Ewert's (1983) work on the use and measurement of self-esteem in the wilderness literature). Naturally, the hypothesis is that participation in a wilderness program has a positive impact on the self-esteem or self-concept of the participant. Unfortunately, some of the studies stated that they used a self-esteem measure, but fail to provide the reader with any information about the scale, including its name. In looking at the literature, one finds that the Lipsett Self-Concept Scale was used (Krieger, 1973), as was the Hudson Index of Self-Esteem (Stich & Sussman, 1981). Kimball (1979) utilized the Tennessee Self-Concept Scale. Finally, the Piers-Harris Self-Esteem Inventory appeared in a few studies (Chenery, 1981; Davis-Berman & Berman, 1989).

It is rather surprising that despite the emphasis on self-esteem and self-concept in these studies, very few standardized instruments were actually used (see Figure 8-1 for information on obtaining instruments). The more common occurrence in the literature was to ask the subjects to provide a rating of their self-image, self-concept, or self-esteem. In this regard, Clifford and Clifford (1967) asked subjects to provide self descriptions, and descriptions of their ideal selves. Likewise, Smith and associates (1975), evaluated subjects based on their self report of their self-esteem, sense of self-awareness, self-assertion, and acceptance of others. Finally, Koepke (1974) included a subjective rating of the real and ideal self in the Outward Bound study.

In addition to self concept or self-esteem, the only other measure that seems to appear across some studies is recidivism. Obviously, the measurement of this variable is found in the evaluation of delinquency studies, and is included in the majority of such studies. It is problematic, however, in that often the operational definitions of this concept differ. Others have criticized the use of this measure as an indicator of success (c.f. Cyntrynbaum & Ken, 1975; Kelly & Baer, 1968, 1971; Willman & Chun, 1973).

Additional variables that are identified in the literature include: behavior change (Berman & Anton, 1988; Cyntrynbaum & Ken, 1975; Krieger, 1973), and change on various personality dimensions (Berman & Anton, 1988; Burdsal & Force, 1983; Shniderman, 1974; Stich & Sussman, 1981). It is interesting and important to note, however, that these examples are isolated studies. There does not appear to be a theoretical or research based rationale for the choice of dependent variables in the evaluation of outdoor programs.

In addition to a lack of consensus on the selection and use of measurement instruments, one finds a number of studies utilizing clinical and subjective ratings of effectiveness of programs. Some interesting examples include clinical impressions of improvement in psychiatric inpatients (Jerstad & Selzer, 1973) and in outpatients (Kaplan, 1974). Subjective ratings of effectiveness were also used by Fletcher (1970) in his evaluation of Outward Bound in Great Britain. Examples of the use of subjective reports can also be

Figure 8-1. Obtaining Standardized Tests

Yet another difficulty with using validated measurement instruments is their accessibility. Some instruments are not copyrighted and can be reproduced with permission from the instrument's author. More often, the copyright for the inventories is owned by a corporation, and permission and often purchase of the tests are required for use.

For example, the copyright for the BSI is owned by National Computer Systems, while information on the Piers-Harris Self-Concept Scale can be obtained through Western Psychological Services. It should be noted, however, that many tests require that the user hold a certain license and/or possess specific educational degrees before being permitted to purchase the tests for clinical or research use.

As a first step toward selecting research instruments, we recommend that you consult either the *Handbook of Mental Measurements* or *Tests in Print* which can be found in the reference section of your library. These sources provide descriptions of tests and copyright information.

seen in the work of Marx (1988) and Sakofs (1992), where they utilized subjective ratings of staff and parents.

Although subjective reports and clinical impressions may indeed be a rich source of data, we often make the mistake of treating this data as though it were quantitative, thus utilizing it to draw conclusions and to make generalizations. It is important to note that subjective reports alone often do not warrant such conclusions, although they do identify interesting and important trends. Levitt (1984) offers a strong critique of the use of anecdotal data, and suggests that research should focus more on quantifiable measures of change. In fact, she argues for the use of traditional research designs, and for the increased use of statistics in the analysis of data.

In contrast to this quantitative view of researchers, some have argued for the increased use of qualitative methods in the evaluation of wilderness programs. Ewert (1989) discusses the qualitative approach, yet argues for the use of both quantitative and qualitative methods. In fact, he appears to advocate most strongly for research that is theoretically based, and thus, contributes to theory building.

In contrast, Rowley (1987) argues for the use of qualitative methods. He asserts that these methods might be especially suited to the evaluation of wilderness programs. He suggests that, "qualitative research offers outdoor adventure educators another important way to substantiate and bring legitimacy to traditional claims, some of which could not be confirmed employing quantitative approaches" (Rowley, 1987, p. 11). In much the same way, Kolb (1991) advocates for the use of qualitative methods, citing personal interviews, participant observation, and journal analysis as being especially appropriate data collection strategies.

Patton's (1980; 1982) work is exemplary in the field of program evaluation in general, and as related to the use of qualitative evaluation. In his books, *Qualitative Evaluation Methods* and *Practical Evaluation,* he reports on a qualitative evaluation of a wilderness program. Unlike studies that simply rely on subjective or clinical impressions as measures, this study was actually designed and executed as a qualitative study. Patton himself conducted the evaluation and served as a participant/observer in the program. The wilderness program was part of the Learninghouse Southwest Field Training Project, and involved the training of staff utilizing various wilderness locations and outdoor modalities over a period of two years. Data was collected by Patton following the first field conference in the Gila Wilderness in New Mexico, following the wilderness experience in the Kofa mountains in Arizona, and after the third and final wilderness excursion, a trip down the San Juan river (Patton, 1980).

Although Patton was part of the experience as an observer and a participant, the research experience was also structured in that a set of basic questions guided the evaluation. Included were the following open-ended questions which comprised the follow-up interviews: (1) How has your participation in the Learninghouse project affected you personally? (2) How has your participation in the Learninghouse project affected you professionally? (3) How has your participation in the Learninghouse project affected your institution? (Patton, 1980, p. 359). Utilizing this information and his own observations of the process on the wilderness trips, Patton attempted to identify common themes and metaphors which emerged during the experience (Patton, 1982).

The use of metaphors was a critical part of both the trip and the evaluation material developed from the trip. In fact, Patton (1982, p. 124) described the project itself as being like a metaphor- an "experimental acting out of what the world could be like." Through the interviews and direct observation, it was determined that five metaphors seemed to be recurrent and characterized the experience of the participants. These included: (1) group cohesion and identity metaphors, (2) life challenge metaphors, (3) process and change metaphors, (4) metaphors of self, and (5) giving special meaning to things and experiences (Patton, 1982, p. 138).

Clearly, this qualitative approach to evaluation focuses more on the process of the program and less on the outcome. In this regard, the program was seen to contribute to the introspection, sense of self, group feeling, and goal setting of the participants. More important than these impressions, however, is the use of a qualitative approach to gathering and analyzing data that is illustrated by this program. Direct observation was combined with a set of questions to serve as a guide for open ended interviews.

A second example of a qualitative evaluation was done by Henderson and Bialeschki (1987). The program was a "women's week" experience, in which women participated in a week of outdoor activity. A sample of women were pre-tested, and all women were part of the study during their experience. The study employed participant/observation method. After analysis of the observer's collected data, Henderson and Bialeschki concluded that the women really enjoyed the choices that they were given regarding the wilderness activities they engaged in, that they enjoyed being out-of-doors, that they appreciated the woman-only nature of the program, that they relished the challenges in the program, and finally, that the women felt that they were able to play (Henderson & Bialeschki, 1987, p. 26-28).

Finally, Kaplan and Kaplan (1989) report on their use of qualitative data collection strategies. Over the course of the 10-year evaluation of the Outdoor Challenge Program, quantitative and qualitative approaches were used. Examples of the qualitative items included asking participants to respond to these questions: "What do you remember most about the Outdoor Challenge? What seems most special about your surroundings there? What was most different from the way things are now?" (Kaplan & Kaplan, 1989, p. 296).

Thus far, we have focused on the dichotomy between quantitative and qualitative methods. We agree, however, with researchers like Ewert (1989) who suggests that a combination of these two approaches might be the most appropriate and efficacious. Evaluators need to become more open and flexible in their research on wilderness programs. In order to examine the effectiveness of the particular program, some sort of quantitative data must be collected utilizing scientific principles.

This is imperative with all therapeutic programs, but especially important with innovative or controversial ones. In addition to data on effectiveness, it would seem that qualitative data describing the process, especially the therapeutic process of wilderness programs would be valuable. The reader may remember previous discussion about the lack of research which describes the therapeutic process in the wilderness, and the few examples of work that does describe this process (e.g., Barley, 1972; Hughes & Dudley, 1973). Without much information on process, the reader is left with impressions about the therapeutic process, and very little real information.

The remainder of this chapter presents suggestions for use in the evaluation of wilderness programs. Some of the ideas contained herein are drawn from the literature, largely from studies that we have discussed. Other suggestions come from our own successes and failures with the Wilderness Therapy Program. It is our hope that these ideas will be presented in a clear, straightforward fashion so that they might be understood and used by a variety of different program types in different practice settings.

Evaluating Wilderness Programs

We note at this point that we do not have the answers for many of the evaluation dilemmas that we have raised in this chapter and elsewhere in the book. In fact, our own research reflects many of the problems that others have encountered in this field. What we do have, however, is a desire to raise these issues and to encourage thinking in the area of evaluation. Finally, we have experience in practice-based research and want to encourage and facilitate the union of research and practice. Prior to actually articulating our ideas for evaluation, a number of underlying assumptions will be presented: (1) All therapeutic programs have the obligation to evaluate their process and their effectiveness; (2) Wilderness programs are unique and often do not fit into a standard evaluation format; (3) All evaluations must be scientifically rigorous, yet allow for the qualitative parts of wilderness programs to be known.

We have talked extensively in this book about the need to evaluate wilderness programs, and believe that this issue is of sufficient importance that we raise it yet again. The reader is referred to some classic sources for involved arguments as to the need for evaluation (Patton, 1980; 1982; 1987; Suchman, 1967). We believe that evaluation becomes even more critical when the clientele are adolescents, and the treatment occurs in a non-traditional setting. This is a scientific as well as a moral imperative. On the scientific front, wilderness programs represent a fairly recent development in the therapeutic literature. As with any innovative approach, a firm commitment must be made to determining the effectiveness of these programs. This is critical to the acceptance of wilderness programs by the professional community and by the clients themselves. In addition to scientific imperatives, we would suggest that the evaluation of wilderness programs also has a moral basis. In defining this moral basis, we are referring to a type of professional responsibility that comes with the provision of human services. As we have discussed, one of the most therapeutic aspects of wilderness programs is their use of the outdoors as an unfamiliar and potentially threatening environment. Adolescents are placed in this foreign setting and realize that their former coping strategies are no longer effective.

When a treatment program removes clients from the familiarity of their everyday lives and exposes them to an unfamiliar environment, one must recognize that there may be inherent risks. In addition, many wilderness programs utilize challenging activities, such as ropes courses, rock climbing, and backpacking which could involve some physical risk to the participants.

Finally, due to the fact that many wilderness treatment programs are conducted in remote areas, modern medical and emergency services are not readily available to the participants should the need for these services arise.

Thus, risk to the participants may increase simply because standard emergency procedures are not readily available to the participants.

It should be noted that the vast majority of programs take these potential risks into account in their program planning, by having medical personnel either on location or easily accessible. Trip leaders are often trained in emergency first aid and wilderness medicine, and are capable of handling injury and illness. Finally, the trip leaders are usually experts in their respective outdoor skills. Thus, the risks are greatly reduced with such experienced and qualified instructors. Nevertheless, given the fact that these types of risk do exist, wilderness programs should be scrutinized to a greater extent and in greater depth than traditional programs.

The second assumption speaks to the argument that wilderness programs are not conducive to the use of standard evaluation methods and procedures. Traditional program evaluation often utilizes established, quantitative approaches to research. Agency records are reviewed, client satisfaction is assessed, the costs and benefits of the service are reviewed, and the efficiency and effectiveness of the program are evaluated. Sometimes this involves collecting data from a number of sources, including clients, other professionals, and by direct assessment of the program itself (Rossi & Freeman, 1982).

Obviously, when a program is being run in a non-traditional setting, the task of data collection becomes quite complicated. It is impossible, for instance, to completely capture the essence of the wilderness trip by reading the progress notes of a therapist who was a participant. Likewise, it is unlikely that one will discover the true meaning of the wilderness experience for the participant by asking him or her to complete a personality inventory or a client satisfaction survey. Finally, it will be very difficult to interview other professionals in the field, asking them for their assessment of the effects of your wilderness program. These types of innovative programs are not commonly seen, and few professionals have had the experience with them to render an informed opinion.

In addition to the general difficulty in applying research methods to wilderness programs, the dedicated traditional researcher will become frustrated with a number of specific research issues. Some of these potential problems areas include the difficulty in securing a control or comparison group, and the problems encountered with administering standardized tests in non-traditional settings. One has to only visualize a group of tired backpackers being asked to fill out paper and pencil surveys as they lean up against a tree at the end of a grueling day. On many occasions, we have had participants become very reluctant, if not hostile about completing forms after their experience.

These potential problems are raised not to discourage the pursuit of methodologically sound research studies, but rather, to build the argument that effective research on wilderness programs must be innovative and creative, yet scientifically sound. We must develop ways to meet scientific criteria yet not compromise the uniqueness of our programs. This, we believe, is one of the major challenges for wilderness programs in the 1990s.

Our third assumption is related to the second, and again calls for the creative evaluation of wilderness programs. We have mentioned some of the criticisms surrounding the lack of both quantitative and qualitative rigor in the literature. Generally, researchers have responded to these critiques by trying to become "more scientific." While this may certainly be an improvement, we are missing an entire dimension of program evaluation. As we and others have argued, the non-traditional nature of wilderness programs may render them especially well suited to such qualitative evaluation. By utilizing these methods, we may begin to understand more about the process of our wilderness programs, as very few studies have provided data on the actual process that takes place in such programs.

Since specific therapeutic approaches have not been developed as wilderness approaches per se, one has little way of determining how these programs are therapeutic. Are there techniques that are used that contribute to their effectiveness? Are there qualities or characteristics of certain wilderness environments that are therapeutic in and of themselves? Do we need to provide traditional counseling or therapy on these trips, and more importantly, are these approaches appropriate for such innovative programs?

These questions and many more must be addressed in the design and conduct of research on wilderness programs if we are to ever develop a solid body of literature on these approaches. With these underlying assumptions in mind, the following section of this chapter presents some evaluation ideas and guidelines. An attempt will be made to present these ideas in as informal a fashion as possible to facilitate their application to a variety of program types.

Preparing for the Evaluation

We begin this section of the chapter discussing some traditional quantitative research issues, such as research design considerations and instrumentation. The final section suggests how evaluation might combine elements of both the quantitative and qualitative approaches to research in evaluating wilderness programs.

Research Design

We have found that it is critical to think about evaluating the program during the actual planning and development phase. In conceptualizing the program from an evaluation perspective, the wilderness experience becomes the intervention or the independent variable. Obviously, one of the research tasks is to measure change caused by this intervention. Planners should thus ask themselves how they will measure change as they design their interventions. Generally, it is wise to consider the use of pre-tests, as they contribute significantly to the internal validity of the study. In our Wilderness Therapy Program, we administer pre-tests at admission to the program and again before the program begins.

Interestingly, we have found some fairly dramatic reductions in self-reported symptoms of distress in the respondents following admission into the program (Davis-Berman & Berman, 1989). The admission portion of the program consists of group meetings to discuss the upcoming program, the development of treatment plans, and the organization of the equipment. It is possible that simply belonging to the program can have an impact on the respondents. This issue is presented by Levitt (1984), and is compared by her to the Hawthorne Effect. On the more therapeutic front, it could also be that the identification of the treatment plan goals begins to encourage the process of change. In our program, these goals are stated verbally by adolescents, parents and therapists. This "uncovering" or public declaration does, indeed, seem to facilitate change. Thus we feel that it would be beneficial to structure pre-tests to include this critical time in program planning, and to capitalize on this use of treatment planning.

To gain a valid representation of the participant's behavior and/or affect immediately prior to the wilderness experience, it is a good idea to pre-test again as the experience begins. This testing can even be done on site, as we have administered our test instruments in base camp on a number of occasions. In this way, the evaluation becomes part of the wilderness program itself, rather than a tedious chore which detracts from the experience.

A cautionary note is in order at this point. When designing testing administration schedules, it is important to take the problem of testing effects into account, as repeated testing can severely compromise the internal validity of the study (Campbell & Stanley, 1963). This issue is especially critical if the instruments are short or easily memorizable. In this event, it may be wise to consider eliminating one of the testing times.

Logically, if one includes a pre-test in the wilderness program evaluation, the inclusion of a post-test of some sort is essential. Once again, we suggest that this post-test occur in a timely fashion, to assure that immediate change is measured. Often this post-testing occurs while still on the trip.

Finally, it is wise to administer the instruments after the completion of the wilderness trip. The issue of follow-up measures has been discussed repeatedly in this book and is a significant problem in the evaluation of wilderness programs. We require that all participants get together two weeks after their experience to "debrief" and to complete the survey instruments again. This testing time is critical in that it represents a measure of short-term change. By the time of this measurement, the adolescents have had a chance to re-enter their peer groups, and have begun to integrate some of the changes experienced on the trip into their daily lives.

In addition to the traditional pre-testing and post-testing, we recommend that follow-up data collection times be established with the design of the program. Throughout this book, we have pointed to the lack of follow-up studies in the literature which has contributed to the methodological problems in evaluating wilderness programs. As part of the program, and a requirement for participation, all of the adolescents should be required to attend follow-up sessions. These sessions can be woven into each program in a unique way, dependent on the nature and length of the program.

Our program is short-term; thus we collect follow-up data at six-month intervals for a period of two years. Generally, we gather all of the past participants for a reunion and a picnic which allows us to keep in touch and collect data.

In summary, we suggest a pre-test post-test design with a two-year follow-up component as a good design to use if possible. We also suggest that this design can be adapted to most program types if the evaluation portion of the program is conceived of as an integral part of the program and is included at even the most fundamental level of program planning. We do realize that with such multiple data collection points, we run the risk of having significant testing effects contaminate the data. However, we have decided that measurement over time and follow-up data are of sufficient importance to justify this risk.

Another essential design recommendation is the use of a control group. Again, the reader is reminded of the discussion throughout this book on the lack of control groups in the literature on wilderness programs. Such an omission has contributed to internal validity problems with many of the studies.

We do recognize that control or comparison groups are often extremely difficult to obtain in clinical settings. Ethical issues regarding the use of such groups must also be considered. Large programs may utilize their waiting lists as potential comparison groups. Smaller programs like ours have a more difficult time selecting a comparison group. Clients from local social service programs may be used as a comparison group if these clients are not receiving wilderness programming. In fact, positive results from the study could then be used to present to the agency where the control group was drawn to encourage them to utilize the wilderness program. In this way, the comparison group may at some time be given access to the treatment. This issue of selecting and using a control group is a difficult one to implement. We still struggle with this, yet we know that innovative solutions to comparison groups must be developed to improve the validity of the research on wilderness programs.

Some of the methodological difficulties discussed throughout this book are specific to wilderness therapy programs; however, many relate more generally to the difficulty in evaluating therapeutic activities. Kazdin (1991) raises a number of these issues and highlights the difficulty in determining the effectiveness of therapy with children and adolescents.

An alternative approach may be to consider the use of quasi-experimental designs, such as single-subject designs. The multiple baseline design eliminates the need for such rigorous control or the need for control groups. For example, wilderness trips can be evaluated at different times with this type of design, with the intervention groups serving as comparison groups for each other (Nelsen, 1988).

Figure 8-2. Multiple Baseline Design

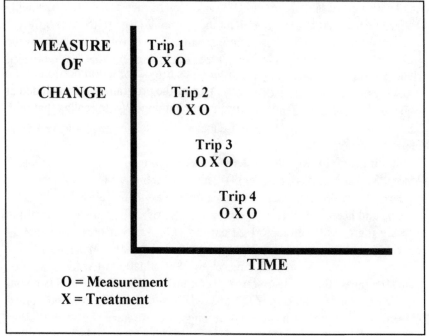

This multiple baseline design allows for the use of standardized measurement instruments, or the specification of target behaviors for change, and eliminates the need for control groups. As each group awaits their program, they are in essence serving as a comparison group for the others. Finally, the multiple baseline design allows for the use of one subject per group or for small groups. Thus, the small sample problems plaguing experimental designs do not apply. Although quasi-experimental designs are not as powerful as experimental designs, they may be more appropriate for use in evaluating therapeutic programs (Nelsen, 1988).

Instrumentation

It is difficult to identify a set of research instruments which are especially appropriate for use in the evaluation of wilderness programs. As has been previously discussed, there are so many different types of programs, focusing on a variety of goals, and working with diverse clientele. However, despite the diversity in the field, we have identified and discussed common instruments that have been reported in the literature. Before we make any recommendations for measurement, however, it is important to stress that standardized instruments should be used. If we are to quantify change in affect, thoughts or behaviors, it is critical that validated instruments be used in the measurement of change.

As with the design of the study, the selection of measurement instruments should take place during program planning. Although we realize that different programs may require that specific instruments be developed for use in the study, we can recommend a number of types of instruments that could be used when examining a therapeutic program.

Self-esteem is a concept that has been measured in numerous studies, and which has been discussed in some detail in this book. For a more detailed discussion of the assessment of self-concept and self-esteem, the reader is referred to Ewert (1983).

In our program, we have had some success in using the Pier-Harris Self Concept Scale (Piers & Harris, 1969). This instrument is easily administered, is geared toward children and adolescents, is very comprehensible by adolescents, and is relatively easy to score. It is also of sufficient length that it is unlikely that it will be memorized on post-test. Another measure which is related to self-concept, but reflects more of a competence measure is self-efficacy. The application of this theory to the evaluation of wilderness programs is fairly recent (Harmon & Templin, 1987), however, the actual formulation of the theory is over 15 years old (Bandura, 1977). A standardized self-efficacy instrument has been developed, and we have seen some rather interesting changes on this measure (Sherer, Maddux, Mercandante, Prentice-Dunn, Jacobs, & Rogers, 1982). Self-efficacy is an interesting measure to use because self-efficacy expectations have been shown to be dependent on experience, and thus are highly amenable to change (Bandura, 1977).

In addition to the more trait oriented measures, we have found it important to measure symptoms of distress, and we have seen decreases in subjective distress following participation in the wilderness program and for up to two

Figure 8-3. The General Self-Efficacy Scale

General Self-Efficacy

Directions: Please indicate if these statements describe your behavior by answering yes or no.

1. When I make plans, I am certain I can make them work.
2. One of my problems is that I cannot get down to work when I should.
3. If I can't do a job the first time, I keep trying until I can.
4. When I set important goals for myself, I rarely achieve them.
5. I give up on things before completing them.
6. I avoid facing difficulties.
7. If something looks too complicated, I will not even bother to try it.
8. When I have something unpleasant to do, I stick to it until I finish it.
9. When I decide to do something, I go right to work on it.
10. When trying to learn something new, I soon give up if I am not initially successful.
11. When unexpected problems occur, I don't handle them well.
12. I avoid trying to learn new things when they look too difficult for me.
13. Failure just makes me try harder.
14. I feel insecure about my ability to do things.
15. I am a self-reliant person.
16. I give up easily.
17. I do not seem capable of dealing with most problems that come up in life.

Reproduced with permission of authors and publisher from: Sherer, M., Maddux, J. E., Mercandante, B., Prentice-Dunn, S., Jacobs, B, & Rogers, R. W. "The Self-Efficacy Scale: Construction and Validation." *Psychological Reports,* 1982, *51*, 663-671. ©

---

years post-test (Berman & Anton, 1988; Davis-Berman & Berman, 1989). We have used the Brief Symptom Inventory as a measure of distress. This inventory is plainly written and easy to comprehend, with respondents simply checking whether or not an item describes them, making this instrument very fast to administer (Derogatis, 1975).

Finally, in addition to general symptoms of distress, programs may wish to measure specific psychological characteristics. Since much of our work is done with troubled adolescents, many of whom are depressed, we have found it logical to utilize a measure of depressive symptomatology. As with the other measures, it is important that this instrument be concise, easily understood, and fairly easy to interpret and score. The Depression Adjective Checklist appears to meet these criteria. This instrument has a number of different forms. Once a form is chosen, the respondent simply indicates if an adjective describes the way that he/she has been feeling in the past week or not (Lubin, 1967). It should be noted that all of these instruments have been validated and

Figure 8-4. Selected Items from the BSI®

Below is a list of problems and complaints that people sometimes have. Read each one carefully, and select one of the numbered descriptions that best describes how much discomfort that problem has caused you during the past 7 days including today.

Descriptors: 0 = not at all;
                            1 = a little bit;
                            2 = moderately;
                            3 = Quite a bit;
                            4 = Extremely

1.   Feeling that most people cannot be trusted.
2.   Feeling inferior to others.
3.   Temper outbursts that you could not control.

The BSI® Leonard R. Derogatis, Ph.D., Reproduced by Permission. National Computer Systems, 5605 Green Circle Drive, Minnetonka, MN 55343

Note: Due to copyright constraints, we were only permitted to reprint three items. For further information contact National Computer Systems.

---

used rather extensively in the research literature.[3]

In addition to the standardized instruments, more subjective measures may be used, and reflect a qualitative dimension in the study. In a later section in this chapter, we will discuss combining quantitative and qualitative approaches in evaluation. At this point, however, we will introduce the reader to the notion of qualitatively oriented measurement.

To meaningfully include qualitative measurement, one must plan and structure such measurement. For example, we develop, in concert with parents and therapists, personalized treatment plan goals for each participant. Prior to the departure of the trip, we ask the participants and their parents to rate the extent to which they are meeting the treatment plan goal at the present time. During the trip, therapists provide ratings of the progress of the participants in meeting these treatment plan goals. These ratings are also provided at post-test. Thus although this is a fairly subjective rating of change, it is structured in such a way that it becomes more than personal opinion, and can be used as a measure of change on the trip.

---

[3] (The reader is reminded of the restrictions on the use of psychological instruments raised in Table 8-1).

Other appropriate subjective measures which are conducive for use in wilderness programs include therapist, group leader and participant ratings. Most studies utilize an open-ended approach to subjective ratings. This approach, unfortunately, makes it impossible to compare ratings across studies, and thus makes it difficult to develop a set of qualitative data.

We suggest that therapists, trip leaders, and participants be asked to keep a daily log or journal and respond to a series of directed questions or items related to the effects of the wilderness program. Examples of some of these items might include the following: (1) Describe your (participant #1) ability to be a leader, (2) Describe your (participant #1) real self/ your ideal self, (3) What are your (participant #1) greatest strengths? (4) What are your (participant #1) greatest weaknesses? By providing such structure, the therapist, trip leader and participants are able to provide daily qualitative data, rich in detail and description. Yet, this data is somewhat structured in the midst of its richness. In addition to these structured questions, all participants could be instructed to keep a daily feeling log to be completed before retiring every night. The purpose of this log is to get in touch with, and record, feelings. This log could also be used as a rich source of qualitative data. By imposing some structure to the ratings and journaling assignments, we move more toward discovering the qualitative as suggested by Kolb (1991), yet we generate a structured data set.

General Research Issues

Following the development of the research design and the selection of standardized instruments, the evaluation is ready to be implemented. As was previously discussed, data collection will take place before, during, and after the trip itself. Probably the most important issue at this point is the need for active participation in the evaluation. Often times, staff members who actually implement programs are not included in program planning. We have discussed the need for the evaluation to be closely aligned with the sponsoring agency, and especially with the staff who are actually participating in the program (Berman & Davis-Berman, 1991).

The involvement of staff in the evaluation of wilderness programs is probably more critical than the need for their involvement in more traditional agency programs. If we are to devise innovative and creative strategies, then these staff members must understand their importance and support them with enthusiasm. It is also helpful if the staff presents the notion of evaluation to the participants as an important part of the entire program.

Likewise, the participants themselves must understand and appreciate the importance of the evaluation to the program. From their admission into the program, they must be told about the evaluative component, and be made aware of its importance. In our program, participants are told about the evaluation and are told when they will be required to complete instruments at the first group meeting. They are also told about the required journal writing on the trip. Participants understand that these evaluation activities are important to the success of the program, and that their participation in the program is contingent on their cooperation with the evaluation efforts.

Finally, the development of the treatment plan goals is done in a group setting, with all of the participants and their family members in attendance. Often, group discussion ensues as adolescents realize that they have many common issues. In this way, evaluation quickly becomes part of the process of the program.

Combining Quantitative and Qualitative Approaches

The reader will recognize one of the recurring themes in this book as the lack of writing which describes the actual therapeutic process of wilderness programs. This has been supported very strongly by Ewert (1989), a demonstrated leader in the evaluation of wilderness programs. Only a few works were cited which even attempted to provide the reader with a "window" on the wilderness experience (Barley, 1972; Hughes & Dudley, 1973; Nadler & Luckner, 1992). Since the need for more qualitative approaches to research has been identified as an assumption of our model, it clearly warrants further discussion.

The majority of evaluation utilizing quantitative research approaches focuses on the evaluation of outcome or effectiveness of the program. These types of studies are data based, often utilize statistical analysis of data, and standardized measurement instruments. Very little mention, if any, is made of the actual process of the program or what goes on within the program, independent of its effectiveness (Rossi & Freeman, 1982). This is not to say that the majority of evaluation studies of wilderness programs take the form of process evaluations. Rather, we suggest that a combination of outcome and process evaluations occur. Since so little is presented in the literature on process evaluation, a brief description is in order.

The major goal of process evaluations is different than the goal of outcome evaluations. Process evaluations focus on the internal workings of the program, rather than on its effectiveness. When evaluating the process of a program, one focuses on the day-to-day operations, desiring to understand the actual "workings" of the program (Patton, 1987). In other words, the process evaluator really makes an attempt to get inside of the program, to see what makes it tick. It appears that the use of this evaluation method may serve to provide us with some of the vital information that we are lacking in the research literature.

This is supported by Warner (1990) in a chapter of an edited volume. In this chapter, he reviews evaluation research in general, and suggests that a combination of quantitative and qualitative approaches is in order, and facilitates the evaluation of program process. He discusses this issue very succinctly when he defends the combination of quantitative and qualitative methods by saying, "In fact, the two approaches complement each other. Behavioral outcome evaluation will only provide meaningful information if it can be connected to information about program processes and experiences in a longitudinal way" (Warner, 1990, p. 314-315).

It can be suggested that wilderness programs are especially well suited for the use of process evaluation. While it may be important to learn that these programs do create change in the participants, and are thus effective, this is not really enough. Before these statements about efficacy can become meaningful, one must know what is causing the change. Thus to ask what occurs, how it occurs, and why it occurs on wilderness trips may certainly be appropriate.

In support of these contentions, Patton (1987, p. 23) suggests that process evaluations be used to begin to explore and answer the following questions: "What are the factors that come together to make this program what it is? What are the strengths and weaknesses of the program? How are clients brought into the program and how do they move through the program once they are participants? and finally, What is the nature of staff-client interactions?" We believe that these items apply in a very specific and meaningful way to wilderness programs.

Obviously, the aim of this chapter is to develop ideas and promote further investigation, rather than to instruct in the process of evaluation research. At this point, however, we would suggest that the evaluator examine the wilderness program as a participant/observer, rather than as an objective researcher. Patton (1982) provides such an example, and the reader will remember our discussion of his observations on the use of metaphors in wilderness programs. We, too, encourage the identification of metaphors which develop in programs. Each participant could be instructed to identify his or her own personal and group metaphors. This data is then used in the group and individual therapy sessions to facilitate change.

The most important contribution of the participant observer, however, is to describe for the lay and professional public the actual process that occurs on the wilderness trips. Important points of observation might include: staff-participant interactions, group formation and solidarity among participants, hostile behaviors, helping behaviors, and a description of the therapeutic techniques which are used in the program.

Since programs differ so greatly, we recognize that these descriptions will vary greatly between programs. However, by collecting this data, we may then begin to describe and compare program types. For example, we might describe the therapeutic approaches used in mental health programs, or in programs serving delinquents. To make these comparisons, however, the collection of qualitative data is essential. Very little actual data has been generated which looks at the process of programs and the differential effect various offerings might have. For example, it could be that certain wilderness modalities in combination with specific therapeutic techniques may facilitate change in selected and specific population groups. These issues have been discussed in a very preliminary fashion (Ewert, 1991; Hazelworth & Wilson, 1990) in the literature, yet require a great deal more research attention. Such qualitative data collection might even involve audio or videotaping the therapeutic sessions taking place on wilderness trips. This would have to take place within the confines of professional regulations about confidentiality. Content analyses could then be performed on these recordings.

In this chapter, an attempt has been made to introduce the reader to the topic of evaluation, to discuss its application to wilderness programs, and to make some suggestions for the future. It is important that these issues be addressed by those involved in wilderness programs. If we are ever able to strengthen the reputation and respect of our programs, we must build evaluation components into them at their inception. This type of approach involves the interest and commitment of planners and of those actually running the programs. If we have encouraged and focused interest on the implementation of evaluation in this chapter, then we have been successful.

In addition to interest, we must evaluate our programs according to accepted research practice. We have seen and discussed common flaws in the current literature, and some design and measurement suggestions were made in this chapter which begin to address some of these problems. One of these suggestions has been that programs consider the use of single-subject designs, especially multiple baseline designs, if appropriate. We must improve the quality of our evaluations if they are to be taken seriously. Shoddy research reflects poorly on the design and integrity of the programs that we are evaluating. Only through well designed and executed studies can the reputations of our programs rest.

Finally, we must consider qualitative aspects of our programs in addition to the more objective, quantitative aspects. We have suggested that evaluation studies make an effort to combine the use of these approaches. Through such a combination, we may develop a well rounded data set. Wilderness programs are innovative and unique in their attempts to facilitate change and growth in their participants. As with any new program types, however, skeptics abound. By describing the process that we engage in on these programs, as well as the outcome, we move toward greater acceptance and toward greater respect of these innovative approaches to change. By pursuing the process of our programs, we also begin to determine which kinds of therapeutic techniques and methods are effective with certain populations. This issue represents our research challenge for the future. We must define and measure our process so we can determine which types of outdoor programs benefit certain client types. We can therefore move away from a generic model of "wilderness change" to more finely tuned, sophisticated programs.

The final chapter briefly summarizes some of the major themes presented in this book. The reader is then challenged to think about some of the critical issues on the forefront of wilderness programming today. Finally, critical practice and research issues for the future are suggested.

References

Bandura, A. (1977). Self-efficacy: Toward a unifying theory of behavioral change. *Psychological Review, 84* (2), 191-215.

Barley, F. (1972). Camp can change campus attitudes. *Camping Magazine, 44* (7), 18.

Berman, D., & Anton, M. (1988). A wilderness therapy program as an alternative to adolescent psychiatric hospitalization. *Residential Treatment for Children and Youth, 5,* 39-52.

Berman, D., & Davis-Berman, J. (1991). Wilderness therapy and adolescent mental health: Administrative and clinical issues. *Administration and Policy in Mental Health, 18* (5), 373-379.

Bernstein, I., & Freeman, H. (1975). *Academic and entrepreneurial research: Consequences of diversity in federal evaluation studies.* New York: Russell Sage.

Burdsal, C., & Force, R.C. (1983). An examination of counselor ratings of behavior problem youth in an early stage, community-based intervention program. *Journal of Clinical Psychology, 39,* 353-360.

Campbell, D., & Stanley, J. (1963). *Experimental and quasi-experimental designs for research.* Boston: Houghton Mifflin Co.

Chenery, M. (1981). Effects of summer camp on child development and contributions of counselors to those effects. *Journal of Leisure Research,* third quarter, 195-207.

Clifford, E., & Clifford, M. (1967). Self-concept before and after survival training. *British Journal of Social and Clinical Psychology, 6,* 241-248.

Cyntrynbaum, S., & Ken, K. (1975). *The Connecticut wilderness program: A preliminary report.* Hartford, CT: State of Connecticut Council on Human Services.

Davis-Berman, J., & Berman, D. (1989). The wilderness therapy program: An empirical study of its effects with adolescents in an outpatient setting. *Journal of Contemporary Psychotherapy, 19* (4), 271-281.

Derogatis, L. (1975). *Brief symptom inventory.* Riverwood, MD: Clinical Psychometric Research.

Dooley, D. (1990). *Social research methods.* Englewood Cliffs: Prentice-Hall.

Ewert, A. (1983). *Outdoor adventure and self-concept: A research analysis.* Eugene, OR: Center for Leisure Studies, University of Oregon.

Ewert, A. (1989). *Outdoor adventure pursuits: Foundations, models, and theories.* Columbus, OH: Publishing Horizons.

Ewert, A. (1991). Revisiting the self-concept: A new twist on an old subject. *The Journal of Experiential Education, 14* (1), 49.

Fletcher, B. (1970). *Students of Outward Bound schools in Great Britain: A followup study.* University of Bristol, School of Education.

Hazelworth, M., & Wilson, B. (1990). The effects of an outdoor adventure camp experience on self-concept. *Journal of Environmental Education, 21* (4), 33-37.

Henderson, K., & Bialeschki, D. (1987). A qualitative evaluation of a women's week experience. *The Journal of Experiential Education, 10* (2), 25-28.

Hornick, J., & Burrows, B. (1988). Program evaluation. In R. Grinnell, (Ed.), *Social work research and evaluation* (pp. 400-420). Itasca, IL: F.E. Peacock Inc.

Hughes, A., & Dudley, H. (1973). An old idea for a new problem: Camping as a treatment for the emotionally disturbed in our state hospitals. *Adolescence, 8,* 43-50.

Jerstad, L., & Selzer, J. (1973). Adventure experiences as treatment for residential mental patients. *Therapeutic Recreation Journal, 1,* 8-11.

Kaplan, R. (1974). Some psychological benefits of an outdoor challenge program. *Environment and Behavior, 6,* 101-115.

Kaplan, R., & Kaplan, S. (1989). *The experience of nature: A psychological perspective.* New York: Cambridge University Press.

Kazdin, A. (1991). Effectiveness of psychotherapy with children and adolescents. *Journal of Consulting and Clinical Psychology, 59* (6), 785-798.

Kelly, F.J., & Baer, D.J. (1968). *Outward Bound schools as an alternative to institutionalization for adolescent delinquent boys.* Boston: Fandel Press.

Kelly, F., & Baer, D. (1971). Physical challenge as a treatment for delinquency. *Crime and Delinquency, 17,* 437-445.

Kimball, R.O. (1979). *Wilderness experience program: Final evaluation report.* Santa Fe: State of New Mexico Forensic System.

Koepke, S. (1974). The effects of Outward Bound participation upon anxiety and self-concept. (Report No. RC 008 234). (ERIC Document Reproduction Service No. ED 099162), 1-7.

Kolb, D. (1991). Meaningful methods: Evaluation without the crunch. *The Journal of Experiential Education, 14* (1), 40-44.

Krieger, W. (1973). Study on self-concept change in campers. *Camping Magazine, 45* (4), 16-17.

Levitt, L. (1984). Research in therapeutic camping: What can we learn from past mistakes? In D. Teschner & J. Wolter, (Eds.), *Wilderness challenge: Outdoor education alternatives for youth in need* (pp. 109-115). Hadlyme, CT: The Institute of Experiential Studies.

Lubin, B. (1967). *Depression adjective checklist.* San Diego: Educational and Industrial Testing Service.

Marx, E. (1988). Camping for crippled children. *Camping Magazine, 16,* 5.

Mills, C. W. (1959). *The sociological imagination.* London: Oxford University Press.

Nadler, R. & Luckner, J. (1992). *Processing the adventure experience: Theory and practice.* Dubuque, IA: Kendall/Hunt.

Nelsen, J. (1988). Single-subject research. In R. Grinnell (Ed.). *Social work research and evaluation.* Itasca, Ill.: F.E. Peacock, 362-399.

Patton, M. (1978). *Utilization-focused evaluation.* Beverly Hills: Sage Publications.

Patton, M. (1980). *Qualitative evaluation methods.* Beverly Hills: Sage Publications.

Patton, M. (1982). *Practical evaluation.* Beverly Hills: Sage Publications.

Piers, E., & Harris, D. (1969). *Manual for the Piers-Harris children's self-concept scale.* Nashville: Counselor Recordings and Texts.

Rossi, P. & Freeman, H. (1982). *Evaluation: A systematic approach.* Beverly Hills: Sage Publications.

Rowley, J. (1987). Adventure education and qualitative research. *Journal of Experiential Education, 10* (2), 8-12.

Sherer, M., Maddux, J., Mercandante, B., Prentice-Dunn, S., Jacobs, B., & Rogers, R. (1982). The self-efficacy scale: Construction and validation. *Psychological Reports, 51,* 663-671.

Shniderman, C. M. (1974). Impact of therapeutic camping. *Social Work, 19,* 354-357.

Smith, M., Gabriel, R., Schott, J., & Padia, W. (1975). *Evaluation of the effects of Outward Bound.* University of Colorado: Bureau of Educational Field Services.

Stich, T., & Sussman, L. (1981). Outward Bound: An adjunctive psychiatric therapy: Preliminary research findings. (Report No. RC 014538). ERIC Document Reproduction Service No. 239791, 1-7.

Suchman, E. (1967). *Evaluative research: Principles and practice in public service and social action programs.* New York: Russell Sage Foundation.

Teschner, D., & Wolter, J. (1984). *Wilderness challenge: Outdoor education alternatives for youth in need.* Hadlyme, CT: The Institute of Experiential Studies.

Warner, A. (1990). Program evaluation: Past, present, and future. In J. Miles & S. Priest, (Eds.), *Adventure education* (pp. 309-321). State College, PA: Venture Publishing, Inc.

Willman, H., & Chun, R. (1973). Homeward bound: An alternative to institutionalization of adjudicated juvenile offenders. *Federal Probation,* September, 52-58.

Chapter Nine ▽

Gaining Perspective

In this final chapter we want to both summarize some of the major points previously made and highlight some of the critical issues in the field of therapeutic wilderness programming. We also hope to forecast the future by identifying which of these issues may play a prominant role in shaping the future of this growing field.

Let us begin our review by recalling how, in order to "set the stage" for our later ideas and discussions, and to establish a rationale for the use of wilderness therapy with adolescents, some general information was introduced. We tried to establish that often the traditional approaches to working with troubled adolescents are not effective, and that innovative alternatives are needed. In this regard, we identified many of the limitations of traditional approaches, and suggested why the use of wilderness therapy serves to overcome many of these obstacles to treatment.

We then began exploring and highlighting various historical influences on the development and refinement of our notions about the wilderness in this country. Drawing on the stories and writings of influential figures, this material provides an exciting background for the remainder of the book. One of the prominent conceptions of the wilderness that developed was that of the wilderness as a healing influence. We traced the development of this belief through the Romantic period to the time of writers like Thoreau. It is through this rich history that we were able to justify the development of therapeutic wilderness programs. Following this introductory material, we reviewed the development and implementation of the earliest therapeutic programs.

In order to ground this history in a context, however, we discussed some of the recreational camps of the early years. Despite the fact that these camps were not decidedly therapeutic, they did attempt to facilitate personal growth among their campers.

The reader will remember that the tone of these early programs shifted with the "tent therapy" programs in the early 1900s, and with the development of Camp Ahmek. Moving into the mid-1900s, we saw increasing sophistication of programs, illustrated by programs such as the Salesmanship Club of Dallas, and by the growth of Outward Bound in America.

Since the time of these early programs, we have become more sophisticated. Equipment and the technical capabilities available to programs and leaders have changed the way programs are designed and implemented. What is surprising, however, is that many of the issues that were being grappled with during the first half of the 20th century are still unresolved today. The reader will remember our early mention of the problem of lack of research, the role of the group in facilitating change, the lack of definition of the term therapeutic, and finally, the lack of consensus on staff qualifications. These issues are still on the forefront of discussion today.

It is this continuity between the past and the present which makes this review of the historical development of wilderness programs so interesting and vital. We continued with this review by presenting programs and discussing issues from the decade of the 1970s to the present day. During this time, we have seen a proliferation of therapeutic programs and writing on wilderness programs, both in the professional and popular literature.

Much of this writing has been geared toward espousing the healing aspects of the wilderness environment itself. As such, there has been debate on the role of reflection, and on the definition of therapeutic. Although this dialogue has helped to define some issues, we have been deficient in identifying and discussing the actual process which occurs in therapeutic wilderness programs, that is, What goes on to make them therapeutic?

A few reports have attempted such a description, but basically, we are left to our own devices. Although some fine studies have been done, many of the old themes continue to emerge. Most work has focused solely on outcome, while ignoring the process of the programs. Additionally, a number of methodological issues have been raised which lessen the validity of the research results, including the lack of control or comparison groups, small sample sizes, and inadequate measurement techniques. Nonetheless, the research looks promising, and suggests that many therapeutic wilderness programs are indeed effective in reducing behavioral symptoms and raising the self-esteem of troubled youth.

In addition to providing the reader with research literature, we wanted to present some examples of programs which were actually indicative of the types of programs currently being offered across the country. As such, representative mental health, court related, school, health, and enrichment programs were described. Importantly, the enrichment programs easily outnumber all of the other types of programs, with the court programs being the most widely researched. The interested reader will find the appendix to this book a source of information on wilderness programs throughout the country.

Following the descriptive nature of the first half of the book, the second half focused more on practical applications, such as the design and development of therapeutic wilderness programs. To set the stage for program design, we discussed the theoretical underpinnings of wilderness programming. As such, the reader was introduced to the nature and importance of theory. Additionally, a number of theories, including systems theory were presented, and many examples were used to illustrate its utility in understanding, designing and implementing wilderness programs.

Next, the practical aspects of designing and implementing wilderness programs were presented, and included very concrete information on selecting staff and participants, the development of the therapeutic component of the trip, and actually conducting therapy. It is our hope that those interested in planning and implementing a therapeutic program found this information especially helpful.

We thought that the evaluation of the process and outcome of the therapeutic program was of sufficient importance to warrant special consideration. Thus after developing a rationale for the importance of research, we discussed both quantitative and qualitative methods, and presented ideas which combine both approaches. It is our hope that readers will not be intimidated by the nature of this topic. In this regard, we have attempted to present all discussions of research in a straightforward, easy to understand fashion.

Following this brief summary of our work to this point, it seems appropriate to end this chapter discussing some of the critical issues currently facing program planners, administrators, and staff. Additionally, it is important to forecast emerging and critical issues for the future. Toward this end, we will discuss professionalization, the need to define and refine the field of therapeutic wilderness programming, and future issues such as accreditation and other credentialing and research needs.

Professionalization

Debates on the professionalization of therapeutic wilderness programming are certainly not new; however, they are still quite salient for our discussions today. Those who support increased professionalism cite the benefits to those involved in the field. For instance, Ewert (1989) suggests that professions fill social needs, and that being professionalized communicates an accepted body of knowledge, literature, and an ethical code of conduct to society. It appears then, that the notion of being a profession helps to impose some consistency, order and at least an implied set of standards on programs. For those of us who object to the wide variety of unregulated wilderness programs, the idea of increased professionalism seems intriguing.

Despite one's own views on this subject, it is difficult to deny that many efforts to increase the professional influence in this field have already taken place. This growth seems to be rooted in two distinct traditions: outdoor education and the mental health profession.

Training organizations based in an outdoor education model have begun to prepare leaders to become wilderness instructors. Organizations like the Wilderness Education Association are involved, with one of their missions being to "promote the professionalization of outdoor leadership and thereby improve the safety of outdoor trips and enhance the conservation of the wild outdoors" (Cockrell & Lupton, 1991, p. 1). To achieve this goal, the WEA has developed a certification curriculum for an outdoor leader called the "National Standard Program" (NSP). Universities are accredited to teach this course, and individuals are certified as "outdoor leaders" (WEA, 1989). They also offer a unique "wilderness stewardship" program that focuses on at least one of the curriculum components of the NSP.

Other organizations offer courses in outdoor leadership, but without the certification. Examples of these organizations include the National Outdoor Leadership School (NOLS) and Outward Bound. Still other organizations are geared less toward training and more toward serving professional interests in the area of outdoor programming. The Association for Experiential Education represents such an organization, encompassing a diverse membership including both individuals and organizations.

The AEE has particular expertise in establishing standards for the use of technical skills in outdoor education. Their *Safety Practices in Adventure Programming* (Priest & Dixon, 1990) is replete with expertise in the "hard skills" involved in outdoor programming. This is an excellent reference for those planning or implementing wilderness therapy programs, in that it helps to ensure that the physical aspects of the programs will be offered in a safe way and in compliance with the most rigorous of physical standards.

Thus, if a program offers cross country skiing, or any of a number of other activities, this manual provides guidelines for equipment and instruction, as well as concerns for participants, the environment and ethical issues. In addition to "hard skills," the AEE distinguishes between "soft skills" and "meta skills," where the former refers to the ability to teach, organize and facilitate the learning of the process, and the latter relates to interpersonal communication and problem solving skills, as well as judgment and leadership style (Priest & Dixon, 1990).

The second major area of professional growth in outdoor programming appears to come from the mental health arena. The reader will remember our earlier presentation of therapeutic programs, where we discussed the "tent therapy" programs, and the importance of Camp Ahmek in the development of therapeutic programs. This therapeutic trend continued so that by the 1940s and 50s, many mental health professionals were consulting in or employed by therapeutic outdoor camps.

With the community mental health centers movement in the 1960s and 1970s, there was impetus given to the idea that the out-of-doors could become an alternative to institution-based services. Programs like those discussed earlier (e.g. Adams, 1970; Jerstad & Selzer, 1973; Kaplan, 1974; Kistler, Bryant & Tucker, 1977) involved taking patients from hospitals and clinics into forests and other rustic settings with praiseworthy reports of their success.

Finally, this trend toward the involvement of the mental health community in outdoor programs has continued to the present day, and in fact, even seems to be on the increase. Recently, we conducted a rather in-depth study of 31 wilderness mental health programs. Although all of these programs identified themselves as being primarily for the provision of mental health services, the diversity in design and implementation of the program offerings was quite interesting. As a result of this research, we have been able to identify a few critical issues related to the professionalization of the field which warrant further discussion. These issues will be discussed under the umbrella of defining the field which includes distinguishing between therapeutic and therapy (Davis-Berman, Berman & Capone, 1992).

Defining the Field

There are a number of different terms or labels used to describe therapeutic wilderness programs. The field has variously been called outdoor education, experiential education, camping therapy, tent therapy, therapeutic wilderness programming, wilderness therapy, and a host of other terms. In fact, at one point, we jokingly referred to this field as "psychoforestry," only to find this label used in a newspaper article reporting on a paper we presented at a conference! The simple truth is that there are no generally accepted basic definitions of therapeutic programs or wilderness therapy.

A recent article (McGowan, 1992, p. 3) defined wilderness therapy as involving the use of outdoor adventure activities "in the treatment and rehabilitation of persons with disabilities" in such a way as to include "juvenile delinquency" and people with a "variety of physical, cognitive and emotional disabilities." This definition reflects the problems that exist in defining the scope of the field. Presumably, as long as the activity involves perceived physical risk and the participants are identified as having a deficiency that the program is addressing, then the activity is wilderness therapy.

We believe that definitions of this sort are too nebulous to be of any help in determining what kinds of activities and programs constitute wilderness therapy. Instead, we view the essential components of wilderness therapy as the following:

> Wilderness therapy involves promoting change in troubled individuals
> through the application of mental health principles and practices in
> outdoor settings.

Let us briefly consider each of the components of our definition: program participants, principles of change, and the outdoor setting.

The vast majority of participants in programs are adolescents, with some residing in hospitals, others in residential centers, some within the juvenile justice system, and still others in outpatient counseling settings. All of these adolescents are deemed to be in need of counseling, and exhibit emotional and/or behavioral problems that can be characterized within the system of standard psychiatric nomenclature (e.g., DSM-III R, 1987). Clearly, the programs being discussed deal with a very high risk population.

Even those programs that do not profess to be mental health in their orientation often claim to improve self-esteem, and toward this end apply mental health principles to their programs. These activities can range from reinforcing positive behaviors to the use of individualized treatment plans. These methods of change are not inconsistent with various definitions of psychotherapy (e.g., Kazdin, 1991).

Finally, our definition states that wilderness therapy activities take place in outdoor settings, with elements of heightened arousal and perceived risk often being a critical part of this experience. In other words, this environment involves being away from the normal living situation, in the outdoors, where physical activity is involved in a challenging way. The reader will remember our previous discussion of programs which suggest that the wilderness environment is therapeutic in and of itself. There remains a great deal of controversy about the definitions of therapy and the distinction between therapy and therapeutic as related to wilderness programs.

When programs are described as therapeutic, it is usually meant that they are helpful in some way. Participants can expect to change as a result of these programs in relatively general ways (e.g., improved self-esteem), but the programs are not geared toward the problems, needs or issues of a specific individual. Many of these programs actually report the changes in self-esteem, and discuss participant satisfaction with the program in their materials. Additionally, most of the programs that we talked to discussed the "naturally" therapeutic qualities of the out-of-doors. In other words, simply "being there" was therapeutic (Davis-Berman, Berman & Capone, 1992).

In contrast to therapeutic, therapy, or in the case of mental health counseling-psychotherapy, involves a planned course of intervention designed to deal with a set of specific individual problems. Therapy is planned and intentional and involves:

> An intervention designed to decrease distress, psychological symptoms, and maladaptive behavior or to improve adaptive and prosocial functioning (Kazdin, 1991, p. 785).

These ends are sought primarily through interpersonal sources of influence such as learning, persuasion, counseling and discussion integrated into a specific treatment plan (Kazdin, 1991, p. 785). We would argue that all wilderness programs should be therapeutic, for if they were not, there would be no rationale for the program. We also strongly suggest that mental health programs must also provide therapy in addition to their therapeutic emphasis.

We have suggested elsewhere (Berman & Davis-Berman, 1992) that it is imperative that planned, deliberate therapy forms the basis of all wilderness programs serving troubled clients. This is especially critical in programs that promote themselves as residential in nature, and as alternatives to psychiatric hospitalization. In our study of mental health programs, essentially all reported that they were targeting adolescents with identified mental health problems including: behavioral, school and family problems, conduct disorders, self-esteem problems, depression, and suicidal ideation (Davis-Berman, Berman & Capone, 1992). Clearly, these programs are serving high-risk clients who fall under the auspices of mental health.

The vast majority of mental health programs that we surveyed were very vague in their discussion of their therapeutic methods. In fact, very few actually referred to organized and systematic therapy. The use of the therapeutic properties of the group seemed to be common among programs. When asked to elaborate, the group was seen as a vehicle for change, but the specific process of this change was not detailed. Finally, many of the programs mentioned that they tried to use the wilderness experience as a metaphor for experiences in other areas of life (Davis-Berman, Berman & Capone, 1992). What this study suggests, then, is that even among programs which identify themselves as having a mental health treatment focus, very little if any systematic, formal therapy is being offered.

Thus far, we have suggested that all outdoor programs should be therapeutic, and all of those serving troubled, high risk adolescents should be based on a solid model of therapy. The next question becomes: What are the characteristics and qualifications of the personnel who should be implementing such programs? It appears that it is a rare individual who possesses all of the requisite skills to provide for the needs of all of the participants. As such, we suggest that three types of individuals are needed to effectively provide wilderness therapy, plus a host of supervisory staff and consultants.

First, wilderness leaders are needed. These are individuals who are trained to provide supervision and direction for the physical aspects of the out-of-doors activities. An example of the type of abilities that one would need in this capacity would be certification from the Wilderness Education Association (WEA) as an outdoor leader. These individuals must be able to:

a) Teach others how to use and enjoy the wilderness with minimum impact, b) Safely lead others in the wild outdoors, c) Exercise good judgement and leadership, to fully recognize his/her leadership abilities and limitations, and d) Demonstrate a basic standard of outdoor knowledge and experience based on the WEA 18 point curriculum (WEA, 1989, p. 5).

These competencies are taught as part of the National Standard Program. The Association for Experiential Education (AEE) possesses similar standards (Priest and Dixon, 1990). Those adhering to these standards would also need to possess the requisite skills to be an accomplished outdoor leader. It should be mentioned, however, that AEE is an organization that does not officially certify or license individuals. Rather, it is an organization for those who, on a voluntary basis, are interested in maintaining safe, environmentally conscious education for outdoor leaders. Additionally, outdoor leaders trained by NOLS, Outward Bound, and some of the other schools would also be well trained. Secondly, in addition to wilderness leaders, there is a need for wilderness therapists. These individuals should have mental health training and experience in providing therapy to individuals with emotional (i.e., psychiatrically diagnosable) disorders. In some cases, the wilderness therapist might also be the wilderness leader. However, this is not necessarily so, and probably represents the exception rather than the rule.

Most, if not all, states and provinces regulate the practice of mental health professions to the point of determining the qualifications required for independent or supervised practice. If program participants are in one location where it is possible for a licensed therapist to provide direct supervision (e.g., to be able to observe a group session), it would seem reasonable to allow less trained staff to provide the counseling. In our view, a licensed, Master's level professional should provide the supervision, or directly provide the counseling (Berman & Davis-Berman, 1992).

When programs include wilderness expeditions of any kind, we believe that the presence of a licensed professional is even more imperative, as the isolation of an expedition makes outside response to a psychiatric emergency extremely difficult (Berman & Davis-Berman, 1992). Our own experiences leading trips with adolescents from juvenile court, inpatient psychiatric hospitals, residential programs, protective services, and outpatient counseling have made us very aware of the mental health problems and opportunities that arise when you are on a trail miles from the nearest road. Examples include knowing how to handle crises, like an adolescent who talks of suicide or has a dissociative reaction. We would assert that only well trained, fully licensed mental health professionals deal with these types of issues and situations.

Interestingly, our survey suggested that programs are not utilizing independently licensed professionals in the implementation of their programs. A little over half of those surveyed said that Master's degreed personnel were part of their programs; however, many of these individuals served as supervisors. When exploring further, we discovered that this supervision did not always follow our recommendation of being direct and on-site, but rather, supervisors were often hundreds of miles away in offices or base camps reviewing case records. As a result, the majority of those working directly with troubled clients had Bachelor's degrees or no degrees, supported by the fact that almost half of the programs did not require a completed degree of any kind as a condition of employment (Davis-Berman, Berman & Capone, 1992).

Finally, in addition to wilderness leaders and therapists, there is often a need for ancillary, supportive staff. These individuals consist of specialists who are needed to provide technical training for activities like rappelling or spelunking. These staff also can serve special needs, such as medical and substance abuse counseling needs.

Thus far, we have suggested that the entire field of therapeutic outdoor programming is in the midst of a redefinition. The number of operating programs has quickly grown and the diversity of program offerings has increased. Logically, with such growth comes the emergence of critical issues and discussion which will begin to shape and refine the field. The professionalization of therapeutic wilderness programs has begun, with organizations like the AEE and the WEA calling for guidelines, standards and general accountability. Other pressure towards increased professionalization comes from some in mental health who insist on professional credentials and standards in the provision of mental health services.

These positions have not been taken without challenge, however. In fact, those from the outdoor and adventure education models sometimes oppose such professionalization. Logically, these differences of opinion within the field translate into debate on the basic definitions of therapeutic and therapy, and the qualifications of the staff needed to deliver the mental health services in the program. We have taken the strong position in favor of increased professionalization of programs-especially mental health oriented programs. Although we have not specifically discussed substance abuse and delinquency programs, we also strongly support their professionalization.

When examining these programs, it becomes clear that in the majority of cases, the participants have either been given a psychiatric diagnosis, or have been labeled as troubled, behavior disordered or very high risk. With this background and our perspective in mind, the remainder of this chapter identifies and discusses critical issues in the field of therapeutic wilderness programming.

Critical Issues and Emerging Trends

We have briefly mentioned the dual roots of therapeutic programs, namely the outdoor adventure and mental health traditions. As a result of this history, there tends to be a great deal of fragmentation in the field, and a lack of understanding and empathy for the "other camp's" position. It is clear that this fragmentation will continue, and will probably grow unless there are increased efforts to address the unique combination of outdoor adventure pursuits and counseling. This new relationship between the mental health orientation toward therapy and the experiential education perspective on adventure-based programs appears to be in the making, and represents an exciting possibility.

One manifestation of this combination could be the cross-training of outdoor education professionals. At this point, it is easier for mental health professionals to be trained in outdoor education by enrolling in courses through Outward Bound, NOLS or similar programs. Aspiring wilderness leaders might also receive training through the WEA certification programs.

There seem to be fewer opportunities for cross-training for those in the field of outdoor education, perhaps because of the educational and training requirements usually associated with the field of mental health counseling. The reader will remember our references to the Master's degree as being the lowest acceptable professional mental health degree. One apparent exception is the field of therapeutic recreation (McGowan, 1992). There is now certification as a therapeutic recreation specialist available from the National Council on Therapeutic Recreation.

In support of this interest in "blending our roots," some of the national outdoor education organizations have begun exploring and further discussing the topic of wilderness therapy. The WEA has published two articles on wilderness therapy in the past 18 months, and has recently called for discussion on wilderness therapy. Additionally, this organization included discussions on this topic at its 1993 National Conference (Berman, 1990; McGowan, 1992). In much the same way, the AEE has continued to dialogue on these issues, and has considered articles and proposals for its annual meeting on wilderness therapy.

If the first approach to arriving at a blending of outdoor education and therapy is through professional cross-training, the second is through the process of regulation. As we have briefly discussed, the issue of regulation has been debated for a number of years (e.g., Ford and Blanchard, 1985), and it appears that it will take center stage in the next few years. Of course, regulation can and does come from a number of different sources. In the field of therapeutic wilderness programming, calls for regulation of some sort seem to be coming from within the profession itself, and from governmental agencies. No doubt the governmental interest is related to allegations of maltreatment of youth in some residential wilderness programs and the deaths of two adolescents in Utah based programs (Matthews, 1991).

Historically, the debate appears to be between those who favor leader certification and those who would rather see program accreditation. A comprehensive study recently asked members of AEE a number of questions regarding their preferences for certification or accreditation. Respondents generally seemed to favor certification and accreditation, with a preference for program accreditation over certification. The difficulty in assessing the "meta skills" was cited as a significant problem in leader certification. Respondents also pointed to the difficulty in assessing staff qualities and competence when asked about their feelings about program accreditation (Bassin, Breault, Fleming, Foell, Neufeld, & Priest, 1992). This study seems to support our call for the rigid adherence to high standards for staff. If staff competency is so difficult to assess in wilderness programs, by requiring a Masters level licensed professional, one is at least assured that the staff person has completed a certain amount of training and formal instruction in therapy, human development, and human behavior.

This study also supports the professionalization of the field in that it suggests that those in the field desire to become more professional. Respondents identified maintaining professional standards, improving public attitudes toward risk activities, and reducing accidents as the three most important influences that leader certification would have on the field (Bassin, Breault, Fleming, Foell, Neufeld, & Priest, 1992, p. 24).

In addition to conducting research to assess the attitudes of its members toward program accreditation and credentialing, the AEE has been examining the issue of the peer review of programs quite extensively. To the present time, some 250 individuals have been included in a peer review directory, and AEE has established a National Task Force on Accreditation. The intent of this kind of review and accreditation process is the improvement and assurance of the continuation of program quality. Importantly, according to AEE, this process is completely voluntary at the present time (AEE, 1992).

It is beyond the scope of this volume, and it is certainly not our intent to comprehensively discuss certification and accreditation issues. We do, however, recognize the importance of the debate over these issues and the research that has been done in this area. As such, we refer the reader to a chapter by David Cockrell (1990). In his work in this volume, Cockrell elegantly presents the history, current debates, and research surrounding outdoor leadership certification.

The examination and accreditation of therapeutic wilderness programs has also been considered by the Council on Accreditation of Services for Families and Children (COA). The COA currently accredits over 500 agencies, providing dozens of specialized services ranging from adoption to protective services, day care for the aging, substance abuse services, and residential treatment programs (COA, 1992). Most recently, this organization began to examine some therapeutic wilderness programs, since it seemed apparent that many of these programs were, in fact, residential in nature. However, they did not fit the traditional model of most residential programs; thus existing accreditation standards were difficult to apply.

One of the first steps in writing standards was the development of a task force whose charge was to draft standards for the accreditation of residentially oriented wilderness programs. When this task force first met, it was realized that AEE was also actively working on the development of accreditation standards. Since AEE has the expertise on technical and safety issues, talk of a partnership between AEE and COA ensued, and at the time of this writing, this partnership, though not formal, exists.

The COA task force has drafted standards, with sections on admission criteria, personnel, group size, client rights, opportunities for growth and learning, and health and safety being included. Of particular interest to this discussion are the sections that might clarify the critical issues raised earlier, especially with regard to definitions of the field, and with the provision of services.

As we have discussed throughout this book, and in this chapter in specific, the parameters of the field of therapeutic wilderness programming are extremely difficult to define and clarify. It appears that this difficulty was also shared by the COA task force. While some COA specialized service areas are clearly marked by their titles, like "resettlement service" or "credit counseling service," the second draft of the task force listed the outdoor program as "Therapeutic Residential Wilderness Camping Programs/Adventure-Based Therapeutic Outdoor Programs" (COA, 1992, p. 1). Following this rather ambiguous title, the beginning of the document was intended to clarify the field, and presented the definition of outdoor programs as attempting:

> To provide therapeutic outdoor physical, environmental education, athletic, or other challenging activities, which involve physical and psychological challenges and which are designed to stimulate competence and personal growth, to expand individual capabilities, to develop self-confidence and insight, and to improve interpersonal skills and relationships (COA, 1992, p. 1).

Clearly, if we are to move toward implementing the examination and eventual accreditation of programs, the actual definition of the program must become more precise.

At the time of this writing, the task force had not finished with its work, yet a number of interesting issues had arisen. Full blown program accreditation is a very time-consuming process which is often quite expensive for the agency seeking such accreditation. Those who have completed this process report a time commitment of approximately two years, and thousands of dollars in agency time devoted to becoming accredited. Given these realities, one wonders if the accreditation process will only be open to the large financially healthy agencies.

Another interesting issue involves the staffing of these residential programs. Although they clearly target troubled, and often psychiatrically troubled adolescents, the emphasis on staff qualifications appears to be on outdoor experience, and in some cases, the attainment of a Bachelor's degree. In the draft of the accreditation standards, Master's degrees were not required for staff directly providing service to, and facilitating group counseling for troubled adolescents (COA, 1992, pp. 2-4). Based on our own orientation presented in this book, we take exception to these staff qualifications, and suggest that they be made more demanding. This is especially important given the fact that many of these residential programs do deal with very disturbed participants, and are often used as a substitute for psychiatric hospitalization.

Along with the issue of staff qualifications comes the provision of service. The draft standards do not provide any specificity on the type of counseling or therapy that must be provided in a good program. Debates reminding us of the early "therapeutic versus therapy" type have been and are still being heard.

Again, we believe that an accreditable program which serves high risk youth should provide therapy for all participants, conducted by Master's level licensed clinicians. This issue becomes even more salient when one considers insurance reimbursement. Although not a present reality, there is some speculation that accreditation will facilitate the process of insurance reimbursement for these residentially based therapeutic wilderness programs. If this is to occur, the treatment standards must be no less rigorous than what one would find in a hospital or other residential setting. These issues are beginning to be discussed and debated (e.g., Berman & Davis-Berman, 1992), and serve to provide for stimulating dialogue. The resolution of these issues is also critically important, as basic definitions, staff qualifications and service delivery models will actually determine the shape of the therapeutic programs of the future.

A final issue that we believe will continue to guide the development of therapeutic wilderness programs is the need for research, and the specific directions that research will move in the future. Throughout this book, we have discussed our interest in and commitment to well designed and implemented research studies. Much of our own work in the area of therapeutic wilderness programs has been and continues to be research based (e.g., Berman & Anton, 1988; Davis-Berman, & Berman, 1989; Davis-Berman, Berman & Capone, 1992). As people who are interested in program development and implementation, we know that all good programs are based in the scientific literature in one way or another, and we also know that all good programs are open to scientific evaluation. We look forward to discussion and the development and implementation of new research strategies.

This emphasis on evaluation is even more important when viewed in the context of increased professionalization and program accreditation. The COA general accreditation standards emphasized the importance of evaluation, and, in fact, required it for accreditation. This will be especially important if and when insurance reimbursement becomes more common. In order for insurance carriers to consider paying for wilderness programs as independent programs or as components of other programs, the effectiveness of these programs must be established through recognized research methods.

This type of recognition relates to the overriding issue of professionalism. Those who operate legitimate programs are always concerned with upholding high standards, and being differentiated from programs that have been identified as irresponsible (Matthews, 1991). They, of course, also have a vested interest in improving the reputation of therapeutic wilderness programs. One of the most effective ways to enhance this professional reputation is through the development of a body of literature which demonstrates the effectiveness of wilderness programs.

Finally, in addition to encouraging the field to engage in greater amounts of research, we must also advocate for increased specificity in research studies. For example, it seems that wilderness programs are currently operating utilizing a number of different outdoor modalities, and serving a wide variety of client types.

In our small study alone, we saw outdoor modalities ranging from the use of a ropes course to extensive backpacking and canoeing, with outdoor games, biking and horseback riding falling somewhere in between (Davis-Berman, Berman, & Capone, 1992). It is naive to think that outdoor experiences will be effective in reaching every type of client. More sophisticated research needs to be done which examines which outdoor modality is most effective with particular types of clients.

In this way, we can move away from damaging generalizations that suggest that simply being in the "wilderness" is therapy or is equally therapeutic for all. This direction has been discussed in a preliminary fashion in the literature (Ewert, 1991; Hazelworth & Wilson, 1990) and promises to be of significance in the years ahead.

This chapter has attempted to highlight some of the salient issues in the field of therapeutic wilderness programming. In this regard, we have discussed the increased professionalization of this field, and the often heated debates which occur on this issue. A component of professionalism is certainly the basic definition of the field itself. It is virtually impossible to forge ahead and develop and refine a professional identity without a clear vision and understanding of the nature of the field itself. However well intentioned, it appears that this is exactly what has happened in this field.

Programs are advertising, being examined for accreditation purposes, and are claiming to effectively raise self-esteem and reduce symptoms without the benefit of a well grounded, well designed and understood foundation. Questions such as: "What is therapy and what is therapeutic?" resound and cast aspersions on the professional nature of these programs. We have made some suggestions which contribute to our bias toward increased profes-sionalization, namely the provision of planned and deliberate therapy by those legally qualified to deliver such service. It is our contention that to ensure the continued success of wilderness programs, we could advocate for nothing less.

In this regard, we agree with our colleagues from the AEE and support the movement toward program accreditation. At the same time, we are wary that such efforts may exclude smaller, well designed programs. We believe that the dialogue on accreditation and the appropriate development of standards has just begun and will guide the development of this field in the years to come.

Finally, we end this chapter, and hence this book, with a few comments on research, specifically process and outcome evaluation. With issues of professionalization and accreditation gaining prominence, research has never been more vital. It is only through the conduct, publication and other dissemination of quality research that the professionalization of our field will become possible.

We hope that through this book we have demonstrated that we love the outdoors, especially the wilderness environment. We also believe (and have personally experienced) that the wilderness can be cleansing and can be a catalyst for change. Based on these underlying propositions, we support the development and implementation of therapeutic wilderness programs for troubled adolescents.

We approach this field from its "mental health" roots, and have advocated rather strongly for the provision of therapy by qualified professionals in all programs serving troubled youth. We are lucky to be involved in the growth and development of such a diverse and exciting field, and we look forward to dialoguing and debating these issues with our colleagues in the AEE and the WEA. If some of our positions are offensive to those of the "outdoor adventure" profession, we welcome debate and discussion, as we truly feel that the ideal state of wilderness therapy will occur when a true merger of these two "camps" begins.

The appendix of this book provides the reader with a listing of some representative outdoor programs throughout the country. After speaking and working with many wonderful people involved in wilderness programs, we were informed that such a compilation was desired. It is not all inclusive, and largely represents those on the AEE institutional membership roster who expressed interest in talking and working with us. We present this appendix to you in the hope that it will help to facilitate networking and will contribute to the further definition and growth of therapeutic wilderness programs for adolescents.

References

Adams, W. (1970). Survival training: Its effects on self-concept and selected personality factors of emotionally disturbed adolescents. (Doctoral Dissertation, University of Utah, 1969). *Dissertation Abstracts International, 31*, 388B.

American Psychiatric Association. (1987). *Diagnostic and Statistical Manual.* 3rd. ed., Revised. Washington, D.C: American Psychiatric Association.

American Psychological Association. (1987). *Diagnostic and statistical manual of mental disorders.* Washington DC: American Psychiatric Association.

Association for Experiential Education, (1992). *The AEE Horizon,* No. 7.

Bassin, Z., Breault, M., Fleming, J., Foell, S., Neufeld, J., & Priest, S. (1992). AEE organizational membership preference for program accreditation. *The Journal of Experiential Education, 15,* (1), 21-26.

Berman, D. (1990). Wilderness therapy: Conceptual and training issues. *WEA Legend,* Summer, 4-5.

Berman, D., & Anton, M. (1988). A wilderness therapy program as an alternative to adolescent psychiatric hospitalization. *Residential Treatment for Children and Youth, 5,* 39-52.

Berman, D., & Davis-Berman, J. (1992). Professionalizing wilderness therapy. Unpublished document.

Cockrell, D. (1990). Outdoor leadership certification. In J. Miles & S. Priest (Eds.), *Adventure Education* (pp. 251-262). State College, PA: Venture Publishing, Inc.

Cockrell, D., & Lupton, F. (1991). An introduction to the Wilderness Education Association. In D. Cockrell, (Ed.), *The wilderness educator: The wilderness education association curriculum guide* (pp. 1-11). Merrillville, IN: ICS Books.

Council on Accreditation for Services to Families and Youth, (1992). Draft of the standards from the wilderness therapy task force. Unpublished document.

Davis-Berman, J., & Berman, D. (1989). The wilderness therapy program: An empirical study of its effects with adolescents in an outpatient setting. *Journal of Contemporary Psychotherapy, 19,* (4), 271-281.

Davis-Berman, J., Berman, D., & Capone, L. (1992). Therapeutic wilderness programs: A national survey of mental health offerings. Unpublished document.

Ewert, A. (1989). *Outdoor adventure pursuits: Foundations, models, and theories.* Columbus, OH: Publishing Horizons.

Ewert, A. (1991). Revisiting the self-concept: A new twist on an old subject. *The Journal of Experiential Education, 14,* (1), 49.

Ford, P., & Blanchard, J. (1985). *Leadership and administration of outdoor pursuits.* State College, PA: Venture Publishing.

Hazelworth, M., & Wilson, B. (1990). The effects of an outdoor adventure camp experience on self-concept. *Journal of Environmental Education, 21,* (4), 33-37.

Jerstad, L., & Selzer, J. (1973). Adventure experiences as treatment for residential mental patients. *Therapeutic Recreation Journal, 1,* 8-11.

Kaplan, R. (1974). Some psychological benefits of an outdoor challenge program. *Environment and Behavior, 6,* 101-115.

Kazdin, A. (1991). Effectiveness of psychotherapy with children and adolescents. *Journal of Consulting and Clinical Psychology, 59,* 785-798.

Kistler, K., Bryant, P., & Tucker, G. (1977). Outward Bound: Providing a therapeutic experience for troubled adolescents. *Hospital and Community Psychiatry, 28* (11), 808-812.

Matthews, M. (1991). Wilderness programs offer promising alternative for some youth: More regulation likely. *Youth Law News, 12,* (6), 12-15.

McGowan, M. (1992). The challenge of wilderness therapy. *WEA Legend,* Winter, 3.

Priest, S., & Dixon, T. (1990). *Safety practices in adventure programming.* Boulder, CO: AEE.

Wilderness Education Association (1989). *The WEA affiliate handbook.* Lake Saranac, NY: The Wilderness Education Association.

Program Resources

This chapter lists and briefly describes a number of wilderness programs operating throughout the United States. As detailed in Chapter 5, the majority of the programs listed replied to a survey we sent to institutional members of the Association for Experiential Education. We have also added others, however, who were not included in this roster.

Those who are interested more in the "professionalization" or training types of outdoor programs are referred to Ewert's (1989) resource listing. He focuses on training opportunities and university programs in far greater depth than we do in this listing. Our resource listing, rather, is designed to assist program administrators and staff in identifying similar programs, and to facilitate communication and cooperation between programs.

To increase the usefulness of this listing as a resource for programs, we decided to place each program into one of five of the following categories:

∇   Mental Health Programs
∇   Enrichment Programs
        Leadership, Personal Growth, and Training
        Executive Programs
        University-Related Programs
∇   Court Programs
∇   School Programs
∇   Health Programs

The reader will recognize that these categories were also used to present the varieties of programs in Chapter 6. Many of the programs we examined easily qualify for inclusion in more than one category. For instance, there may be considerable overlap in mental health and court-related programs. We decided, however, to the best of our ability, to place each program into only one category based on its primary emphasis.

Once again, we want to reiterate that this resource listing is not comprehensive. However, it does represent a compilation of varied, interesting programs committed to the use of outdoor experience in their approach to working with people of various ages and levels of functioning. It is our hope that programs will continue to contact us, so that we might update this resources chapter on an ongoing basis.

We can be reached at:

1698 Forestdale Avenue
Dayton, OH 45432
(513) 426-2079
(513) 426-0211 (fax)

▽ **Mental Health Programs** ▽

Adolescent Behavioral Change
SUWS, Inc.
P.O. Box 171
Redmond, WA 98073
206-881-7173
    A private wilderness program which takes adolescents who have "oppositional attitudes," motivational problems, drug or alcohol dependency, or who resist treatment for such dependency, and requires them to live in the back country with minimal equipment for 21 days. ABC uses a neurolinguistic approach and often works with private therapists in order to "crack through" and make patients more receptive to the therapeutic process.

Adventure/Discovery, Inc.
319 N. Humphreys
Flagstaff, AZ 86001
602-774-1926
    A private non-profit organization which offers therapy to youth referred by the Department of Corrections or Children's Services. Students work on a forestry service conservation crew, live in a forest service station-made-lodge, and take periodic eight-day trips into the back country.

Appalachian Mountain Teen Project
P.O. Box 1597
Wolfeboro, NH 03894
603-569-2705
    Provides wilderness trips for at-risk youth ranging in length from 1-30 days, involving cross-country travel, hosteling, and a variety of outdoor recreational skills. All trips involve adventure, community service, and cross-cultural experience. Staff try to provide an environment conducive to bonding and disclosure between students, many of whom come from poor or abusive families, and encourage students to lean on one another for emotional support rather than offering traditional "counseling."

Austin Child Guidance Center
810 West 45th St.
Austin, TX 78751
512-451-2242

Provides educational assistance, therapy, and psychiatric evaluation to children and the families of children suffering from emotional problems, difficulties in family communication, or the aftermath of abuse. A ropes/challenge course at the center assists participants as well as community organizations and private groups in the acquisition of cooperative skills, enhancement of self esteem, and goal setting.

Austin Wilderness Counseling Services
1300 West Lynn St., Suite 200
Austin, TX 78703
512-472-2927

Offers group counseling and in-school counseling for at-risk youth at all grade levels, as well as parenting courses for parents. Activities include visits to parks and preserves in the Austin area, hiking, and group initiative exercises.

Beech Hill/Outward Bound
P.O. Box 254
Dublin, N.H. 03444
800-438-0200

A joint venture between Beech Hill Hospital and Hurricane Island Outward Bound. This chemical dependency program is approximately one month long, with an aftercare component. This program involves wilderness living and multi-element outdoor experience.

Catherine Freer Survival School
1230 Pulver Lane NW
Albany, Oregon 97321
503-967-8722

Students with emotional or behavioral difficulties spend 21 days in the mountains of the Northwest or the desert, building their own shelters, cooking their own food, backpacking, and engaging in individual therapy with trained counselors. The course involves a 3 day solo component. Staff prefer to work with clients from intact families and use a family systems approach, although clients with drug or alcohol problems use the 12-step model.

Centennial Peaks Hospital
2255 South 88th St.
Louisville, Co 80027
800-842-HOPE

A private psychiatric hospital using ropes courses with all patients in order to symbolize issues or group dynamics of relevance to the individual client. The hospital also offers ropes courses to community or corporate management groups, as well as a program for high-risk youth in high schools.

Childrens Square USA
North 6th St. and Avenue E
P.O. Box 8-C
Council Bluffs, IA 51502-3008
712-322-3700

A private organization offering a wide range of services such as emergency shelters for children, a therapeutic foster care program, daycare and afterschool activities for children in protective custody, and family counseling. Childrens Square also operates a residential facility for extremely behaviorally disturbed children, usually with a history of psychiatric placements or legal problems, which uses ropes and other experiential techniques as part of its therapy programming.

Circle S Recovery Ranch
12000 Sunitsch Canyon Road
Leavenworth, WA 98826
1-800-544-1668

A 20-bed residential chemical dependency treatment program for young men between the ages of 14 and 24, which uses meditation, wilderness expeditions, and ropes courses as techniques in conjunction with a strong twelve-step therapeutic process. Wilderness trips are usually 16 days in length and allow the participants to explore the direct consequences of actions, to engage in reflection, and to learn problem solving skills.

Eagle Mountain Outpost Ranch School
P.O. Box 1506
Sandpoint, ID 83864-0867
208-263-3447

An accredited residential Special Purpose School for adolescent boys experiencing academic difficulties, family problems, and low self-esteem. Outdoor adventure activities are designed to promote a feeling of accomplishment, to help participants identify personal therapeutic issues, and to learn to cope more effectively using the wilderness as a model for everyday life. Adventure activities include skiing, rock-climbing, and horseback riding.

Eagleville Hospital—Adventure Based Therapy
100 Eagleville Road
Eagleville, PA 19408
215-539-6000

Eagleville Hospital is the only facility in Pennsylvania to specialize entirely in drug and alcohol dependency treatment. Eagleville uses Project Adventure's model for metaphor therapy with low ropes courses, in conjunction with the 12-step model of addiction treatment.

Elmcrest Therapeutic Adventure Program
25 Marlborough St.
Portland, CT 06480
203-342-0480

A private hospital specializing primarily in inpatient care for children, adolescents, and chemically dependent adolescents. Patients and often their families participate in ropes activities with a metaphor therapy focus.

Escape to Reality
Experiential Therapists, Inc.
P.O. Box 55821
Houston, TX 77255-5821
713-467-9751

Escape to Reality is a training facility instructing therapists in the development and implementation of outdoor therapeutic modalities. This program serves mental health facilities nationwide and offers services to diverse patient groups.

Exodus
241 High St.
New Wilmington, PA 16142
412-946-2838

An indoor experiential education facility which provides activities designed to address relationship and behavior qualities in individuals, families, and groups. Exodus offers ground-level cooperative group activities, low initiatives activities, and high ropes individual and group initiatives for a variety of purposes, including behavior assessment, educational therapy, educational counseling, and recreation or adventure.

Florida Sherriffs' Youth Ranches—Caruth Camp
Boys Ranch, Florida 32060
904-842-5501

A residential program for at-risk youth. While most students live in ranch-type group homes, a wilderness camp has been established for the most difficult students. Residents live in cabins, participate in a wide variety of outdoor activities including long-term treks into back country, and learn academic subjects in a practical, task-oriented context.

Girls' Adventure Trails
3626 Cole Ave.
Dallas, TX 75204
214-522-9200

A prevention and early-intervention program for at-risk girls referred by schools, churches, and agencies. Girls' Adventure Trails places a strong emphasis on family therapy. The clients undertake an 8-day wilderness trip during the course of an 8-week group family therapy program. Families engage in a shorter camping trip together, and family counseling continues for up to five months after the completion of this primary phase.

Glenwood Mental Health Services, Inc.
150 Glenwood Lane
Birmingham, Alabama 35242
205-969-2880

A private treatment program for emotionally disturbed youth which operates a year-round therapeutic wilderness camp for adolescent boys as an alternative to residential placement. Academic classwork and both individual and group counseling are important components of treatment. The wilderness setting provides a context in which to learn individual and group responsibility and to increase self-esteem.

The Green Mountain Wilderness Foundation
P.O. Box 125
Waitsfield, VT 05673
802-496-5300

Offers an intensive wilderness survival experience for drug-and-alcohol-dependent adolescents. Students develop greater self-esteem and a sense of community interdependence as a result of living with natural rather than social limitations. Therapy is based on the 12-step model.

Griffith Center
P.O. Box 95
Larkspur, CO 80118
303-681-2400

A private residential ranch, housing male youth with behavioral and social problems. Students stay with Griffith Center for 1-3 years, hiking for up to a month at a time and participating in individual and group therapy.

Heights Psychiatric Hospital—Stepping Out Program
103 Hospital Loop NE
Albuquerque, NM 87109
505-883-8777

A private hospital which includes ropes courses and short hiking expeditions as part of the normal course of treatment. Heights also offers ropes courses to local agencies, outpatients, business groups, and schools.

Hope Center
4115 Yoakum
Houston, TX 77006
713-526-4673

Offers residential programs for adolescents engaged in social or family conflict or substance abuse, as well as victims of abuse or neglect. Residents live in outdoor camps, sharing living responsibilities, engaging in group, individual, and family therapy, and attending a year-round academic program. In addition, Hope Center operates an Alternative School, serving emotionally handicapped youth from the greater Houston area.

Hurricane Island Outward Bound
Rt. 2, Box 237-E
Yulee, FL 32097
904-261-4021

Operates six programs which provide wilderness experiences to youth at-risk as well as to members of the general population. One program offers 30-day expeditions for troubled adolescents and another is conducted primarily on-site at a state residential facility for delinquent males.

Inner Harbour Psychiatric Hospitals, Ltd.
4685 Dorsett Shoals Road
Douglasville, GA 30135
800-255-8657

Inner Harbour operates three hospitals (two in Georgia and one in Florida) specializing in the care of emotionally troubled adolescents. After an initial closed-unit observation period, clients participate in a series of adventure learning modules, live in cabins, and take responsibility for many everyday living needs. Activities include camping, horseback riding, group initiatives, and a sailing course leading to certification.

Inward Bound
Windsor Psychiatric Hospital
115 E. Summit St.
Chagrin Falls, Ohio 44022
800-542-5432

A facility serving adolescents and adults suffering from depression, eating disorders, behavior problems, or recovering from abuse. Ropes experiences and initiatives games are integrated twice weekly into the therapy in order to increase trust and self-esteem. Windsor also offers ropes courses to corporate groups and holds workshops frequently in the city school system.

Interventions
5701 South Wood St.
Chicago, IL 60636
312-737-4600

An extensive network of mental health and chemical dependency programs located in Wisconsin, Illinois, and Indiana, integrating all types of outdoor recreation and wilderness experiences into the recovery process. Length of participation ranges from 1-6 months, during which clients undertake 5 or 6 two-week trips throughout the US.

John de la Howe School
Route 1, Box 154
McCormick, SC 29835
803-391-2131

A state-supported boarding school for emotionally handicapped youth experiencing minor legal problems, abuse, or academic difficulty. Students build their own dwellings and are responsible for maintenance as well as meal planning and preparation on weekends. Counseling emphasizes the role of peer pressure in forming a socially functional identity.

Life Adventure Camp
1122 Oak Hill Drive
Lexington, KY 40505
606-252-4733

Provides five-day camping excursions for children and adolescents with emotional and behavioral problems; a day camp for children 8-10, and a more advanced camping experience involving backpacking and training in wilderness living skills for adolescents 10-18. Close-knit living situations give students an opportunity to develop cooperative skills, self-esteem, problem-solving abilities, and respect for the natural environment.

Life Development Center
8560 Kingston Pike, Suite D201
Knoxville, TN 37919
615-693-9672

Coordinates adventure programs involving ropes, group initiatives, caving, rock climbing, and rafting for agencies in East Tennessee who contract with the state for alcohol and drug rehabilitation. Courses can be designed for both agency clientele and staff, not only to assist in emotional growth and the overcoming of addiction but also to establish more productive working relationships within the agency structure itself.

Long Lane School Youth Challenge
Box 882
Middletown, CT 06457-0882
203-344-2811

Includes a variety of outdoor programs geared toward at-risk youth. The program utilizes a number of outdoor modalities to facilitate the development of responsible and socially acceptable behaviors in youth.

Looking Up
P.O. Box K
Augusta, Maine 04332-0470
207-626-3402

Counseling program to rebuild self-esteem and a sense of agency in male and female non-offending victims and survivors of incest of all ages. Programming options include retreats and workshops as well as wilderness trips of varying lengths, undertaken in a variety of locations.

New Dominion School, Inc.
P.O. Box 540
Dillwyn, VA 23936
804-983-2051

Year-round residential camp for male youth with emotional problems who experience school failure but have average or better intellectual ability. Students build their own shelters and plan meals, learning to live creatively within limited resources. Programming features small class size and daily group counseling to build self-esteem and trust.

New Life Treatment Center Wilderness Program
570 Glenneyre, Suite 107
Laguna Beach, CA 92651
800-332-TEEN

A private Christian organization offering mental health treatment to the disabled, depressed, youth-at-risk, abused persons, and persons with drug and alcohol dependencies. This program uses the staff and services of Summit Adventure, a wilderness "management" organization which coordinates trips for client agencies. The program, which lasts for 21 days, uses a version of the 12-step model with a scriptural emphasis, and focuses on improving its clients' self-esteem.

Northwest Passage
Box 349
Webster, WI 54893
715-866-8301

A residential treatment center providing intensive individual counseling, special education and personalized therapeutic services for male delinquents. Participants are referred by school and social service agencies and undertake vocational training as well as academic classes. The Ventures Program, which offers ropes courses and canoeing and backpacking stress-challenge experiences, is a standard part of every resident's program and teaches interpersonal and practical skills.

The Oaks
1407 W. Stassney Lane
Austin, TX 70745
512-444-9561

A long-term psychiatric facility serving adolescents, which uses experiential education as part of the normal treatment process. The Oaks periodically engages patients in outdoor activities such as hiking, fishing, rock climbing, and rappelling, although the primary emphasis is on weekly ropes experiences. Therapy sessions for groups and families are also available on the ropes course.

On Belay Youth and Family Services, Inc.
1902 East Washington Ave.
Madison, WI 53703
608-241-1214

A private organization offering therapeutic and recreational programming for youth referred by city agencies, usually in connection with minor legal problems or family conflicts. Although some clients are in transition from shelters to home, most live with their parents. The program lasts for 6-9 months and involves weekly recreational activities around town, including a nine-week experiential education program during the summer.

Pressley Ridge School
Box 25, Rd. #1
Ohiopyle, PA 15470
412-329-8300

A school for boys with emotional and conduct problems which uses an experiential approach to education. Boys live on-campus in tents or cabins and take numerous short trips into the back country to practice outdoor skills and explore strengths and weaknesses. Students plan their own trips and are encouraged to put their experiences into words through the writing of letters and book reports.

Project Adventure—Challenge Program
P.O. Box 100
Hamilton, MA 01936
508-468-7981

Trains educators, mental health professionals, and various educational leaders to administer adventure programs within their own agencies. Courses are taught on-site and focus primarily on the use of ropes; students are shown how to provide experiences which can convince clients that they are more physically or emotionally capable than they had ever before believed.

Raven's Way
Southeast Alaska Regional Health Corporation
Sitka, AL 99835
800-478-2451

A 60-day alcohol and drug treatment program which involves ropes activities and a three-week wilderness experience. Students live communally in a large farmhouse and learn independent living and cooperative skills.

Salesmanship Club Therapeutic Camps
Route 1, Box 305
Hawkins, Texas 75765
214-948-1818

A boys' camp and girls' camp each provide residential, therapeutic programs for younger adolescents in a wilderness camp setting. Students build and rebuild their own shelters and learn basic living skills. The programming, which usually extends for six to nine months, includes group and family counseling, three hours of for-credit academic classwork per day, and extended camping and backpacking trips.

Seneca
P.O. Box 971
Orem, Utah, 84059
801-226-0090

Two-month survival experience for rebellious adolescents involves seven day camp and "solo" week, as well as instruction in mountaineering skills and wildlife studies. Staff include ex-military personnel, paramedics, and Native Americans who teach "primitive ways".

S.O.A.R. (Special Outdoor Adventure Resources)
Warren Township Youth Services
17801 West Washington St.
Gurnee, IL 60031-2598
708-244-1105

Engages youth in activities such as rock climbing, backpacking, caving, canoeing, and white-water rafting in order to build feelings of self-esteem and confidence. Group process and counseling are an important part of the program.

The St. Francis Academy Passport to Adventure Program
509 East Elm St.
P.O. Box 1340
Salina, KS 67402-1340
800-423-1342

A program for 4th, 5th, and 6th grade children considered "at-risk" by teachers or counselors, consisting of 3 two-week camping trips with a week between for the child to visit home. On the first trip, students learn to live in tents, cook their own food, and participate in group initiatives. During later trips, students undertake extensive backpacking or canoeing experiences. Staff follow-up on each student with a visit to the parents and school personnel.

St. Helena Hospital—Challenge Course Program
Deer Park, California 94576
707-963-6553

A low ropes course serving inpatients of St. Helena Hospital, business groups, and local agencies. Treatment uses a structural family therapy model, and encourages the client to use ropes experiences to represent the family dynamics encountered in real-life.

Summit Quest
P.O. Box 50567
Provo, Utah 84605
801-489-5119

Nine-week residential inpatient wilderness program for self-destructive or defiant adolescents provides intensive individual counseling and group therapy, with an emphasis on instilling traditional values and personal responsibility. The course includes an impact "boot camp" phase, a three-day solo experience, frontier living skills (hard labor) and a full ropes course.

Vista Youth and Family Center
Route 4, Box 230
Chickamauga, GA 30707
404-539-2228

A residential chemical dependency treatment program which uses individual and group therapy, training in living skills, and recreational therapy.

West Pines Psychiatric Hospital
3400 Lutheran Parkway
Wheat Ridge, CO 80033
303-239-4000

Offers the Discovery Program, a ropes and initiatives program for patients, school groups, families, and corporate teams. The primary goal of the Discovery Program is to place individuals in physically, intellectually, and emotionally demanding situations where skills of cooperation, problem-solving, goal-setting, and self-awareness are rapidly developed.

Wilderness Academy
P.O. Box 50148
Provo, Utah 84605
800-283-8334

8-week survival training for adolescents embroiled in family conflict; designed to build self-discipline, cooperative attitudes, and a sense of responsibility. Reality therapy takes adolescents out of self-destructive environments in order to face them with natural limits.

Wilderness Conquest Inc.
P.O. Box 12
Monticello, Utah 84535
208-522-1080

Takes youth with self-esteem problems, depression, or symptoms of withdrawal into the wilderness for 38 days. Once in the back country, there is no "control" placed on clients other than the requirements of survival. Counseling introduces the twelve-step model in order to provide a starting point for subsequent therapy.

Wilderness School
P.O. Box 298
East Hartland, CT 06027
203-566-4146

The Wilderness School was created as an alternative social services program for troubled youth. The School works closely with the referring agency and the family, and involves a 20-day wilderness trip. This program involves orientation and post-expedition counseling.

Wilderness Therapy Program
1698 Forestdale Ave.
Dayton, Ohio 45432
513-426-2079

A component of Lifespan Counseling Associates, the private counseling practice of Drs. Dene Berman and Jennifer Davis-Berman. The WTP provides troubled youth with intensive counseling in out-of-doors settings. Populations served have included adolescents from inpatient and outpatient settings, and juvenile court and Childrens' Services residential programs.

Woodside Trails
P.O. Box 999
Smithville, TX 78957
512-237-4602

A private agency serving the State of Texas Department of Human Services. Woodside Trails offers a residential treatment program to boys with a history of abuse, neglect, or conduct disorders. Students cut down trees to build their own shelters and participate in a variety of outdoor recreational activities.

Wilderness Treatment Centers
200 Hubbart Dam Road
Marion, Montana 59925
406-854-2832

Offers both drug and alcohol rehabilitation programs as well as professional renewal courses using a wilderness model. The drug and alcohol dependency program is aimed at men aged 14-24 years old, and lasts approximately 60 days. Patients spend 30 days in an inpatient setting, and then progress to a 16-21 day wilderness trip.

YMCA Juvenile Crisis Program
2859 El Cajon Blvd.
San Diego, CA 92104
619-284-0361

A program for families with youth who have run away from home or who experience serious difficulties with conflict resolution. Youth are given counseling and may spend up to two weeks in a foster home, and the reunited family receives intensive counseling in order to prevent further problems. The Outdoor Adventure Program is a drug abuse prevention program which involves youth in day trips, short camping trips, youth camps, and weekend family retreats.

∇ Enrichment Programs ∇

Leadership, Personal Growth, and Training Programs

Action Quest
P.O. Box 5507
Sarasota, FL 34277
813-924-6789

Summer programs in the British Virgin Islands and Leeward Islands provide men and women ages 13-19 with sailing and diving certification and leadership training. Participants from many countries live aboard sailing yachts for 2-6 weeks. Noncompetitive atmosphere is centered around hands-on shipsmanship and the development of group support skills.

Adventure Associates
P.O. Box 16304
Seattle, WA 98116
206-932-8352

Offers co-ed and men or women-only adventure expeditions and outdoor workshops in the United States and overseas. Experiences emphasize not only outdoor skills, but also self-understanding, ecological awareness, and an appreciation for cultural diversity.

Adventures Rolling Cross-Country, Inc.
P.O. Box 2337
Mill Valley, CA 94942
800-767-ARCC
415-381-1030

An adventure program for youth 13-18 years of age which coordinates 15-28 day expeditions to locations in the West. Students develop teamwork skills as well as an ability to handle various modes of transport/recreation such as kayaking, cycling, rafting, snorkeling and mountain climbing.

Adventureworks, Inc.
1300 Narrows of the Harpeth
Kingston Springs, TN 37082
615-297-2250

Offers initiatives and wilderness expeditions to individuals, groups, and corporate teams for the purpose of building trust, communication skills, personal empowerment, a sense of community, and the ability to take creative risks.

American Leadership Forum
1800 Grant Street, Suite 550
Denver, Colorado 80220
303-831-1010

This non-profit national organization is devoted to developing leadership skills and public responsibility in professionals and leaders from different fields. Each year, the program involves 20 community leaders in a 22-day program to develop skills in collaboration, consensus-building, and conflict resolution, to explore the nature of leadership, and to develop an understanding of ethical and political ideals. Participants undertake a six-day wilderness experience to teach risk-taking and vision, and later make a commitment to a community project.

Appalachian Mountain Club
Youth Opportunities Program
School Program
5 Joy Street
Boston, MA 02108
617-523-0636

Provides an opportunity for inner-city youth to explore mountain environments and develop an appreciation of the natural environment. The Youth Opportunities Program trains older youth, employed and school-age, to become youth leaders for wilderness expeditions.

Associates for Youth Development, Inc.
P.O. Box 36748
Tuscon, AZ 85740
602-292-9767

A national educational and technical assistance organization which seeks to foster a positive culture of youth work by developing the educational potential of communities. Workshops, books, and training materials are available.

Austin Young Men's Business League
P.O. Box 5702
Austin, TX 78763

Offers summer camp programs for at-risk children from low-income families in the greater Austin area. Camp experiences include swimming, hiking, nature walks, ropes courses, and responsibility-building exercises such as putting up tents and cooking meals. Programming stresses self-esteem, trust, and group building.

Baltimore (City of)
Carrie Murray Outdoor Education Campus
1901 Ridgetop Road
Baltimore, Maryland 21207
301-396-0808
Provides classes and programs in wildlife conservation and live animal study as well as group initiatives, climbing, and adventure activities for all age levels within the community. Programming makes optimal use of the variety of environments available and provides camps for children of all ages and maintains trails for hikers and naturalists.

Bear Mountain Outdoor School
Hightown, Virginia 24444
703-468-2700
Presents week-long and weekend programs involving the outdoors for individuals, families, and organized groups of all ages. Options include carpentry instruction, rural living skills, adventure programs and education in wildlife lore and ecology.

Bicycle Adventures
P.O. Box 7875
Olympia, Washington 98507
206-786-0989
Arranges 6-8 day bicycle tours of the Pacific Northwest for cyclists of varying strength and experience. Tours are designed to maximize scenic and environmental variety and beauty.

The Biking Expedition, Inc.
P.O. Box 547
Henniker, New Hampshire 03242
1-800-245-4649
Provides students with bicycling tours of various length and difficulty, giving them an opportunity to learn about themselves, develop self-sufficiency, and explore new places. Students camp and hostel, cook their own food, and provide for most basic living needs on the road, under the advising of two adult leaders trained in group dynamics management.

Birch Trail Camp for Girls
5146 N. Woodburn
Whitefish Bay, WI 53217
414-962-2548
(Summer) Minong, WI 54859
715-466-2216

Offers traditional camp experiences involving sports, crafts, and horseback riding in a non-competitive context for girls ages 8-15. All trips last at least three days, and more advanced campers can undertake extended expeditions involving minimal impact camping, canoeing, and kayaking.

Boys Town
Boys Town, Nebraska 68010
402-498-1111

This program provides recreational activities for the residents at Father Flanagan's campus. Although they are outdoor activities, they are not specifically wilderness-oriented in nature.

Michael H. Brown Counseling and Psychological Services
4889 Finlay St.
Richmond, VA 23231
804-222-0483

Coordinates and guides wilderness trips either as independent experiences or as part of ongoing counseling for the purpose of self-development. Programming attempts to increase self esteem, enhance communication skills, and develop latent strengths using a variety of conventional therapeutic techniques as well as artistic and spiritual practices.

Camp Broadstone
Appalachian State University
Rt. 4 Box 92
Banner Elk, NC 28604
704-262-3045

Coordinates seasonal programs using the out-of-doors as a context for developing group interaction skills and learning about ecology and natural environments. A special two-week Summer Enrichment Program is available for talented and gifted 4th-9th graders, enabling them to participate in adventure and nature education while living on-site.

Camp High Rocks
P.O. Box 127
Cedar Mountain, NC 28718
704-885-2153

Provides two, three, and four week camping experiences for boys of various ages, on 1100 acres of wooded mountain terrain. Boys live in cabins and engage in climbing, horseback riding, canoeing, and other on-site activities.

Camp Huston
P.O. Box 140
Gold Bar, WA 98125
206-793-0441

An outreach program of the Episcopal Diocese of Olympia, Camp Huston provides youth with short camping experiences with a Christian Community focus. Students are encouraged to think about their relationship with God and develop self-esteem in relation to the natural environment.

Camp Livingston
Jewish Community Center
1580 Summit Road
Cincinnati, Ohio 45237
513-761-7500

Provides camping experiences for Jewish children of all ages which involve a focus on Jewish heritage and culture in addition to the traditional camping activities. The camp has facilities for a full range of recreational activities and runs 4-8 week summer sessions.

Camp Rising Sun
The Louis August Jonas Foundation
2 Rhinebeck Savings Village Plaza
Rhinebeck, NY 12572
914-876-4331

Provides full scholarships to an eight-week summer camp experience for men and women ages 16-18. Students are chosen on the basis of character, intelligence, and leadership potential, and although the participants live in tents, the campsite includes opportunities for swimming and boating as well as libraries, computer facilities, and scheduled cultural events.

Challenge Sonoma Adventure Ropes Course

P.O. Box 12

Eldridge, CA 95431

707-938-6579

Provides ropes course experiences to professional development teams, individuals, and human service agencies serving the juvenile court system and schools.

Charlotte Outdoor Adventure Center

2601 E. 7th St.

Charlotte, NC 28204

704-334-4631

Provides teambuilding and personal development experiences to corporations, businesses, community programs, and family and youth services. Programs utilize ropes and challenge courses and focus on trust building, group cohesion, and problem solving skills.

Chesapeake Bay Foundation

162 Prince George St.

Annapolis, MD 21401

301-268-8816

A private conservation organization which operates programs in environmental education, environmental defense, and land conservancy. Provides training for environmental lawyers as well as 1-3 day programs for students interested in the ecology, economics, and politics of wetlands exploitation and conservation.

Christodora-Manice Education Center

666 Broadway—Suite 515

New York, NY 10012

212-529-6868

A small, residential educational facility located in the mountains of Massachusetts, which provides New York City youth with an opportunity to engage in adventure activities, environmental education, and leadership training. The goal of the Manice Center is to encourage minority participation and leadership in the conservation movement, especially among lower-income youth who are primarily familiar with urban environments.

Colorado Outward Bound School
945 Pennsylvania St.
Denver, Colorado 80203-3198
303-837-0880

Offers courses in outdoor living and recreational skills, using the variety of natural environments in the American West, Alaska, the Soviet Union, and Nepal. Special programs are available for youth, women, recovering alcoholics and addicts, and cancer patients, in addition to college credit courses in leadership development.

Deer Hill Summer Expeditions
P.O. Box 180
Mancos, CO 81328
303-533-7492

Offers youth the opportunity to undertake expeditions in the American Southwest with a focus on environmental awareness and the history of native peoples of the region. Participants engage in outdoor activities such as camping, rafting, backpacking, service and conservation work on reservations.

Eagle's Nest Camp
633 Summit Street
Winston-Salem, NC 27101
919-761-1040 (winter) 704-877-4349 (summer)

Provides traditional camping and wilderness experiences for boys and girls aged 7-17. Eagle's Nest tries to provide campers with a racially and culturally diverse experience which replaces sex-stereotypes and competition with friendship and equality.

Educo International
4817 North Country Road 29
Loveland, CO 80538
303-679-4294

A joint American/Canadian organization which provides youth with opportunities for experiential education regarding other countries and allows them to undertake educational expeditions throughout the world. Offers a Rite of Passage wilderness experience for young men ages 13-18 for purposes of inner growth, self-discovery, and reflection.

Farm and Wilderness Summer Camps
HCR 70 Box 27
Plymouth, VT 0506-7916
802-422-3761

A camping and educational association founded on Quaker principles which provides a variety of experiences for children and families. Children engage in farmwork, crafts, and outdoor recreation in an ecologically conscious community setting.

For the Love of Children
1711 Fourteenth St, NW
Washington, DC 20009
202-462-8686

Provides personal growth and summer programs for local youth. One of their programs focuses specifically on the development of leadership skills.

Forty Legends
Route 2, Box 836
Washington, MO 63090
314-239-6087

Provides 3-week camping experiences including horseback riding, woodworking and other craft skills, canoeing, and hiking. Forty Legends cultivates a large organic garden, raises small farm animals and teaches composting, in keeping with its attempt to develop and teach patterns of living that will lead to an ecologically sustainable lifestyle.

Four Winds, Inc.
2339 Copperfield Dr.
Santa Rosa, CA 95401
707-576-8022

Offers ropes courses, adventure experiences, and initiatives to educators, corporate teams, political organizations, and individuals or families. Programs specifically centering on awareness of mens' issues, women's spirituality, peer counseling education, and self-esteem enhancement and positive decision making for adolescents are available.

Foxfire Teacher Outreach
P.O. Box Box B
Rabun, GA 30568
404-746-5318

Trains high school teachers to use innovative techniques with students from low-income or other disadvantaged backgrounds in order to increase motivation and enhance the students' feeling of purpose and accomplishment in learning.

Genessee Valley Outdoor Learning Center
1700 Rayville Road
Parkton, MD 21120
301-343-0101

Provides outdoor programming for schools, teams of individuals seeking self-empowerment, and professional development teams. Activities include ropes, canoeing, fishing, and kayaking, environmental studies, and farm work experiences.

Girl Scout Council of the Nation's Capital
2233 Wisconsin Ave. NW
Washington, DC 20007
202-337-4300

Coordinates a variety of different camp programs with specialized themes as well as traditional camp experiences for girls of all ages. Summer day programs and 1-2 week resident camps are available.

Hoover Outdoor Education Center
11285A Fox Road
Yorkville, IL 60560
312-553-7361

This center is a barrier-free recreational facility for use by schools, residential centers, health and human services agencies, church groups, nursing homes, and a variety of other community organizations. Swimming, sports, nature study, camping, and programs emphasizing living skills and the ethnic heritage of the Fox Valley are available to all age groups.

Inner Quest, Inc.
220 Queen St., NW
Leesburg, VA 22075
703-478-1078

Provides adventure experiences for children of all ages. Leadership-building trips are available for older adolescents, as well as one-day trips, ropes and initiatives workshops, trips focusing on the development of a specific skills like kayaking or mountaineering, and an "Urban Quest" expedition.

Insight!
P.O. Box 12436
Portland, OR 97212
503-249-0688

Provides adventure based programs for personal and professional development, 1/2 to 5 days in length, for groups and/or individuals. Programs allow participants to view the direct results of decision making processes, to explore group dynamics and leadership techniques, and to develop a commitment to common goals based on appreciation of diversity.

Institute for Creative Living
3630 Fairmount Blvd.
Cleveland, Ohio 44118
216-932-3785

Offers ropes and initiatives courses, wilderness expeditions, urban explorations, and consultation services to individuals, schools, churches, agencies, and corporations. Provides people with the skills to engage in socially constructive and creative efforts in both their personal life and their work.

Interlocken
RR #2, Box 165
Hillsboro
Upper Village, New Hampshire 03244
603-478-3166

Coordinates experiential travel programs for children of all ages around the world. High-school age students can participate in community service projects in Kenya or Thailand. Also provides a traditional summer camp experience in New Hampshire for younger children from all countries.

Kent Mountain Adventure Center
PO Box 835
Estes Park, CO 80517
303-586-5990

Provides a variety of intensive wilderness experiences which teach primitive living skills and low-impact camping. Also offers adventure programs in wilderness settings for youth, which teach self-esteem, decision-making skills, and respect for the environment. Some specialized programs for the disabled or students with emotional problems are also available.

Kiwanis Camp Wyman
600 Kiwanis Drive
Eureka, MO 63025
314-938-5245

Provides experiential education programs including a summer camp for disadvantaged youth referred by agencies and schools. The summer camp attempts to intervene in the lives of at-risk youth, many from violent or poor families, in order to provide them with a respite from their everyday environment and to teach them conflict resolution, problem-solving, prejudice-reduction, and self-esteem skills.

Learning Forum
1725 South Hill St.
Oceanside, CA 92054
619-722-0072

Provides educational materials and training seminars in experiential and intensive education techniques. Learning Forum also sponsors Supercamp, a ten-day program designed to foster enthusiasm for learning and teach intensive study, learning, and communication skills.

Marimed Foundation
1050 Ala Moana Boulevard, Building D.
Honolulu, Hawaii 96814
808-537-5586

Owns and operates Tole Mour, a 156 foot square topsail schooner, Sailing School Vessel, and health and human services support ship for the Marshall Islands. This ship carries volunteer health professionals from Hawaii and among the Marshall Islands, enabling them to provide medical assistance to the largely poverty-stricken population. The Ocean Skills and Education Program for Youth gives Hawaiian and Marshallese youth an opportunity to assist health workers, learn sailing in a positive and socially useful environment.

Meet the Wilderness
P.O. Box 468
130 Stetson Drive
Edwards, Colorado 81632
303-926-2010

Sponsored by the Mission of Our Lady of Mercy in Chicago, this program gives youth from low-income areas in Chicago, as well as some students from Denver and Vail, an opportunity to explore personal growth in a wilderness setting.

Nantahala Outdoor Center
41 US Hwy 19 West
Bryson City, NC 28713
704-488-2175

Provides short training courses in outdoor and adventure skills, mostly on-site, with regularly scheduled trips to other parts of the country for advanced students. Activities include whitewater rafting, kayaking, and climbing.

National Indian Youth Leadership Development Project, Inc.
650 Vanden Bosch Parkway
Gallup, NM 87301
505-722-9176

Assists Native American communities nationwide with the development of curricula, teacher education, and organization of community service and learning programs. Summer camps and year-round programs are available for Native American youth in 6th through 8th grade, involving canoeing, camping, rappelling, ropes courses, and an emphasis on leadership skills and personal development.

National Outdoor Leadership School
P.O. Box AA
Lander, Wyoming 82520-0579
307-332-6973

Provides intensive 14, 30, and 75-day wilderness trips which train students in outdoor skills, environmental awareness, and leadership and judgement development. Programs are conducted in American national parks as well as in Kenya, Chile, and other locations around the world.

National Wildlife Federation
1400 16th St., NW
Washington, D.C. 20036-2266
800-432-6564

Provides camp experiences, leadership training programs, and educational "summits" for people of all ages. NWF offers workshops and materials to educators who wish to enhance their ability to teach students about nature or to use experiential techniques in their curricula.

National Youth Leadership Council
1910 W. County Road B
Roseville, MN 55113
800-366-6952

Promotes youth service and encourages the use of student-empowering educational techniques in schools. NYLC offers programs which train educators to use hands-on learning techniques which may be more suited to the needs of students than the lecture-test method.

Natural Bridge Learning Center
HC 62 Box 103
Natural Bridge Station, Virginia 24579-9411
703-291-2129

A campsite and recreation center built by youth under the direction of the Virginia Department of Youth and Family Services, offering day hikes, swimming, backpacking, canoeing, ropes courses, and some extended wilderness experiences to youth from around the state.

Nobles Day Camp
507 Bridge St.
Dedham, MA 02026-4198
617-326-3700

A day camp with programs for younger and older children, offering traditional recreational activities, as well as specialties like carpentry and education in Indian lore. Eighth graders can participate in additional activities such as spelunking and nature observation or fishing at the beach.

North Carolina Outward Bound School
121 N. Sterling St.
Morgantown, NC 28655-3443
704-437-6112

Offers backpacking and whitewater canoeing expeditions into the Blue Ridge and Smoky Mountains, as well as warm-weather trips into the Everglades and Big Cypress National Park in Florida. Programs are available for educators, social services professionals, women over 30, the hearing impaired, youth, executives, and older adults. NCOBS also provides training for professionals and volunteers in the field of experiential education.

On Belay
514 E. 40th St.
Austin, TX 78751
512-454-1746

Assists organizations in the construction and operation of ropes courses, trains ropes instructors, and teaches therapists and other educational or social service personnel how to integrate ropes courses into their own programming.

Outdoor Discoveries
P.O. Box 7687
Tacoma, WA 98407
206-759-6555

Offers expeditions to locations around the world, accessible to people with varying degrees of physical strength and outdoor experience, as well as family trips, adventure quests for teams of individuals, custom-designed expeditions for therapists and educators, and courses specializing in specific outdoor skills. Provides teambuilding and development workshops for public and private organizations and community groups of varying lengths.

Outdoor Leadership Training Seminar
P.O. Box 20281
Denver, CO 80220
800-331-7238

Provides self-development programs which emphasize leadership training and ecological consciousness through such activities as whitewater rafting, rockclimbing, and mountaineering. Many of the courses involve explorations of Native American spirituality as well as more traditional techniques of community building and communication development. Programs are available for corporate teams, individuals, or educators seeking specific training in outdoor skills.

Outward Bound, USA
384 Field Point Road
Greenwich, CT 06830
203-661-0797

Outward Bound is the oldest and largest adventure-based education program in the world. Courses focus on self-exploration and are designed to be accessible to all ages and to groups with varying interests, including Vietnam veterans, people with diabetes, cancer survivors, addiction recovery groups and women's empowerment teams. Programs involve sailing, canoeing, mountaineering, rafting, and skiing and are located throughout the United States.

Pacific Crest Outward Bound School
0110 SW Bancroft St.
Portland, OR 97201-4050
800-547-3312

Provides wilderness courses of various lengths to men and women ages 14 and older. Programs focus on the development of outdoor living skills, personal qualities such as resourcefulness and cooperative decision-making, and self-development, especially during the "solo" phase.

Paradigm Ventures
PO Box 6032
Santa Fe, NM 87502
505-988-1813

Offers personal and team development experiences using the wilderness as a context for risk-taking and creativity enhancement. One-day programs as well as extended trips are possible.

Pennsylvania Conservation Corps
Room 1304 Labor and Industry Building
Harrisburg, PA 17120
717-783-6385

Aims to develop participants' workplace skills, instill an ethic of citizenship, and accomplish significant conservation and historical work on projects of benefit to the public. Participants are between the ages of 18 and 25, with preference given to the economically disadvantaged.

Pine Ridge Adventure Center
1079 Williston Road
Williston, VT 05495
802-434-5294

Provides adventure experiences for individuals and business teams, as well as colleges, human service agencies, and schools. Programs can be tailored to the interests and abilities of the participants.

Pocono Environmental Education Center
Rd. 2, Box 1010
Dingmans Ferry, PA 18328
717-828-2319

Serves as an educational facility and research center for environmental studies. The Center has accomodations for weekend visits and frequently hosts environmental conferences in addition to its programming for the public.

Project S.O.A.R.
P.O. Box 388
Balsam, NC 28707
704-456-3435

An adventure-based program for students of average or above-average intelligence who have not succeeded academically due to learning disabilities, ADD, or a variety of factors. Participants are grouped by age and ability level, and emphasis is placed upon self-esteem and problem-solving skills. Expeditions travel to various sites throughout the US, and last from 12-27 days, although weekend adventures are also available.

Rock Eagle 4-H Center
Outdoor and Environmental Education Program
350 Rock Eagle Road, NW
Eatonton, GA 31024-9998
404-485-2831

Provides hands-on environmental education for elementary and middle school children throughout the school year. Rock Eagle has a residential facility, attempts to use the outdoors in teaching all educational subjects, and can tailor programs to the curriculum of client schools.

Roland and Associates, Inc.
67 Emerald St.
Keene, NH 03431
603-357-2181

Provides equipment and training services to mental health professionals or facilities interested in incorporating a challenge or adventure element into their regular programming. Offers seminars and workshops in safety and effective use of the new techniques.

The Seven Hills Schools
5400 Red Bank Road
Cincinnati, Ohio 45227-1198
513-271-9027

Coordinates one-day, weekend, and weeklong expeditions which enable young people to explore their own strengths and weaknesses through contact with the natural environment. Students develop an understanding of community through group effort.

Sierra Club Inner City Outings
730 Polk St.
San Francisco, CA 94109
415-776-2211
Trains volunteers in recreational and safety skills, so they can then act as leaders for back-country expeditions involving people from urban environments. In most cases, the volunteers make their expertise available to community agencies dealing with youth, seniors, or the physically disabled.

Solo
RFD 1, Box 163, Tasker Hill
Conway, NH 03818
603-447-6711
Provides wilderness and emergency medicine instruction to guides and personnel from mountain rescue teams and organizations such as Outward Bound and the National Audubon Society. Courses are taught by practicing paramedics and mountain rescue personnel.

Step Inc.
P.O. Box 1328
Lincoln St.
Williamsport, PA 17703-1328
717-326-0587
Offers on-site and back-country adventure experiences for both individuals and organizations. Weekends, bed-and-breakfast ski and bike tours, and "trial size" courses are also available.

Storer Camps YMCA
7260 South Stony Lake Road
Jackson, MI 49201
517-536-8607
Offers summer camps, including specialized camps for asthmatic children, wilderness trips, challenge courses, leadership training seminars for adolescents, and a variety of longer adventures focused on specific outdoor skills.

Three Oaks Adventure Center
P.O. Box 4881
Florence, SC 29502
803-665-9349

Offers 1/2 and 1-day ropes courses in conjunction with Circle Park Family Counseling and Addiction Services, as well as to individuals, school groups, and corporate teams.

Trailmark Outdoor Adventures
155 Schuyler Road
Nyack, NY 10960
800-229-0262

Enables teenagers to travel to the American Southwest, the Pacific Coast, Nova Scotia, and New England, take part in outdoor or adventure activities and sports suited to the region, and explore local scenery and life.

Tulare County Conservation Corps
120 North M St.
Tulare, CA 93275
209-685-0839

Offers valuable work experience to low income men and women between the ages of 18-23. Participants engage in public service, conservation, and emergency relief work. A similar program for high school students provides a two-week volunteer experience in Sequoia National Park.

Ultimate Adventures, Inc.
2853 Valley View Ave.
Salt Lake City, Utah 84117
801-278-5233

Operates ropes workshops for individuals and groups within the community, trains ropes staff, and assists in the design and construction of courses for outside agencies.

United Charities Camp Algonquin
1889 Cary Road
Algonquin, IL 60102
708-658-8212

Offers camp experiences for low-income families, children, teens, and senior citizens from the Chicago area. Participants live in cabins, and camp experiences include a variety of traditional activities. The camp seeks to provide family members with a retreat from the stresses of the urban environment and to promote communication and decision-making patterns.

Voyageur Outward Bound School
10900 Cedar Lake Road
Minnetonka, MN 55343
800-328-2943

Offers 15 and 22-day canoe expeditions into the Minnesota Boundary Waters and the White Otter Wilderness Region in Canada. The journey is intended to develop strength, confidence, and safety skills for people interested in outdoor adventure.

Washington Rock Girl Scout Council
201 Grove St. East
Westfield, NJ 07090
908-232-3236

Provides a range of year-round activities and camps for girls ages 5-17, helping them to develop character, sound values, confidence and self worth.

Wilderness Education Association
20 Winona Ave., Box 89
Saranac Lake, NY 12983
518-891-2915 EXT 254

The purpose of the WEA is to promote the professionalization of outdoor leadership and to thereby improve the safety and quality of outdoor trips and protect the lands which have been set aside for conservation and recreation purposes. Offers courses and certification in leadership and outdoor instruction, provides job referrals for professional outdoor positions, and has internship positions.

The Wilderness Institute
28118 Agoura Road
Agoura Hills, CA 93101
818-991-7327

Coordinates educational hikes which train participants in outdoor skills, safety and emergency medical techniques, and nature observation and appreciation.

Wilderness Southeast
711 Sandtown Road
Savannah, GA 31410
912-897-5108

Provides group trips to locations in the US and around the world for teens and adults. Trips involve specific outdoor/transport skills but focus intensely upon observation of natural surroundings and awareness of the region's cultural context.

Wolfcreek Wilderness School
Route 1, Box 1190
Blairsville, GA 30512
404-745-5553

Offers wilderness trips for adolescents, corporate training seminars, ropes and challenge experiences, and educational programs in outdoor safety and skills. Purpose is to provide non-traditional education which promotes an awareness of the link between humanity and nature.

Woodswomen
25 West Diamond Lake Road
Minneapolis, MN 55419
612-822-3809

Provides wilderness trips, leadership training, and confidence building experiences for women in eight countries and throughout the US. Some trips are specialized for women offenders, recovering victims of sexual abuse, and gay and lesbian young adults.

YMCA Camp Widjiwagan
Midway YMCA
1761 University Ave.
St. Paul, MN 55104
612-645-6605

Outfits wilderness travelers and offers camping, backpacking, canoeing, and kayaking expeditions within the Boundary Waters and the Great Lakes area.

YMCA of the Rockies
Snow Mountain Ranch
P.O. Box 169
Winter Park, CO 80482
303-887-2152
Estes Park Center
Estes Park, CO 80511-2550
303-586-3341

Offers a wide variety of summer and winter sports to members of the YMCA from around the country. Also has challenge courses for individual or team self-development and facilities for conferences and retreats.

Youth Service International
301 N. Blount St.
Raleigh, NC 27601-1007
Offers youth ages 17-25 the opportunity to participate in human service and environmental conservation expeditions in the US and in developing nations.

Executive Programs

Career Resources, Inc.
34 N. Main St., Suite 1245
Dayton, Ohio 45402
Offers consulting services to individuals who have suffered job displacement, persons seeking career changes, advancement, or better definition, and corporate teams interested in improving leadership and goal-setting skills.

Catalyst Consulting Team
P.O. Box 1389
Soquel, CA 95073
408-479-0222
Assists in the development and implementation of teamwork programs for business and industry. Ropes courses are the major outdoor modality.

Changeworks
Harmon, Kloth, and Associates
3440 Olentangy River Road
Suite 103
Columbus, Ohio 43202-1556
614-263-7093
Coordinates out-of-doors and ropes experiences for businesses and human service agencies.

Cheyenne Mountain Conference Resort
3225 Broadmoor Valley Road
Colorado Springs, CO 80906
1-800-428-8886
A conference center with guest accomodations and complete recreational facilities, including an 18-hole golf course and fitness center. Offers an Executive Team Challenge program involving ropes courses and initiatives.

Cornerstone
1014 N. Weber
Colorado Springs, CO 80903
719-634-1825

Offers experiential workshops for corporate teams, health care professionals, schools, youth at risk, and people recovering from emotional and/or physical addictions.

Corporate Adventure
P.O. Box 2723
Reston, VA 22090
703-471-7745

Provides customized team training programs and outdoor simulations.

Cradlerock Outdoor Network
Box 1431
Princeton, NJ 08542
609-924-2919

Offers outdoor programs for local schools, training for outdoor instructors, and a range of corporate enrichment activities. Several adventure programs are open to the public, including rock climbing, caving, and white water rafting.

Earthwalk
Kenneth Meyer, Ph.D.
227 Grove St.
Mt. Kisco, NY 10549
914-241-3506

Provides management training and team-building programs which develop group skills by placing participants in a wilderness environment and requiring them to find their way as a group with minimal orienteering equipment.

Executive Adventure, Inc
2030 Powers Ferry Road, Suite 444
Atlanta, GA 30339
404-955-0071

Uses experience based outdoor activities to reinforce the development of teamwork, leadership, and planning skills. Programs and activities can be tailored to group needs.

Executive Expeditions
131 Village Parkway, Suite 4
Marietta, GA 30067
404-951-2173

Specializes in the design and application of outdoor experience-based simulations which reflect the situations encountered by client corporate teams and develop the skills needed to succeed in those situations.

Millvale Plantation
Rembert, SC 29128
803-432-7129

A restored Southern plantation house offering conference facilities and guest quarters to corporate and managerial teams. Consulting services are available for needs assessment and skill building, as well as ropes courses and orienteering exercises.

Peak Performance
219 W. Colorado Ave., Suite 204
Colorado Springs, CO 80903
719-633-0804

Offers and assists in the engineering of innovative audience-participation workshops designed to enhance productivity and organizational effectiveness. Participatory educational techniques, ropes courses, and cliff scaling are some of the activity contexts.

Pecos River Learning Centers
1800 Old Pecos Trail
Santa Fe, NM 87501
505-989-9101

Offers management training programs to business enterprises of all sizes, involving experiential and wilderness components. The focus is on "changing the game;" training managers to create and to thrive in an atmosphere of continuous improvement, especially with an eye to effective competition in a multinational market.

Performance Dynamics Group
256 N. Sam Houston Parkway E., #135
Houston, TX 77060
713-820-6707

Offers experientially-based programs to corporate teams to develop such skills as accurate and creative personality assessment, leadership, strategic planning, and self-marketing. Ropes courses are available and some programs are geared specifically toward women professionals.

Renaissance Leadership
17 Cook Ave.
Madison, NJ 07940
201-966-1795
Offers corporate development programs with an experiential focus. Programs utilize golf, sailing, orienteering, rafting, mountaineering, and ropes to symbolize and address issues of communication, morale, and goal setting.

Vision Us, Inc.
Rt. 3, Box 265
Stillwater, OK 74074
Offers ropes and initiatives programs for individuals and teams to shape personal goals, find new sources of inner strength and capability, develop communication skills and cooperation, and enhance leadership.

Waterhouse Center
P.O. Box 953
Monroe, Washington 98272
206-794-0415
Offers team development programs tailored to the needs of the client organization. Participants undertake a variety of challenge exercises leading to a greater sense of self-esteem and faith in the positive power of group support and cooperation.

University-Related Programs

University of Alaska at Anchorage
3211 Providence Drive
Anchorage, Alaska 99508
907-786-1468
The Alaska Wilderness Studies program is the academic outdoor arm of the University of Alaska at Anchorage, teaching outdoor skills to students, citizens, and tourists. Courses are organized around weekend field sessions and are designed to be convenient for working adults.

Bemidji State University
Outdoor Program Center
Hobson Memorial Union
Bemidji, MN 56601
218-755-3764

Provides equipment and training to students and members of the general public interested in canoeing, backpacking, rock-climbing, and other outdoor activities. The Outdoor Program Center also runs summer programs for "youth at risk."

Berry College
Winshape Wilderness Education Centre
9 Berry College
Mount Berry, GA 30149
1-800-448-6955

Offers wilderness and adventure programs for corporations, schools, churches, hospitals, and colleges. Programs include rock climbing, ropes courses, backpacking trips, and white-water rafting.

Bloomsburg University—Quest
Corporate Institute
Simon Hall
Bloomsburg University
Bloomsburg, PA 17815
717-389-4323

Provides corporate team development programs designed to build communication skills and develop group dynamics which capitalize on individual strengths. Optional environments include rock and mountain climbing, sea kayaking, and shorter initiatives on-site at the Bloomsburg University campus.

Bradford Woods
5040 St. Road 67 North
Martinsville, IN 46151
812-855-0227

Indiana University's outdoor education, recreation, and leadership-training center, which provides summer camping, outdoor education for school-age children, and opportunities for leadership development and applied research.

College of DuPage Field Studies Program
Glen Ellyn, IL 60137
708-858-2800

Provides a variety of travel experiences throughout North America, including archeological education tours. A special Vision Quest program takes students into the Canadian wilderness to practice traditional Native American solo, fasting, and sweat lodge rituals.

Cornell Outdoor Education
Department of Physical Education and Athletics
P.O. Box 729
Ithaca, NY 14851
607-255-6415

Provides courses in outdoor adventure skills such as rock climbing, caving, and skiing, using on-site facilities as well as environments in the New York state park system and the Finger Lakes.

Dartmouth Outing Club
H.B. 6142
Hanover, NH 03755
603-646-2428

An organization of specialized outdoor clubs featuring winter sports, canoeing, mountaineering, and trap and skeet shooting.

Earlham College
August Wilderness Program
Box 87
Richmond, Indiana 47374
317-983-1327

Offers students the opportunity to engage in either a canoe trip or a mountaineering expedition. Students travel with faculty from a variety of disciplines and receive training in outdoor skills, local history, communication and decision-making techniques.

Garrett Community College Adventure Sports Program
P.O. Box 151, Mosser Rd.
McHenry, MD 21541
1-800-695-4221

Students are trained to become experts in the development and management of adventure sports and tourism.

George Williams College
P.O. Box 210
Williams Bay, Wisconsin 53191
414-245-5531

Provides non-traditional education for human services professionals and the general public. Most of the courses involve outdoor experiences as part of the curriculum.

Great Hollow Wilderness School
Wesleyan University
Wesleyan Station
Middletown, Connecticutt 06457-6056
203-347-9411

Provides opportunities for individual and group development through planned and systematic experiences in the wilderness. Students practice minimum-impact camping, orienteering, solo, and a variety of skill-building challenge exercises.

University of Kentucky Team Challenge
4th Floor Central Library Building
140 E. Main St.
Lexington, KY 40507-1376
800-325-2766

Training program for businesses, educational groups, and other professional organizations. Although its target audience is usually adult groups, they are branching out into programs for at-risk youth.

The Leisure Connection
5828 Hardy Avenue
San Diego State University
San Diego, CA 92182
619-594-6994

Coordinates low-impact camping and other outdoor activities for San Diego State students and members of the community. Outings are designed to enhance appreciation of the environment.

Maine Bound
Memorial Union, University of Maine
Orono, Maine 04469
207-581-1794

Offers outdoor recreation and skills workshops and courses, as well as training for leaders of outdoor expeditions and ropes facilitators.

Mankato State University
Department of Experiential Education
MSU Box 52
P.O. Box 8400
Mankato, Minnesota 56002-8400
507-389-1005

Offers a Master of Science degree in Experiential Education, including training in counseling, leadership skills, and outdoor skills. Also operates a ropes course for other students within the university, and provides specialized experiential programming for community agencies.

Middle Tennessee State University
Murfreesboro, TN 37132
615-898-2104

Coordinates weekend rafting and camping trips for students, primarily as a recreational break from study.

University of Minnesota
4-H Youth Development
1420 Eckles Hall
St. Paul, MN 55108
612-625-9719

Sponsors biking and bike safety programs for youth. The Pedal Power program trains youth in bike safety techniques, enabling them to train others in the community.

National Audubon Society Expedition Institute
P.O. Box 67
Mt. Vernon, ME 04352
207-685-3111

Offers B.S. and M.S. degrees in Environmental Education in conjunction with Lesley College, Massachusetts, as well as various programs at the high school level. Undergraduate courses focus on American anthropology and the political contours of the environmental problem. Graduate students receive advanced training in counseling and education, and are given the opportunity to undertake wilderness expeditions.

University of Nebraska at Lincoln
Office of Campus Recreation
55 Campus Recreation Center
Lincoln, NE 68588-0232
402-472-3467

Coordinates small-group adventure trips, trains students in outdoor skills, and provides equipment to student groups interested in outdoor recreation.

University of New Hampshire
Department of Physical Education
New Hampshire Hall
Durham, NH 03824-3559
603-862-2070

Offers an undergraduate degree in Outdoor Education. Each student specializes in a current professional application such as education, business, or therapy.

University of North Carolina at Charlotte
Venture Program
Charlotte, NC 28223
704-547-2521

Offers weekend workshops in outdoor skills, courses for credit in Physical Education, a Group Initiatives course, a Ropes Course, and leadership development workshops.

Northeastern Illinois University
T.E.A.M
5500 North St. Louis Ave.
Chicago, IL 60625-4699
312-794-2885

Informs professionals and educators involved with experiential education as to changes and advances in experiential methodology, upcoming conferences, new literature, and programs throughout Illinois.

Northern Illinois University
College of Continuing Education
DeKalb, Illinois 60115-2860
815-753-6923

Provides teachers and facilities for corporate training and technical development seminars. A wide variety of program options are available, including an on-site initiatives course.

Touch of Nature Environmental Center
Southern Illinois University at Carbondale
Carbondale, IL 62901-6623
618-453-1121

This facility is well equipped both for visiting conferences and for camping or challenge-style programs. Offers a range of camping and nature-oriented experiences for disabled people of all ages, as well as educational and traditional camps.

University of Pittsburgh—Semester at Sea
811 William Pitt Union
Pittsburgh, PA 15260
412-648-7490

Enables 500 students per semester to take a 12-15 hour course load while traveling for 100 days on board the S.S. Universe. Students spend approximately 50 days of the semester onshore, where they can travel and gain field experience in different countries for 3-seven days per port of call.

Prescott College
Environmental Studies Program
220 Grove Ave.
Prescott, AZ 86301
602-778-2090

A private college offering degrees in environmental studies as well as other liberal arts concentrations taught from an environmental perspective.

Texas A & M University
Outdoor Education Institute
College Station, Texas 77843-4243
409-845-3458

Provides outdoor education and challenge opportunities to students from the university at large in addition to offering undergraduate and graduate degrees in outdoor education.

Tomball College
30555 Tomball Parkway
Tomball, TX 77375-4036
713-351-3300

Offers a course entitled Venture Dynamics, whose goal is to allow students to explore inter and intra-personal relationships through the medium of outdoor adventure activities.

Washington State University
Outdoor Recreation Center
Compton Union Building, B-22
Pullman, WA 99164-7204
509-335-2651

Offers non-credit courses in outdoor skills, coordinates trips, and rents equipment to students, faculty, and staff. A riding therapy program for mentally and/or physically disabled persons is also available on campus, although separate from the ORC.

Western State College of Colorado
Wilderness Pursuits Program
Gunnison, CO 82131
303-943-7051

Provides a variety of land and water-based trips. Activities include skiing, skydiving, backpacking and rafting.

∇ Court Programs ∇

Camp Woodson
741 Old US Highway 70
Swannanoa, NC 28778
704-628-9933

Designed to facilitate personal growth and social adjustment for adjudicated delinquent youth. Participants are prepared for the 8-week program by several weeks of therapy and physical conditioning. Group and individualized therapy is used, with emphasis on role modeling, field activity processing, small group interaction, and primary supportive counseling.

Eckard Family Youth Alternative
RR 1, Box 607A
Exeter, RI 02822
800-554-HELP

Operates residential wilderness rehabilitation programs in six states for mildly delinquent or non-adjudicated but at-risk youth, challenge programs for first-time adjudicated youth, a program run jointly with Florida Conservation Corps for unemployed or underemployed at-risk youth, and an incarceration facility for juvenile felons in Florida. Programs are generally 12-14 months long with an intensive six-month aftercare.

Lloyd McCorkle Training School
Box 70
County Route 601
Skillman, NJ 08558
609-466-2200

A training school for incarcerated adolescents, with a curriculum combining traditional academic subjects and outdoor adventure education. The program generally lasts from 1-9 months, depending on the availability of community placements.

Nokomis Challenge Program
6300 S. Reserve Rd. #G
Prudenville, MI 48651
517-366-5368

An alternative to traditional training schools for adjudicated adolescent male felons, which involves a short but intensive wilderness component and a longer community-based reintegration and surveillance procedure.

Passages to Adventure
Route 19 Hinkle Road
P.O. Box 71
Fayetteville, WV 25840
800-634-3785

Offers wilderness programs for adjudicated youth as well as members of the community and corporate training teams. Uses physical challenges as a teaching analogy for emotional or social challenges.

Project U.S.E.—Urban Suburban Environments
P.O. Box 3315
Long Branch, NJ
908-870-6650

Provides wilderness programs for adjudicated youth in transition from training schools back into their home community, as well as courses for the general public in outdoor skills, high impact training for corporate teams, and environmental education.

Sprite Program
State of Wisconsin—Department of Health and Human Services
Department of Youth Services
1 West Wilson St.
PO Box 8930
Madison, WI 53708-8930
608-266-9342

Teaches awareness and skills which facilitate the rehabilitation of delinquent youth and their reintegration into their home communities or aftercare placements. Outdoor advanture activities provide participants with training in decision making and everyday living and independence skills.

Telos Youth Outposts, Inc.
5020 Truscott Lane
Diamond Springs, CA 95619
916-626-0345

A residential treatment facility for adjudicated and other WIC-status problem males aged 12-17, providing education, therapy, and wilderness experiences in a group home setting.

TresslerCare Wilderness School
P.O. Box 10
Boiling Springs, PA 17007
717-258-3168

Offers residential programs and 30-day wilderness courses for adjudicated youth between the ages of 13 and 17. The residential option involves placement in a TresslerCare foster care home. Participants undertake two wilderness trips.

VisionQuest National, Ltd.
P.O. Box 12906
Tucson, AZ 85732-2906
602-881-3950

Contracts with public agencies to provide rehabilitation programs for adjudicated youth. Wagon trains simulating Old West living conditions encourage the development of cooperative skills. The purpose of the program is to break patterns of defiance and "conning" in order to resocialize youth into an ethic of interdependence and responsibility.

Wilderness Challenge School
119B Tilden Ave.
Chesapeake, VA 23320
804-547-0117

Works with the courts, social services, family, and school system to prevent recidivism and subsequent incarceration of ajudicated youth. Includes a 10-day wilderness component. Youth participate in several weekend wilderness trips after their return to the community, and participate in family counseling.

Working Alternative
Milton Township Committee on Youth
1492 N. Main St.
Wheaton, IL 60187
665-7213

A six-week program for first and second-time juvenile offenders which requires them to engage in community service as an alternative to further court action or incarceration. Includes a 12-20 hour outdoor adventure education program.

▽ School Programs ▽

Albuquerque Academy
6400 Wyoming Blvd. NE
Albuquerque, NM 87109
505-828-3262

A day school for students in grades 6 through 12. Trips range in length from two days to a week, and include hiking, camping, exploration of ghost towns, and farming.

The Athenian School
2100 Mt. Diablo Scenic Blvd.
P.O. Box 6000
Danville, CA 94526
415-837-5375

A Wilderness Experience course is a four week program required of all students prior to their senior academic year. Activities include backpacking; map and compass navigation; group meetings, journal writing, and readings; appreciation of the natural environment, a solo experience, and service projects.

BACSTOP Program
Dearborn Public Schools
18700 Audette Ave.
Dearborn, MI 48124
313-730-3023

Junior high school students engage in a three-day ropes course experience, a winter camping trip, and a backpacking expedition. A resident camping experience for younger students is also offered.

Boojum Wilderness Institute
P.O. Box 687
Idyll Wild, CA 92349
714-659-6250

Provides experiential and environmental education to school children, businesses, and the public. Summer adventure programs are available, as well as courses in outdoor skills, environmental studies, and team work (initiatives courses). Courses are taught in various national parks throughout the West.

The Cambridge School of Weston
Georgian Road
Weston, MA 02193
617-642-8600

A private day and boarding college preparatory school, which offers wilderness expeditions seven times a year during school holiday periods. Trips are primarily oriented around the activities of cycling, camping, white-water canoeing, and hiking.

Camp Grady Spruce
YMCA of Metropolitan Dallas
601 N. Ackard
Dallas, TX 75201
214-954-0647

Offers a challenge course for contract to outside agencies such as drug rehabilitation programs, corporations, high-school leadership groups, and family counselors. An outdoor education program is available for 5th and 6th graders, who live in cabins for a week. Provides teacher training to those educators interested in bringing their students to the outdoor education center.

Cascade School Wilderness Program
P.O. Box 9
Whitmore, CA 96096
916-472-3031

A wilderness component is part of the personal growth curriculum of this school. This program is geared toward the growth and maturity of the student.

Close-Up Foundation—CAAP
44 Canal Center Plaza
Alexandria, VA 22314
703-706-3300

Provides materials and an incentive program to aid 5th-8th grade teachers in the teaching of knowledge, skills, and values necessary for responsible and competent participation in a democratic society. Recent materials have focused on environmental preservation.

Delaware Valley Friends School
Post Office Box 71
Bryn Mawr, PA 19010-0071
215-526-9595

A Quaker institution serving the academic needs of students whose school performance falls below their potential. Offers courses on decision-making and values clarification and provides outdoor adventure courses.

The Discovery Program—Camp Allen
Rt. 1, Box 426
Navasota, TX 77868
800-447-9685

Provides students with hands-on exploration of the environment, the food chain, and the relationship between humans and the wilderness. Students participate in activities under the direction of a staff professional who works to integrate the Discovery Program's resources with the teacher's curricular needs.

Echo Hill Outdoor School
Worton, MD 21678
301-348-5880

Offers residential and daytime courses in natural sciences, history and social sciences, and individual and group development. Students are able to explore a variety of natural terrains, and develop confidence skills using an on-site ropes course.

El Camino Pines Outdoor School
Star Rt. Box 9995
Frazier Park, CA 93225
805-245-3519

Offers 3-5 day residential, academic, and community building experiences to schools. Available courses focus on the natural sciences, social studies, community dynamics, and personal challenge and self-concept.

Elon Homes for Children
P.O. Box 157
Elon College, North Carolina 27244
919-584-0091

Provides residential group care for dependent children and young people. While they provide a supportive atmosphere for students in their care, Elon also offers family counseling and consultation and tries to involve a resident's family as much as possible in his or her campus life.

Episcopal School
4100 Merrell Road
Dallas, TX 75229
214-358-4368

Students from fifth grade through high school participate in a series of yearly hikes and overnight excursions involving increasing levels of skill challenge and environmental education. High school students are encouraged to assist in the planning and leadership of underclassmen expeditions as part of a leadership development program.

Experiential Learning Center
Birmingham Public Schools
20500 West 13 Mile Road
Birmingham, MI 48010
313-433-8775

Provides programs aimed at increasing self-awareness, appreciation of fellow students, and commitment to teamwork. The Center uses wilderness and urban environments as a context for this process. Adventure trips involving environmental education and/or recreational skills are available during the summer months.

Horizons for Youth
121 Lakeview St.
Sharon, Massachusetts 02067
617-828-7550

Provides both summer camp experiences and hands-on experiential programs for schools interested in enhancing or supplementing their natural science courses. Children can live on-site at the Horizon's facility for week-long intensive education in ecology, take a one-day visit to the center, or receive in-class instruction from staff educators.

Maryland State Department of Education
200 West Baltimore St.
Baltimore, Maryland 21201-2595
301-333-2427

Coordinates volunteer efforts among high school and grade school students and provides resources, training, and technical assistance to schools seeking to implement community service projects within their own student populations.

Michael A. LaCava Nature Center
Cooperstown Central School
Cooperstown, NY 13326
607-547-8181

Involves middle and high school students in a series of group adventure activities culminating in the performance of a research service project. Students engage in rock climbing, ropes, and back country travel.

Mount Bachelor Academy
P.O. Box 7468
Bend, Oregon 97708-7468
800-462-3404

An experientially based residential secondary school which incorporates outdoor education into most aspects of the curriculum. Courses provide as much individualized attention as possible.

Mountain Classroom
Proctor Academy
Andover, NH 03216
603-735-5126

Offers a nine-week learning experience for high school sophomores, juniors, and seniors, involving both academic work and a five-week field trip to a historically or environmentally sigificant site in the United States. Field trips involve backpacking, nature study, and visits to historical sites and museums.

New Hampshire Conservation Corps
PO Box 550
Charlestown, NH 03603-0550
603-826-4301

Involves disadvantaged and at-risk high-school youth in a residential summer program combining job training, full-time work, remedial math and reading instruction, environmental education, and communication and independent living skills.

New York City Outward Bound
140 West St., Suite 2626
New York, NY 10007
212-608-8899

Provides at-risk youth with an opportunity to improve self-esteem and motivation, strengthen physical fitness, ease racial tension, improve literacy, and promote group compassion and sharing by engaging them in adventures using the City's parks.

The Northwest School
1415 Summit Avenue
Seattle, WA 98122
206-682-7309

Offers classes in hiking, bicycling, camping, orienteering, snow cave and igloo building, and other outdoor living or recreational skills along with a usual curriculum.

Outdoor Education Center
Houston Independent School District
Rt. 2, Box 25-B
Trinity, Texas 75862
409-594-7074

One of 63 magnet schools in the Houston Independent School District. It provides 4-day outdoor experiences to fifth graders from the Houston area. Students learn about the importance of adaptation and conservation, and participate in a variety of outdoor recreational activities.

The Pike School, Inc.
P.O. Box 101
Haverhill, NH 03765
603-989-5862

Uses experiential techniques to teach learning disabled and emotionally handicapped young men. The school is located on a working farm and students are involved in its maintenance. Students also participate in numerous day trips involving different outdoor environments and recreational skills.

Pretty Lake Adventure Centre
9310 West R Avenue
Kalamazoo, MI 49009
616-375-1664

A private corporation providing ropes courses and ropes training to educators and therapists at a wide variety of institutions throughout the Midwest. The Center also runs programs for correctional institutions, mental health agencies, substance abuse organizations, and emotionally impaired and learning disabled classrooms.

Project Pride
New Haven Public Schools
72 Westminster St.
Hamden, CT 06518
203-248-5297

An in-school program that attempts to provide youth with high risk/high reward activities that could replace less rewarding, socially destructive behaviors. Small groups of students participate in experiential exercises to build trust and communication skills. Students also spend a weekend using Springfield College's outdoor ropes and challenge courses.

The Rockport Apprenticeshop Programs
PO Box 539, Sea Street
Rockport, ME 04856
207-236-6071

Provides six-week internships and apprenticeships to people interested in learning to refurbish and build boats in the traditional manner.

Rocky Mountain Academy
Route 1
Bonners Ferry, Idaho 83805
208-267-7522

A private academy for high-school students who have academic or emotional difficulties, providing individualized high-quality education at a variety of ability levels. Group discussions regarding personal development and a number of outdoor or wilderness-oriented activities provide recreational and social growth experiences.

Southwest Open High School
PO Box 1420
Cortez, CO 81321
303-565-1150

A nontraditional school for high school students who have dropped out or are at risk of dropping out. A teen parenting program and daycare are available for students.

Stream
1315 Ann Ave.
St. Louis, MO 63104
314-772-9002
   Coordinates the implementation of experiential education and adventure programming in the St. Louis area by training teachers, providing equipment, and welcoming students and the public to its own facilities.

Thompson Island Outward Bound Education Center
Thompson Island
Boston, MA 02127-0002
617-328-3900
   Attempts to inspire Boston's inner-city youth with a love of learning and character traits such as self-esteem, empathy for others, and taking responsibility for the environment. Provides a variety of educational programs. Utilizing the island and the harbor as a laboratory for studying environmental issues, natural history, and the development of social skills.

The Westminster Schools
1424 West Paces Ferry Road, NW
Atlanta, GA 30327
404-355-8673
   Incorporates wilderness and challenge education as a required part of the curriculum.

White Mountain School
West Farm Road
Littleton, NH 03561
603-444-2928
   A small co-educational school whose curriculum includes recycling and work programs as well as wilderness exploration. 2-4 day expeditions involving biking, backpacking, and whitewater rafting are scheduled at regular intervals throughout the school year.

∇ Health Programs ∇

Accessible Adventures
250 NE Tomahawk Island Drive, #309
Portland, OR 97217
503-789-1019

Designs and constructs challenge and ropes courses for organizations and institutions which are accessible to all clients regardless of disability. Offers consultation services and customized training for users and course facilitators.

Breckenridge Outdoor Education Center
P.O. Box 697
Breckenridge, CO 80424
303-453-6422

Offers a wide range of outdoor recreational and challenge programs for people with physical disabilities, visual or hearing impairments, developmental disabilities, cancer patients, and organizations which work with the disabled. Activities include skiing, camping, snow shoeing, rock climbing, fishing, ropes course, and white water rafting.

Challenge Alaska
Box 110065
Anchorage, Alaska 99511
907-563-2658

Provides recreational opportunities for individuals experiencing physical disabilities, information on accesible recreation sites throughout the state, and technical assistance to outside agencies and programs serving the disabled. Activities include skiing, camping, rafting, wheelchair hiking, and tennis.

Challenge Rehabilitation, Inc.
105 E. Vermijo, Ste. 600
Colorado Springs, CO 80903
719-633-1082

Provides a confidence building experience for individuals injured in auto accidents, especially those with head injuries or chronic pain. Ropes courses are designed to be accessible to persons with physical disabilities.

ETC—Environmental Traveling Companions
Ft. Mason Center Landmark Building C
San Francisco, CA 94123
415-474-7662

Provides whitewater rafting, cross-country skiing, and sea kayaking programs for the visually or hearing impaired; the physically, emotionally, or developmentally disabled; and disadvantaged youth and school groups.

Green Chimneys
Putnam Lake Road
Brewster, NY 10509
914-279-2996

A small school for children with behavioral and/or academic difficulties, situated on a working farm and wildlife rehabilitation center. Offers weekend programming, including camping trips and horseback riding for physically handicapped adults and children.

Lewis Wetzel Personal Care Home
P. O. Box 428
80 E. Benjamin Drive
New Martinsville, WV 26155
304-455-5666

A community house accomodating 50 disabled, elderly, or mentally troubled adults. Residents carry out their ordinary living patterns in community, and are given the opportunity to develop traditional Appalachian craft skills. This home is an alternative to institutionalization for elderly or mentally troubled patients who cannot live alone and nevertheless are capable of relative independence and self-fulfillment.

Magic Me
808 N. Charles St.
Baltimore, MD 21201
301-837-0900

Attempts to motivate and educate at-risk or disillusioned youth by involving them in long-term service to the elderly, mentally retarded, and handicapped. Participating youth develop personal relationships with clients in these settings and engage in weekly recreational and educational activities with their partners.

S'Plore
27 West 3300 South
Salt Lake City, Utah 84115
801-484-4128

Offers a variety of outdoor education and adventure programs to physically, emotionally, or intellectually disabled persons. Most of S'Plore's clients are adult, but programs are available for adolescent psychiatric patients, juvenile offenders, and economically disadvantaged persons.

Appendix B ▽

Index of Programs

Accessible Adventures, 270
Action Quest, 227
Adolescent Behavioral Change, 213
Adventure Associates, 227
Adventure/Discovery, Inc., 213
Adventures Rolling Cross-Country, Inc., 227
Adventureworks, Inc., 227
Albuquerque Academy, 262
American Leadership Forum, 228
Appalachian Mountain Club, 228
Appalachian Mountain Teen Project, 213
Associates for Youth Development, Inc., 228
Athenian School, The, 262
Austin Child Guidance Center, 214
Austin Wilderness Counseling Services, 214
Austin Young Men's Business League, 228
BACSTOP Program, 262
Baltimore (City of) Carrie Murray Outdoor
    Education Campus, 229
Bear Mountain Outdoor School, 229
Beech Hill/Outward Bound, 214
Bemidji State University, 251
Berry College, 251
Bicycle Adventures, 229
Biking Expedition, Inc., The, 229
Birch Trail Camp for Girls, 230
Bloomsburg University—Quest, 251
Boojum Wilderness Institute, 262
Boys Town, 230
Bradford Woods, 251
Breckenridge Outdoor Education Center, 270
Michael H. Brown Counseling and
    Psychological Services, 230
Cambridge School of Weston, The, 263
Camp Broadstone, 230
Camp Grady Spruce, 263
Camp High Rocks, 231
Camp Huston, 231
Camp Livingston, 231
Camp Rising Sun, 231
Camp Woodson, 258
Career Resources, Inc., 247

Cascade School Wilderness Program, 263
Catalyst Consulting Team, 247
Catherine Freer Survival School, 214
Centennial Peaks Hospital, 215
Challenge Alaska, 270
Challenge Rehabilitation, Inc., 270
Challenge Sonoma Adventure Ropes Course,
    232
Changeworks, 247
Charlotte Outdoor Adventure Center, 232
Chesapeake Bay Foundation, 232
Cheyenne Mountain Conference Resort, 247
Childrens Square USA, 215
Christodora-Manice Education Center, 232
    Circle S Recovery Ranch, 215
Close-Up Foundation—CAAP, 263
College of DuPage Field Studies Program,
    252
Colorado Outward Bound School, 233
Cornell Outdoor Education, 252
Cornerstone, 248
Corporate Adventure, 248
Cradlerock Outdoor Network, 248
Dartmouth Outing Club, 252
Deer Hill Summer Expeditions, 233
Delaware Valley Friends School, 264
Discovery Program—Camp Allen, The, 264
Eagle Mountain Outpost Ranch School, 215
Eagle's Nest Camp, 233
Eagleville   Hospital—Adventure   Based
    Therapy, 216
Earlham College, 252
Earthwalk, 248
Echo Hill Outdoor School, 264
Eckard Family Youth Alternative, 258
Educo International, 233
El Camino Pines Outdoor School, 264
Elmcrest Therapeutic Adventure Program,
    216
Elon Homes for Children, 264
Episcopal School, 265
Escape to Reality, 216

ETC—Environmental Traveling Companions, 271
Executive Adventure, Inc., 248
Executive Expeditions, 249
Exodus, 216
Experiential Learning Center, 265
Farm and Wilderness Summer Camps, 234
Florida Sherriffs' Youth Ranches—Caruth Camp, 217
For the Love of Children, 234
Forty Legends, 234
Four Winds, Inc., 234
Foxfire Teacher Outreach, 234
Garrett Community College Adventure Sports Program, 252
Genessee Valley Outdoor Learning Center, 235
George Williams College, 253
Girl Scout Council of the Nation's Capital, 235
Girls' Adventure Trails, 217
Glenwood Mental Health Services, Inc., 217
Great Hollow Wilderness School, 253
Green Chimneys, 271
Green Mountain Wilderness Foundation, The, 217
Griffith Center, 218
Heights Psychiatric Hospital—Stepping Out Program, 218
Hoover Outdoor Education Center, 235
Hope Center, 218
Horizons for Youth, 265
Hurricane Island Outward Bound, 218
Inner Harbour Psychiatric Hospitals, Ltd., 218
Inner Quest, Inc., 235
Insight!, 236
Institute for Creative Living, 236
Interlocken, 236
Interventions, 219
Inward Bound, 219
John de la Howe School, 219
Kent Mountain Adventure Center, 236
Kiwanis Camp Wyman, 237
Michael A. LaCava Nature Center, 266
Learning Forum, 237
Leisure Connection, The, 253
Lewis Wetzel Personal Care Home, 271
Life Adventure Camp, 219
Life Development Center, 220
Lloyd McCorkle Training School, 258
Long Lane School Youth Challenge, 220

Looking Up, 220
Magic Me, 271
Maine Bound, 253
Mankato State University, 254
Marimed Foundation, 237
Maryland State Department of Education, 265
Meet the Wilderness, 237
Middle Tennessee State University, 254
Millvale Plantation, 249
Mount Bachelor Academy, 266
Mountain Classroom, 266
Nantahala Outdoor Center, 238
National Audubon Society Expedition Institute, 254
National Indian Youth Leadership Development Project, Inc., 238
National Outdoor Leadership School, 238
National Wildlife Federation, 238
National Youth Leadership Council, 239
Natural Bridge Learning Center, 239
New Dominion School, Inc., 220
New Hampshire Conservation Corps, 266
New Life Treatment Center Wilderness Program, 221
New York City Outward Bound, 266
Nobles Day Camp, 239
Nokomis Challenge Program, 259
North Carolina Outward Bound School, 239
Northeastern Illinois University, 255
Northern Illinois University, 255
Northwest Passage, 221
Northwest School, The, 267
Oaks, The, 221
On Belay, 240
On Belay Youth and Family Services, Inc., 221
Outdoor Discoveries, 240
Outdoor Education Center, 267
Outdoor Leadership Training Seminar, 240
Outward Bound, USA, 240
Pacific Crest Outward Bound School, 241
Paradigm Ventures, 241
Passages to Adventure, 259
Peak Performance, 249
Pecos River Learning Centers, 249
Pennsylvania Conservation Corps, 241
Performance Dynamics Group, 249
Pike School, Inc., The, 267
Pine Ridge Adventure Center, 241
Pocono Environmental Education Center, 241

Prescott College, 256
Pressley Ridge School, 222
Pretty Lake Adventure Centre, 267
Project Adventure—Challenge Program, 222
Project Pride, 268
Project S.O.A.R., 242
Project U.S.E.—Urban Suburban
  Environments, 259
Raven's Way, 222
Renaissance Leadership, 250
Rock Eagle 4-H Center, 242
Rockport Apprenticeshop Programs, The,
  268
Rocky Mountain Academy, 268
Roland and Associates, Inc., 242
Salesmanship Club Therapeutic Camps, 222
St. Francis Academy Passport to Adventure
  Program, The, 223
St. Helena Hospital—Challenge Course
  Program, 223
Seneca, 223
Seven Hills Schools, The, 242
Sierra Club Inner City Outings, 243
S.O.A.R. (Special Outdoor Adventure
  Resources), 223
Solo, 243
Southwest Open High School, 268
S'Plore, 272
Sprite Program, 259
Step Inc., 243
Storer Camps YMCA, 243
Stream, 269
Summit Quest, 224
Telos Youth Outposts, Inc., 260
Texas A & M University, 260
Thompson Island Outward Bound Education
  Center, 269
Three Oaks Adventure Center, 244
Tomball College, 256
Touch of Nature Environmental Center, 256
Trailmark Outdoor Adventures, 244
TresslerCare Wilderness School, 260
Tulare County Conservation Corps, 244
Ultimate Adventures, Inc., 244
United Charities Camp Algonquin, 244
University of Alaska at Anchorage, 250
University of Kentucky Team Challenge, 253
University of Minnesota, 254
University of Nebraska at Lincoln, 255
University of New Hampshire, 255
University of North Carolina at Charlotte,
  255

University of Pittsburgh—Semester at Sea,
  256
Vision Us, Inc., 250
VisionQuest National, Ltd., 260
Vista Youth and Family Center, 224
Voyageur Outward Bound School, 245
Washington Rock Girl Scout Council, 245
Washington State University, 257
Waterhouse Center, 250
West Pines Psychiatric Hospital, 224
Western State College of Colorado, 257
Westminster Schools, The, 269
White Mountain School, 269
Wilderness Academy, 224
Wilderness Challenge School, 260
Wilderness Conquest Inc., 224
Wilderness Education Association, 245
Wilderness Institute, The, 245
Wilderness School, 225
Wilderness Southeast, 245
Wilderness Therapy Program, 225
Wilderness Treatment Centers, 225
Wolfcreek Wilderness School, 246
Woodside Trails, 225
Woodswomen, 246
Working Alternative, 261
YMCA Camp Widjiwagan, 246
YMCA Juvenile Crisis Program, 226
YMCA of the Rockies, 246
Youth Service International, 247

Index ▽

Abbey, Edward, 20
Accessible Adventures program, 99
Accreditation standards, 140-144
Activities
    adventure education, 13
    goals of, 13
    outdoor, 13
    recreational, 13
    (See also **Backpacking; Canoeing; Kayaking; Rappelling; Rock climbing; Ropes courses; Skiing; Wilderness activities**)
Adirondacks, 27
Adolescence, 3
    adjustment factors of, 2
    developmental stages of, 4-5
    psychological growth factors of, 4
    psychoanalytic theory of, 4
    theoretical accounts of, 3-6
Adolescent chemical dependency program, 89
Adolescent turbulence, 4, 6 (See also *Sturm und drang*)
Adolescents, 2
    first guidance center for, 3
    negative identity in, 5
    psychiatric problems in, 6-7
    social institutions for, 3
    turbulence in, 6
    variety of psychological problems in, 6
Adventure
    activities, 13
    definition of, 13
    games, 13
    pursuits, 2-3
Adventure Based Counseling, 96
American Leadership Forum, 102 (See also **Wilderness Challenge**)
Appalachian Mountain Club, 29
Archetypes, 129
Assessment of applicants, 153-157 (See also **Designing programs**)
Association for Experiential Education, 197

Awareness Adventure Program, 63-64
Backpacking, 13, 87, 93, 177
Baden-Powell, Robert, 42
Balch, Ernest Berkely, 41
Beech Hill Hospital, 89
Bierstadt, Albert, 23
Blos, Peter, 4, 6
Boy Scouts of America, 35, 42-43
    Handbook, 33, 35
Boys Club camp, 42
Bradford, William, 21
Breckenridge Outdoor Education Center, 99
Broadview Farm Camps, The, 46
Brown, T., 12
Burnt Island Camp, 41
Camp Ahmek, 44-46
Camp Baldhead, 41
Camp Dudley, 41
Camp Fire Girls, 42
Camp Kehonka for Girls, 42
Camp Shand, 42
Camping
    as therapeutic, 46-47, 98
    for the emotionally troubled, 49
    for physically challenged children, 46, 99
    for those with mental health needs, 46-47 (See also **Tent therapy**)
    value of, 63-66
Canoeing, 13, 88, 93, 141
Catalyst Consulting Team programs, 102
Certification programs for outdoor leaders, 140-141
Challenge courses (See **Ropes courses**)
Challenge Rehabilitation program, 99
Church, Frederic, 23
Circle processing, 88
Civilian Conservation Corps (CCC), 35
Client needs, 138-140
Client population, defining, 144-145
Clinical ratings of program effectiveness, 173
COA standards, 140, 204-205
Colorado Outward Bound program, 98

Conflicts, pre-adolescent, 5
Coolidge, Calvin, 34
Cooper, James Fenimore, 26
Corporate Adventure programs, 102
Council on Accreditation of Services for Families and Children, 140, 204-205
Court programs, 90-94
Delinquency programs, 77-80, 90-94 (See also **Court programs; Recidivism rate**)
Depression Adjective Checklist, 184
Designing programs, 138-164
Discovery Program at Camp Allen, 96
Dudley, Sumner, 41
DSM-IIIR, 6
Earth Day, 20
Eckard Family Youth Alternative Programs, 94
Effectance Motivation, 122-123
Ego functions, 4
Emerson, Ralph Waldo, 26
Enrichment programs, 100-105
Environmental Traveling Companions program, 99-100
Epigenetic principle, 5
Epileptics, 57
Erikson, Erik, 4-5
Evaluation of programs (See **Program evaluation**)
Evaluation research (See **Program evaluation**)
Executive Expeditions program, 102
Executive programs, 101-102
Experiential learning, 94-95
Experiential Learning Center, 96
Field Studies program at College of Dupage, 103-104
Fresh Air Camp, 40
Friedrick, Caspar David, 22
Funding a program, 162-163
GIG program (See **Group and Individual Growth program**)
Girl Scouts, 42
Good Will Farm for Boys, 41
Gregory, Henry, 29
Group and Individual Growth (GIG) program, 92-93
Group psychotherapy, 13
Guidance centers, 3
Gulick, Luther Halsey, 41
Gunn, Frederick William, 40
Gunnery School for Boys, 40

Hahn, Dr. Kurt, 52-53
Hall, G. Stanley, 3-4
Harms, Dr. Ernest, 46
Health care programs, 97-100
Hetch Hetchy, 28-30, 34
Hiawatha, 25
Hinckley, Rev. George W., 41
Holding, Thomas Hiram, 40
Individual treatment plans (ITP), 146-148
Individuation, 4
Inner Harbour Hospital, 89
Inpatient
    camping programs, 56-57, 87
    mental health services, 8-9
Institute for Juvenile Research, 3
Interventions program, 88
John De La Howe School, 89-90
Johnson, Robert Underwood, 28
Juvenile courts, 3
Juvenile Psychopathic Institute, 3
Kayaking, 13, 99
Knowles, Joseph, 30-34
Langford, Nathaniel, 27
Leadership and training programs, 100-101
Learned helplessness, 9
Learninghouse Southwest Field Training Project, 174-175
Leopold, Aldo, 34
Lincoln, Abraham, 27
Literature on wilderness programs, 62-72
Longfellow, Henry Wadsworth, 24
Loughmiller, Campbell, 49-50
Maintaining long-term change, 161-162
Mandala, 29
Marketing a program, 163-164
Marshall, Robert, 11
Maslow, Abraham, 123-125
Massachusetts Bay Colony, 21
Mattoon, Laura, 42
McFarland, J. Horace, 29
Mental health programs, 86-90
Mental health services, 6, 8-10
    inpatient 8-9
        limitations to 9
    outpatient 8, 10
    limitations to traditional services 9-10
Menu planning, 151-153
Metaphoric Curriculum approach, 72
Monk By the Sea, 22
Monkey Wrench Gang, The, 20
"Mountains Speak for Themselves" (MST), 53-55

MST, 53-55
Muir, John, 28, 30
Multiple baseline design, 181-182
National Audubon Society Expedition Institute, 101
National Conference on Outdoor Recreation (NCOR), 34
National Council on Therapeutic Recreation, 203
National Outdoor Leadership School, 100-101, 197
National Park Service, 30
National Standard Program (NSP), 196
National Wilderness Preservation System, 35
National Wildlife Federation Camp, 101
NatureQuest program, 101
NCOR, 34
Negative identity, 5
New York City Outward Bound Center, 97
NOLS, 100-101, 197
North Carolina Outward Bound program, 98
North Mountain School of Physical Culture, 40
NSP, 196
On Belay Youth and Family Services, 88
Oregon Trail, 23
Outdoor Action program at Prescott College, 103
Outdoor activities (See **Activities**)
Outdoor Adventures program at U. of Nebraska, 103
Outdoor Adventures program at Washington State U., 103
Outdoor adventure pursuits, 13-14
physical challenge, 13
Outdoor Education Center at Cornell U., 103
Outdoor Education programs at George Williams College, 104
Outdoor Education Project, 56
Outdoor program (See **Wilderness**)
Outpatient counseling, 10
Outpatient
mental health services, 8-10
program, 87-88
Outward Bound, 46, 52-56, 57, 36, 72-77, 97-98
Adolescent Chemical Dependency Program, 89
as effective deliquency program, 77-80
chronology of development, 53-55
Discovery Learning model, 72
early program research, 55

goal setting, 53
goals, 53, 54, 73
instructors' leadership qualities, 76, 196
Metaphoric Curriculum, 72
philosophies of, 53-55
program evaluation, 73-76
research on, 72-77
trip leaders, 54
Partial hospitalization, 8
Physical challenge, 13
Pieh, Jerry, 95
Pier-Harris Self Concept Scale, 182
Pilgrims, 21
Pinchot, Gifford, 28
Problem-solving skills, 13
Professional development seminars, 98
Professionalization, 196-198
Program design (See **Designing programs**)
Program evaluation, 168-189
clinical ratings of effectiveness, 173
combining quantitative and qualitative approaches, 186-189
control groups in, 180-181
current research in, 171-176
general research issues on, 185-186
instrumentation, 182-185
of wilderness programs, 176-186
preparing for the evaluation, 178-186
problems, 177-178
process evaluations, 186-188
qualitative approach to, 170-171, 173-174, 175
active participation in, 174
holistic orientation in, 174
inductive approach in, 174
naturalistic emphasis in, 174
(See also **Learninghouse Southwest...**)
quantitative method of, 170, 171-172, 173, 177
research defined, 168-169
research design, 178-182
subjective ratings of effectiveness, 173, 184-185
typologies for, 169-170
Project Adventure program, 95-96
Project Pride program, 96
Psychiatric emergencies in the field, 143
Psychoanalytic theory of adolescence, 4 (See also *Sturm und drang*)
Psychophysiological disorders, 6
Psychotherapy, 2-3, 13-14

Qualitative method of program evaluation
(See *Program evaluation*)
Quantitative method of program evaluation
(See *Program evaluation*)
Quaternity, 129
Rappelling, 88
Recidivism rate
as a measure of program success, 172
effect of wilderness programs on, 77-80, 93
Regard from others, 125-127
conditional positive, 126
unconditional positive, 127
Research design, 178-182
Residential treatment centers, 8
Rock climbing, 88, 93, 102, 177
Rocky Mountain Academy, 97
Rogers, C., 125-127
Romantic movement, 22-27
Romanticism, 22-27
Roosevelt, Theodore, 29
Ropes courses, 89, 91, 99, 177
Rothrock, Joseph Trimble, 40-41
Rustrum, Calvin, 36
Salesmanship Club of Dallas, 48-51, 57
Salesmanship Club Boys Camp, 49-50
Salesmanship Club Youth and Family Center
in Dallas, 90
Santa Fe Mountain Center, 92
School programs, 94-97
Sea Rest, 40
Self-actualization, 123-125
Self-concept (See *Self-esteem*)
Self-efficacy, 182-183
scale, 183
Self-esteem, 121-122, 172, 195
measures of, 172, 182
Self-regard, 125-127
Self theory, 125-127
Sexual drive, 4
Sierra Club, 28-29, 30, 35
Skiing, 88, 99, 4197
adaptive program, 99
(See also *Breckenridge Outdoor
Education Center*)
Socialization of the camper, 44-45
Song of Myself, 25
Song of the Open Road, 25-26
Staff requirements, 140-142
Staff-to-participant ratios, 151
Staffing patterns, 150-151
Standardized tests

obtaining tests, 173
Standards of technical skills in outdoor
education, 197
Stewart, Dr. J.W., 42
Sturm und drang, 4, 6
Subjective ratings of program effectiveness,
173, 184-185
Suicide, 7
Systems theory, 131-132
Talk therapy, 54
Tent therapy, 43-44
Theories
applying criteria for evaluating, 132-133
evaluation of, 113-114
importance of, 110-113
prediction of behavior and, 111
restorative environment, 114-117
social learning, 117-121
relating to self-esteem, 121-127
relating to symbols of transformation,
128-131
systems theory, 131-132
transpersonal theories, 127-131
understanding, 111
Therapy
definition of, 11
Therapy/counseling planning, 157-160
Therapeutic approaches, early, 44-48, 57
Therapeutic moments, 142
Therapeutic Residential Wilderness Camping
Programs/Adventure-Based Therapeutic
Outdoor Programs, 205
Thompson Island Outward Bound program,
97
Thoreau, Henry David, 26
Training for health care professionals, 98
Transcendentalism, 26
Transpersonal Psychology, 127-131
Transpersonal theories, 127-131
Treatment planning, 147 (See **Individual
treatment planning**)
TresslerCare Wilderness School, 93-94
Trip leaders, 54, 177
Trip length, 149-150
Trip location, 150
Trip planning, 148-150
Typologies for program evaluation, 169-170
University of Michigan Fresh Air Camp, 48-49
University programs, 102-105
Vision Quest Program, 91-92
Walden pond, 26-27

White, Robert, 122-123
Whitman, Walt, 24-25
Wilderness
    activities, 13, 200-201, 207
    adventure, defined, 13
    restorative powers of, 48, 114-117
    therapeutic effects of, 48, 54, 62, 73,
        127, 194, 195, 201, 207
    as unique environment, 48
    ethic, 20
    figurative definition of, 12
    healing powers, 48, 57, 195
    literal definition of, 11-12
    preservation of, 27-30
    program design (See **Designing**
        programs)
    program evaluation (See **Program**
        evaluation)
    therapy, 2, 10-11, 13-14, 36, 198, 199,
        203
    therapy for troubled youth 9, 11, 13-14,
        198, 199-200
Wilderness Act of 1964, 12, 35
Wilderness Challenge, 102
Wilderness Challenge School, 93
Wilderness Conquest program, 88
Wilderness counseling
    incorporation into a traditional practice,
        138-164
Wilderness Education Association, 101, 196
Wilderness program classifications, 90-105
    court programs, 90-94
        Eckard Family Youth Alternative
          Programs, 94
        for delinquents, 90-91
        Group and Individual Growth
          (GIG) Program, 92-93
        Santa Fe Mountain Center, 92
        TresslerCare Wilderness School,
          93-94
        Vision Quest Program, 91-92
        Wilderness Challenge School, 93
    enrichment programs, 100-105
        defined, 100
        executive programs, 101-102
          Corporate Adventure, 102
          Executive Expeditions, 102
        leadership and training programs,
          100-101
          American Leadership Forum,
            102

          Catalyst Consulting Team
            programs, 102
        National Outdoor Leadership
          School, 100-101
        National Wildlife Federation
          Camp, 101
        Outward Bound schools, 100
    university programs, 102-105
        Corporate Adventure, 103
        Outdoor Education Center at
          Cornell U., 103
        Field Studies program at
          College of Dupage, 103
        Outdoor Action program at
          Prescott College, 103
        Outdoor Adventures program
          at U. of Nebraska, 103
        Outdoor Adventures program
          at Washington State U.,
          103
        Outdoor Education programs
          at George Williams
          College, 104
    health care programs, 97-100
        Accessible Adventures program,
          99
        Breckenridge Outdoor Education
          Center, 99
        Challenge Rehabilitation program,
          99
        Colorado Outward Bound
          program, 98
        Environmental Traveling
          Companions program, 99
        for the physically disabled, 97-98
        North Carolina Outward Bound
          program, 98
    mental health programs, 86-90
        inpatient programs, 86-87
          Beech Hill Hospital, 89
          Outward Bound Adolescent
            Chemical Dependency
            Program, 89
          Inner Harbour Hospital, 89
          John De La Howe School,
            89-90
          Salesmanship Club Youth
            and Family Center in
            Dallas, 90
        outpatient programs, 87-88
          Wilderness Conquest
            program, 88

On Belay Youth and Family
Services, 88
Interventions program, 88
school programs, 94-97
Discovery Program Camp Allen,
96
Experiential Learning Center, 96
New York City Outward Bound
Center, 97
Project Adventure program, 95-96
Project Pride program, 96
Rocky Mountain Academy, 97
Thompson Island Outward Bound
program, 97
Wilderness programs
accreditation, 203-204, 205-206, 208
as effective delinquency programs, 77-
80
critical issues/emerging trends on, 202-
208
defining the field of, 198-202
design (See **Designing programs**)
early programs, 40-58
early therapeutic approaches, 44-48
(See also **Camp Ahmek; Tent
therapy**)
evaluation (See **Program evaluation**)
general philosophy of, 63-66
leader certification, 203-204
leaders, 200-201
regulation of, 203-204
research on, 62-80
support staff, 202, 205-206
therapy, 2, 10-11, 13-14, 36, 198, 199,
203
therapists, 200-201
theoretical accounts of success of, 110-
133
varieties of, 86-105
Wilderness therapy checklist, 154
Wilderness therapy, conducting, 157-160
Wilderness Therapy Practicum, 98
Wilderness Therapy Program, The, 68-69
Wilson, Woodrow, 30
Yellowstone National Park, 27
Yosemite National Park, 28-29
Yosemite Valley, 27